Enterprise Integration with Ruby

A Pragmatic Guide

Enterprise Integration with Ruby

A Pragmatic Guide

Maik Schmidt

The Pragmatic Bookshelf

Raleigh, North Carolina   Dallas, Texas

Our Pragmatic courses, workshops, and other products can help you and your team create better software and have more fun. For more information, as well as the latest Pragmatic titles, please visit us at

http://www.pragmaticprogrammer.com

Printed in the United States of America.

ISBN 0-9766940-6-9

Printed on acid-free paper with 85% recycled, 30% post-consumer content.

Second printing, July 2006

Version: 2006-6-16

Für meine Eltern.
Ihr seid die Giganten, auf deren Schultern ich stehe!

For my parents.
You are the giants on whose shoulders I stand!

Contents

Foreword   **ix**

1 Introduction   **1**
   1.1   What Is Enterprise Software?   2
   1.2   What Is Enterprise Integration?   3
   1.3   Why Ruby?   3
   1.4   Who Should Read This Book?   5
   1.5   PragBouquet   5
   1.6   Acknowledgments   6

2 Databases   **9**
   2.1   The Coupon Application   10
   2.2   Database Interface (DBI)   26
   2.3   Object-Relational Mappers   29
   2.4   Lightweight Directory Access Protocol (LDAP)   52

3 Processing XML   **81**
   3.1   A Short XML Reminder   83
   3.2   Generating XML Documents   85
   3.3   Processing XML Documents   97
   3.4   Validating XML Documents   129
   3.5   Are There Alternatives to XML?   134

4 Low-Ceremony Distributed Applications   **147**
   4.1   "I'd Rather Use a Socket"   148
   4.2   Remote Procedure Calls Using HTTP   161

5 Distributed Applications with RPC   **181**
   5.1   Another Day, Another Protocol   181
   5.2   We Will Take No REST, Will We?   191
   5.3   SOAP   202
   5.4   CORBA, RMI, and Friends   223

6 Tools and Techniques   **243**
   6.1 Internationalization and Localization 243
   6.2 Logging 264
   6.3 Creating Daemons and Services 282
   6.4 Build and Deployment Process 289
   6.5 Project Automation with Rake 306
   6.6 Testing Legacy Applications 317

A Resources   **325**
   A.1 Bibliography 325

Foreword

A few years ago, I came across the Ruby programming language, and I fell in love. Somehow, it just seemed to work the way my brain works—I can express myself in Ruby more naturally and with less intervening fluff than in any other language I know. I liked it so much I persuaded Andy Hunt to coauthor a book about it.

That was back in 1999. Since then, a lot has happened in the Ruby world. The language went from release 1.6 to 1.8, and the standard library matured into something world class. It gained a standardized documentation system, a standard library distribution mechanism, and a fine build tool. I produced a second edition of *Programming Ruby* to celebrate.

And now, for the first time, I can seriously say that Ruby is ready for the enterprise. The language is stable, the libraries are great, and there is a growing pool of talented and enthusiastic Ruby developers, all rising to the challenge. We see companies such as Amazon and EarthLink using Ruby for both internal- and external-facing projects.

The problem is that—until now—there wasn't much documentation on using Ruby in the enterprise. Sure, you can always find the API documentation for a library, but that doesn't really explain the *how* and the *why*.

Now the situation has changed. With *Enterprise Integration with Ruby*, Maik has done something I would have thought impossible. Not only has he documented just how to use Ruby to create new enterprise solutions and to knit together existing applications, but he has also documented the backgrounds to all the technologies, along with how and when to use each.

I consider this book a worthy partner to *Programming Ruby*. With it, you'll exploit the power and flexibility of Ruby to create new solutions for your company in record time.

And, just as importantly, you'll have fun.

Dave Thomas
The Pragmatic Programmers

Chapter 1

Introduction

Have you ever worked for a big enterprise? Do you remember your expectations as you walked into work on that first day? Whistling as the sun shone brightly, you might have been thinking, "It will be great to work for <company name here>. They will have a professional environment where coffee is free and where every system has been specified accurately, implemented carefully, and tested thoroughly. Hmmmm... I wonder which database and programming language they use."

After your fifth cup of free coffee (around 9:07) you came to realize that the real world looks completely different from your expectations. Typical enterprises use dozens, hundreds, and sometimes even thousands of applications, components, services, and databases. Many of them were custom-built in-house or by third parties, some were bought, others are based on open source projects, and the origin of a few—usually the most critical ones—is completely unknown. A lot of applications are very old, some are fairly new, and seemingly no two of them were written using the same tools. They run on heterogeneous operating systems and hardware, they use databases and messaging systems from various vendors, and they were written in completely different programming languages.

The reasons for this are manifold. You can find countless books that explain why the situation is so bad. You can even find books claiming that they help you prevent such chaos. This book uses another approach. We will not help you clean up this mess, but we will help you deal with the problems pragmatically. Instead of complaining that valuable data is spread across different database schemas or across databases from several vendors, we will write code that integrates it. We will take it even a step further and write new applications that aggregate *all* your existing resources. It doesn't matter if we have to use relational databases, LDAP repositories, XML files, or web services based on different protocol standards. We will blend data from multiple, disparate databases to create new business knowledge.

Along the way we'll show you how to solve all the small day-to-day problems. These are the issues that occur over and over again, especially when developing enterprise software. We will access relational databases such as Oracle and MySQL, and we will work with LDAP repositories. We'll show you how to do application logging, how to deploy your software, how to automate tedious and error-prone tasks, and how to survive in an international environment. Oh, and as you might have guessed already from the book's title, we will use Ruby to accomplish all these feats.

1.1 What Is Enterprise Software?

In *Patterns of Enterprise Application Architecture* [Fow03], Martin Fowler writes, "Enterprise applications are about the display, manipulation, and storage of large amounts of often complex data and the support or automation of business processes with that data."

That's a concise but nevertheless abstract definition, because every nontrivial piece of software has to store, manipulate, and display data. Video games do nothing else (and modern video games also need huge amounts of data that often can get complex). The key point in the previous definition is the second part: the data in enterprise applications is used for business processes and not for rendering alien spaceships.

Unsurprisingly, there are more differences between enterprise applications and other types of software. For example, enterprise applications are often created only for a small user group that is in close contact with the development team, implying the developers know their customers very well. In extreme cases programs are written for only a single person (special report generators for the CEO, for example).

Enterprise software demands a certain set of tools. Large amounts of data—complex or not—have to be stored somehow and somewhere. Often it is stored in relational databases, but it can also be in plain-text files or LDAP repositories. In addition, modern enterprise software is often based on distributed architectures consisting of many small to midsize components that perform specialized tasks and that are connected by some kind of middleware such as CORBA, RMI, SOAP, and XML-RPC.

Obviously, as an enterprise software developer, you're better off if you know how to deal with such technologies. You shouldn't be troubled by the details of reading from a relational database or accessing an LDAP repository. Mastering skills such as these help you concentrate on the fun stuff—the application itself.

1.2 What Is Enterprise Integration?

Enterprise integration is a rather vague term and cannot be defined in a strict mathematical sense. Simply put, it happens whenever you use an existing enterprise resource to achieve some results. If you use an existing database or web service in your application, you're performing enterprise integration. If you build a new component that is used by other pieces of your existing architecture, you're doing enterprise integration, too.

Integration needn't just happen inside a single enterprise. It's quite possible—and not too unusual—that the software or data of two different enterprises has to be integrated. If you're using a payment gateway to bill your customers, for example, you're effectively integrating enterprise software.

You might ask yourself whether every development activity in an enterprise environment is some kind of enterprise integration. There are a few exceptions. Enterprise integration does not happen when you build a completely new piece of software from scratch, for example. In reality this case is rare, but from a theoretical point of view this is the only clear exception.

Enterprise integration often means integration with standard software such as databases, LDAP repositories, message queues, ERM systems, and so on. If you're using one of these technologies, chances are good that you're doing some enterprise integration.

1.3 Why Ruby?

Most enterprise software running today was written in languages such as COBOL, C/C++, and Java. Because of its distributed nature, enterprise software often makes it easy to use new tools and programming languages. When you have to create a small stand-alone application—one that relies only upon an existing database, SOAP service, or LDAP repository—it almost doesn't seem to matter whether you were to write it in C++, Java, or Ruby. But if you look into it more deeply, dynamic languages such as Perl, Python, and Ruby have many advantages, especially in enterprise environments:

- They are interpreted and do not need a compile phase, which increases development speed tremendously. After editing your program, you can see the results of your changes immediately.

- Enterprise software is about munging data. Dynamic languages are designed to handle data and include high-level data types such as hashes.

- Memory management is dealt with by the language. This is a great advantage over languages such as C++ where you have to specify the length of each string you read from a database. Dynamic languages prevent waste and result in more concise, more robust, and more secure software.

- Software written in dynamic languages is installed as source code, so you always know exactly which version is currently running on your production system. Gone are the days when you had to guess whether a certain binary executable is the right one.

We will show you Ruby's strengths and how Ruby helps you accomplish many tasks much faster, more elegantly, and with more fun than with any other programming language available today. But, even more important, we will also tell you about Ruby's weaknesses. Ruby is comparatively young, and although the core of the language is mature and lots of excellent libraries are available, many features are still missing or incomplete.

Although there is no industry standard for enterprise programming with Ruby (as there is with J2EE or .NET), everything you need is readily available. The most important libraries come with every Ruby distribution, and the standard distribution has grown rapidly over the last years. All the other stuff can be found in public places such as RubyForge[1] or the Ruby Application Archive.[2]

---

[1]http://www.rubyforge.org
[2]http://raa.ruby-lang.org

1.4 Who Should Read This Book?

This book was written for experienced enterprise developers who know Java, C#, or C++ but don't know much Ruby (although you should probably have read *Programming Ruby* [TFH05]). We assume you are familiar with relational databases and have at least an idea of what LDAP is. Maybe you do not know RELAX NG, but you understand the concepts of XML and what *well-formed*, *SAX2*, and *DOM* mean.

You've probably used tools such as object-relational mappers. Maybe you're familiar with Enterprise Java Beans (EJB), Java Data Objects (JDO), and so on. Maybe you're fed up with editing configuration files instead of coding. You are looking for better ways to integrate the existing resources in your company, and you are looking for better ways to quickly create new and fancy applications based on all the wonderful stuff you already have.

Depending on the tools you've used to build your architecture, different choices are available for the integration process. If you're using message queues, you have a lot of freedom and flexibility for integrating your services and software with others. The same holds true for all kinds of web service protocols. It's slightly different with databases, because they usually do not offer interfaces as clean as message-based systems do. Sometimes you have to access tables directly, and sometimes you have to use a set of stored procedures written in a proprietary database programming language.

In this book we do not talk about sophisticated messaging patterns. Instead, we cover the basics. We show you how to use databases, web services, XML files, and all the other legacy stuff you want to combine for building new applications.

1.5 PragBouquet

To make things more interesting and tangible, we've founded an imaginary company called *PragBouquet*. It sells flowers from a web shop. Customers from all over the world can order flowers and send them to people living in the United States.

PragBouquet's business demands a lot of components and services. It depends on several partners, too. Their current infrastructure is shown in Figure 1.1, on the following page. Customers place orders in the web shop. The shop communicates with the central order system. Because

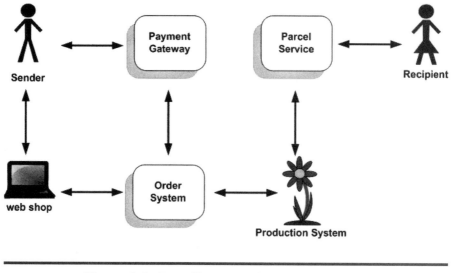

Figure 1.1: PRAGBOUQUET INFRASTRUCTURE

PragBouquet has no billing system, the order system uses an external payment gateway to charge orders. In parallel, the production system is informed of new orders, and busy florists create wonderful bunches of flowers. Eventually, the floral goods are picked up by a parcel service and are delivered to the happy recipient.

This is only a rough overview. We'll show single components in more detail when necessary.

1.6 Acknowledgments

First, I'd like to thank Dave Thomas and Andy Hunt for giving me the opportunity to write this book for the Pragmatic Bookshelf. Working with them has been both an honor and a pleasure. I couldn't imagine better or more professional working conditions.

It would be impossible to write a book about software for enterprise integration without the software itself. The following gentlemen kindly made their ingenious work public for free and have always responded quickly and accurately to all my questions: Yukihiro "Matz" Matsumoto, Will Drewry, arton (the author of Rjb), Sean Russel, Ian Macdonald, Takaaki Tateishi, Thomas Uehlinger, Jim Weirich, Nikolai Lugovoi, Matt Mower, Daniel Berger, *why the lucky stiff*, Minero Aoki, Michael Neumann, Kubo Takehiro, Tomita Masahiro, David Heinemeier Hansson, Hiroshi Nakamura, John W. Small, Takahashi Masayoshi, Gotou Yuuzou, Yoshida Masato, and Grant McLean.

Please join me in thanking my reviewers: Frank Tewissen, Matthias "Matze" Klame, Uwe Simon, and Kaan Karaca did an awesome job! Without their corrections and suggestions this book wouldn't be half as good.

A loud "Thank you very much!!!" goes to all the people who sent errata and suggestions during the beta book process: Lee Grey, Hoang Uong, Ola Bini, Ron Lusk, John Athayde, Blair Zajac, Jim Weirich, Pat Podenski, Gregory Brown, Lachlan Dowding, Sean, Eldon, Henry Chiu, Stuart Halloway, Raymond Brigleb, Ken Barker, Peter Morelli, Eric-Olivier Lamey, Jim Kimball, Wilson Bilkovich, John Douthat, Remco van 't Veer, Mark Mayo, Joe Duhamel, Carl Graf, Adam Keys, Manirith Nuth, Andres Paglayan, Dána Watanabe, Mike Stok, Eric Kramer, and Urban Hafner.

Perhaps there are authors who write books in isolation under a rock or on a lonesome island. Fortunately, I didn't, and I got invaluable support from a lot of wonderful people. I am deeply grateful to my parents (this one is for you); my sister, Yvonne Janka (yet another book you won't read?); my brother, André Schmidt (for relaxing shopping/running tours and even more relaxing evenings with "the boys"); Christian and Agnieszka Rattat (for being true friends when I needed them most); Frank Tewissen (for listening patiently and for advising carefully); Manu (for being "die Manu"! Heja BVB!); AleX Reinartz (I'm looking forward to the next decades); Bettina Hamidian and Corinna Lorscheid (for insightful talks and lots of fun); Katja Wevelsiep (let's have a coffee tomorrow, OK?); Frank Möcke (for giving me the opportunity to publish texts in my mother tongue); Dr. Andreas Kötz (for your appreciation); and the "gleis drei" staff (for providing a perfect proofreading environment).

Mia: I promise to write until I finally learn to clearly express how exciting and wonderful the last months have been.

Chapter 2

Databases

Database management systems are one of the oldest and most widely used applications in information technology—they are indispensable to enterprises. It's nearly impossible to do some serious enterprise integration without touching some kind of database directly or indirectly. Various types exist (relational databases, object-oriented databases, directory services, XML databases, and hash databases such as Berkeley DB). They differ mainly in the way data is organized and accessed internally. Under the hood, though, they are all similar: data is stored in some kind of file system and is accessed through a special layer, often over a network. You can find one or more of the different types in every company, but relational databases are by far the most popular ones in use today.

Although it's often tedious, repetitive, and error-prone work, accessing databases is, in principle, easy. You open a connection, create and execute some statements, read and process some data, and finally free all resources occupied. At least, that's how the Gods Of Persistence wanted it to be. But real life in our sinful world looks different. Information and business logic are often spread across different schemas and databases. To make things even worse, many companies use products from multiple vendors. This happens for various reasons: they want to prevent vendor lock-in, the company is the product of a corporate merger, different departments prefer different tools, and so on.

Unfortunately, PragBouquet is no exception. Its data is stored in both Oracle and MySQL databases. In this chapter we will show you not only how to directly manipulate different types of databases but also how to access them using more advanced tools such as object-relational mappers and database abstraction layers.

2.1 The Coupon Application

PragBouquet's business has been doing well, but business can always be better, can't it? To boost sales, the marketing department wants to send a coupon to every customer who has used the online store but hasn't used it in the last six months. People who asked not to receive e-mail from us should not get an e-mail.

That does not sound too difficult. PragBouquet already has a mass-mailing program that expects a CSV (Comma-Separated Values) file containing e-mail addresses, customer names, and text to be sent. The problem becomes selecting names and e-mail addresses of all customers who did not place an order in the last six months, filtering out those who do not want to be e-mailed, and writing the rest to the CSV file.

Instantly you've fired up your favorite text editor thinking that this is a great opportunity to strengthen your Ruby skills. Creating CSV files is a breeze, and selecting some data sets from a database should not be a problem either. So you ask your database administrator where you can

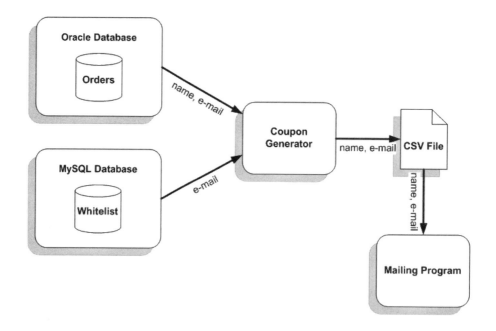

Figure 2.1: COUPON APPLICATION WORKFLOW

find the information you need, and he takes you down a peg or two. He tells you that for historical reasons (a euphemism for "Nobody knows why") the information you need is spread across two databases. Customer data and order data are stored in an Oracle database, but the white list containing the e-mail addresses of all customers who want to receive e-mail from PragBouquet is stored in the web shop's MySQL database. You scribble a bit on your notepad and realize that the system architecture has to look like Figure 2.1, on the preceding page.

Exploring the Environment

You decide to start with the Oracle part. Before moving on, you want to take a closer look at the structure of the order database. Your database administrator told you that the relevant tables are called customers and orders. He gave you plenty of Microsoft Word documents describing every single table in the order database. Despite this you look at the current state of affairs yourself using SQL*Plus, Oracle's SQL shell:

```
C:\> sqlplus scott

SQL*Plus: Release 9.2.0.1.0 - Production on Sat Jun 4 16:00:04 2005

Copyright (c) 1982, 2002, Oracle Corporation.  All rights reserved.

Enter password:

Connected to:
Personal Oracle9i Release 9.2.0.1.0 - Production
With the Partitioning, OLAP and Oracle Data Mining options
JServer Release 9.2.0.1.0 - Production

SQL> describe customers
 Name                                      Null?    Type
 ----------------------------------------- -------- -------------------
 ID                                        NOT NULL NUMBER(38)
 NAME                                      NOT NULL VARCHAR2(64)
 SURNAME                                   NOT NULL VARCHAR2(128)
 STREET                                    NOT NULL VARCHAR2(128)
 HOUSE_NUMBER                              NOT NULL VARCHAR2(10)
 POSTAL_CODE                               NOT NULL VARCHAR2(10)
 CITY                                      NOT NULL VARCHAR2(128)
 STATE                                              VARCHAR2(20)
 COUNTRY_CODE                              NOT NULL VARCHAR2(2)
 EMAIL                                     NOT NULL VARCHAR2(128)
 CREATED                                            DATE
```

> ### Why Didn't We Use a Standard Product?
>
> You might be asking yourself whether it's a good idea for PragBouquet to have created its own customer and order database. Wouldn't it be much easier to buy a solution off the shelf? Customer data is at the core of every enterprise, and many processes rely upon it. It's needed for billing, for statistics, for troubleshooting, and so on. Although many big companies offer software for customer relationship management, it's never a bad idea to think about building your own customer database. No product will fit your needs better than your own, and no product will ever be as flexible as yours.

```
SQL> describe orders
Name                                       Null?    Type
----------------------------------------- -------- -------------------
ID                                        NOT NULL NUMBER(38)
CUSTOMER_ID                               NOT NULL NUMBER(38)
STATE                                     NOT NULL NUMBER(38)
CREATED                                            TIMESTAMP(6)
```

No big surprises here. Obviously, customers are characterized mainly by their address data, and we guess that the tables are connected using column customer_id in table orders.

Determine the Winners

If we're going to use a Ruby program to extract information from an Oracle database, we'll need a library that connects our code to the underlying Oracle API. There are currently three different Ruby modules for Oracle:

- *Oracle* by Yoshida Masato[1]

- *Ruby/OCI8* by Kubo Takehiro[2]

- *Ruby9i* by Jim Kain[3]

The main difference between these libraries is their support (or lack thereof) for new data types. Gone are the days when you could store

---

[1] http://raa.ruby-lang.org/project/oracle
[2] http://rubyforge.org/projects/ruby-oci8
[3] http://rubyforge.org/projects/ruby9i

Storing Addresses—A Plea from the Rest of the World

Even though addresses are critical for many purposes, their data representation is often performed carelessly and without foresight. In particular, aspects of internationalization are often forgotten, because designers and developers normally do not know a lot about the administrative characteristics of their neighbors.

For example, Germany is a federal country divided into 16 states, but to the Germans the different states do not mean a lot. They aren't part of an address, they do not occur on envelopes, and you do not have to put them into a web form when ordering something from an Internet shop. It's not surprising that German customers get annoyed by web forms insisting on a state. When working in an international environment, it's better to make the state optional.

There is no international standard for the representation of an address. In Germany, for example, a street address is the street name followed by a blank followed by the house number. In Italy, there's a comma between the street name and the house number. Other countries put the number before the name.

It's nearly impossible to automatically separate street names and house numbers afterward, because house numbers can contain nearly arbitrary characters.

Another aspect of addresses that is forgotten surprisingly often in this context is that addresses represent geographical objects. Geographical objects have coordinates, locations that are becoming increasingly important as we move into a world using location-based services. If you want to offer location-based services to your customers some day, you'll have to determine the geographical position of their addresses. For many cities it's possible to locate an object down to the individual house number.

Please, don't misunderstand me: you should not try to come up with a solution that will work with every possible address format in the world (I think that would probably be impossible), but you should at least take a closer look at the countries you're potentially working in.

only small strings and numbers in your database. Nowadays you can store complete books or MP3 files in CLOB (*Character Large Object*) or BLOB (*Binary Large Object*) columns. Major versions of the *Oracle Call Interface* (OCI) also differ in other areas, such as security and performance.

Character Large Object

Binary Large Object

Oracle Call Interface

In this book we'll use Kubo Takehiro's Ruby/OCI8 driver—it's actively maintained, it runs on many platforms, and it provides a lot of functionality. It comes in two flavors: a low-level and a high-level API. The low-level API directly reflects the Oracle C library, and we won't show its usage, because the high-level API is probably more convenient to use.

Let's dive into Ruby now and see how we can identify the customers who should get a coupon:

File 16

```
Line 1    require 'oci8'
  -
  -       connection = OCI8.new('maik', 'maik')
  -       cursor = connection.exec(<<-SQL)
  5       select  a.id, a.name, a.surname, a.email
  -       from    customers a, orders b
  -       where   a.id = b.customer_id
  -       and     b.created < sysdate - 180
  -       and     b.created = (
 10         select  max(created)
  -         from    orders
  -         where   customer_id = a.id
  -       )
  -       SQL
 15
  -       while row = cursor.fetch do
  -         puts row[3]
  -       end
  -
 20       cursor.close
  -       connection.logoff
```

This code produces something like this:

```
homer@example.com
seymour@example.com
```

Here we have a typical example of accessing a database. It would look similar in every modern programming language. First we establish a database connection by calling the new() method of class OCI8 (connect() would have been a much better name, but for the moment we have to live with it). The new() method returns a connection object that can be used to communicate with the database server and to create other database objects, such as statements and cursors.

The SQL statement joins the tables customers and orders and returns only those customers whose last order is older than 180 days. The sub-select identifies the most current entry for each customer and makes sure that every customer is returned only once.

As you can see, SQL statements can be executed directly by calling the exec() method of an OCI8 connection. For SELECT statements, exec() returns a so-called cursor representing a result set on the database server. Clients can move through a result set by calling fetch() on the cursor object. After the last row has been read from the cursor, fetch() returns nil.

Finally, we close our cursor to free valuable resources on the database server. Cursors are resources like file handles and are in limited supply. If you're a bad citizen and fail to free these resources, Oracle will raise an exception sooner or later.

Admittedly, our example is concise and expressive, but using Ruby's iterators automatically leads you to a more elegant solution with less explicit resource management:

ile 17

```
Line 1    require 'oci8'
    -
    -     connection = OCI8.new('maik', 'maik')
    -     sql = <<-SQL
    5     select a.id, a.name, a.surname, a.email
    -     from    customers a, orders b
    -     where   a.id = b.customer_id
    -     and     b.created < sysdate - 180
    -     and     b.created = (
   10       select max(created)
    -        from    orders
    -        where   customer_id = a.id
    -     )
    -     SQL
   15
    -
    -     num_customers = connection.exec(sql) do |row|
    -       puts row[3]
    -     end
   20
    -
    -     puts "Found #{num_customers} coupon recipients."
    -     connection.logoff
```

This code produces the following:

```
homer@example.com
seymour@example.com
Found 2 coupon recipients.
```

When exec() is called as an iterator—with a code block—it returns the number of rows selected. The code block automatically gets each row fetched as a parameter, and you no longer have to close the cursor explicitly. Actually, you don't even notice that you're working with a cursor.

Enhancing Flexibility

OK, our first example works. We know where to get the data from and we know how to get it, so let's turn our little script into software. Now we have to replace the constant 180 days with something more dynamic. To do this, we could create the string containing the SQL statement on the fly, substituting in the time value, but this approach has some serious drawbacks.

As we already know, the SQL statement gets transferred over the network to the database server whenever we call exec(). Then it gets parsed, analyzed, optimized, and executed, and eventually the result is sent back to the client.

query execution plan Actually, modern database servers try to optimize a lot. Part of this process is the creation of a *query execution plan* for every statement they receive. Current Oracle versions even try to compress the result sets before sending them back to the client to decrease bandwidth and processing time. For SQL statements that are executed often, this means we could gain a lot if the statement could be parsed, analyzed, and optimized only once.

Furthermore, building SQL statements on the fly often creates dangerous security holes. What if someone uses a web form to pass us the following string for the number of days?

```
'180; delete from customers; commit;'
```

In the worst case, the database server will happily execute the malicious statement, giving you an excellent opportunity to check whether your backup system is working properly. This common kind of attack is *SQL injection* called *SQL injection*.

prepared statements Fortunately, it is possible to circumvent all these disadvantages by using *prepared statements*. We transmit a statement template to the server, where it is parsed, analyzed, and optimized. The server then sends back a statement handle. All the dynamic portions of our statement are replaced by placeholders. Whenever we want to execute our statement, we send the server only the handle and the actual values for our placeholders:

```
require 'oci8'

Customer = Struct.new(:id, :name, :surname, :email)

class CustomerFinder
  def initialize(connection)
    @find_stmt = connection.parse(<<-SQL)
    select a.id, a.name, a.surname, a.email
    from    customers a, orders b
    where   a.id = b.customer_id
    and     b.created < sysdate - :days
    and     b.created = (
      select max(created)
      from    orders
      where   customer_id = a.id
    )
    SQL
  end

  def find(days)
    @find_stmt.bind_param(':days', days)
    @find_stmt.exec
    customers = []
    while row = @find_stmt.fetch do
      customers << Customer.new(*row)
    end
    customers
  end
end
```

First of all, we have inserted a placeholder (:days) into the SELECT statement. Second of all, we have created a prepared statement by calling parse(sql) on our connection. This method returns a handle identifying our statement on the server.

Calling bind_param() in line 17 binds the :days placeholder to its actual value, and in the following line we finally execute the SELECT statement, to which @find_stmt is referring. The rest is business as usual. Using the CustomerFinder looks like this:

```
ora_connection = OCI8.new('maik', 'maik')
finder = CustomerFinder.new(ora_connection)
customers = finder.find(180)
customers.each { |c| puts c.email }
ora_connection.logoff
```

Respecting Customer Privacy

So far, so good. We can create a list of all customers who should potentially get a coupon, but we still have to sort out those who do not want
to receive e-mails from PragBouquet. As we've already learned, this
information is stored in the web shop's MySQL database. There we can
find a table called whitelist containing a list of all e-mail addresses that
we are allowed to use.

MySQL, created by Monty Widenius, is one of the most popular open
source databases at the moment. It started as a thin wrapper for the
mSQL database and has grown over the years into a full-blown transactional database management system. MySQL support in Ruby was
made possible by the great work of Tomita Masahiro. He has developed
both a C library binding called MySQL/Ruby[4] and a pure Ruby binding called Ruby/MySQL.[5] Thanks to a patch written by Matt Mower,
Ruby/MySQL now also works with MySQL version 4.1.1 and later.[6]

In this book we'll use the pure Ruby implementation (for no special
reason). As with our order database we first examine the webshop
database using the MySQL shell:

```
C:\>mysql webshop
Welcome to the MySQL monitor.  Commands end with ; or \g.
Your MySQL connection id is 3 to server version: 4.0.22-nt

Type 'help;' or '\h' for help. Type '\c' to clear the buffer.

mysql> describe whitelist;
+---------+------------------+------+-----+---------+-------+
| Field   | Type             | Null | Key | Default | Extra |
+---------+------------------+------+-----+---------+-------+
| id      | int(10) unsigned |      | PRI | 0       |       |
| email   | varchar(255)     |      | UNI |         |       |
| created | timestamp(14)    | YES  |     | NULL    |       |
+---------+------------------+------+-----+---------+-------+
3 rows in set (0.16 sec)

mysql>
```

As a first exercise we try to connect to the MySQL server and print the
whole whitelist.

---

[4]http://tmtm.org/en/mysql/ruby/README.html
[5]http://tmtm.org/en/ruby/mysql/README_en.html
[6]This patch is part of Rails' ActiveRecord module. See http://lists.rubyonrails.
org/pipermail/rails-core/2005-November/000195.html if you want to install the
patch separately.

```
Line 1   require 'mysql'
    -    connection = Mysql.new('localhost', '', '', 'webshop')
    -    whitelist = connection.query('select * from whitelist');
    -    whitelist.each_hash { |h| puts h['email'] }
    5    connection.close
```

This code produces something like this:

```
homer@example.com
info@example.net
...
c-m-burns@example.org
```

Here we have a textbook example of database use: create a connection, execute a query, print its result, and finally close the connection. What more could we say that hasn't already been expressed in the code? All right, we have some details for you. Calling the query(sql) method returns an object of class Mysql::Result that represents a complete result set. You can read the single rows of a result set using various methods—here we chose each_hash(). It returns a hash for every row where the column names are the hash keys with the data as the corresponding values.

Printing the whole whitelist was not exactly what we wanted. Instead we have to check whether a certain e-mail address is contained in the whitelist. That means we have to execute a statement such as:

```
select count(*)
  from whitelist
 where email = 'email@example.com'
```

and see whether it returns 1. Obviously, the e-mail address in the where clause of our statement is variable, and from what we've learned in Section 2.1, *Enhancing Flexibility*, on page 16, you might assume it would be a good idea to use a prepared statement for this purpose. You are absolutely right: but unfortunately support for prepared statements in MySQL is a rather new feature. It was introduced in version 4.1, and the current Ruby drivers do not support it:

```
Line 1   require 'mysql'
    -    class Whitelist
    -      def initialize(connection) @connection = connection; end
    -      def contains?(email)
    5        sql = "select * from whitelist where email = '#{email}'"
    -        result = @connection.query(sql)
    -        result.num_rows == 1
    -      end
    -    end
```

Obviously, num_rows() returns the number of rows in a result set (which is what we wanted to determine). In use, our Whitelist class looks as follows:

File 22

```
Line 1   connection = Mysql.new('localhost', '', '', 'webshop')
  -      whitelist = Whitelist.new(connection)
  -      puts whitelist.contains?('homer@example.com')
  -      puts whitelist.contains?('unknown_address')
  5      connection.close
```

This code produces the following:

```
true
false
```

We've created our SQL statement using strings. Does it make you feel comfortable? Although the coupon application is an internal project, the e-mail addresses come from an external source, so you should never trust them. In addition, it's really wasteful to execute a SQL statement for every single e-mail address. So, we will trade some space for time and read all e-mail addresses into a hash initially.

File 21

```
Line 1   require 'mysql'
  -
  -      class Whitelist
  -        def initialize(connection)
  5          @whitelist = {}
  -          result = connection.query('select email from whitelist');
  -          result.each_hash { |h| @whitelist[h['email']] = true }
  -        end
  -
  10       def contains?(email)
  -          @whitelist.has_key?(email)
  -        end
  -      end
```

That's a really good compromise. Even if we have to read several thousand e-mail addresses into memory, it's still a low price for the performance and security we get.

Joining Forces

We have everything available now to create the list of our lucky coupon recipients: we can read all potential customers from the Oracle order database and can look them up on the white list stored in the MySQL webshop database. Because the mailing program expects data as CSV (comma-separated values), we reopen the Customer class and add an appropriate method (see Section 3.5, *Comma-Separated Values (CSV)*, on page 135, to learn more about Ruby's CSV library):

File 15
```
require 'csv'
class Customer
  def to_csv(del = ',')
    str = ''
    CSV::Writer.generate(str, del) do |csv|
      csv << [name, surname, email]
    end
    str
  end
end
```

The following program then prints CSV data to the console so it can be easily redirected to the mass-mailing program:

File 13
```
Line 1   require 'cusfinder'
    -    require 'whitelist'
    -
    -    # Read all potential customers
    5    ora_connection = OCI8.new('maik', 'maik')
    -    finder = CustomerFinder.new(ora_connection)
    -    customers = finder.find(180)
    -    ora_connection.logoff
    -
   10    # Sort out customers not in whitelist
    -    mysql_connection = Mysql.new('localhost', '', '', 'webshop')
    -    whitelist = Whitelist.new(mysql_connection)
    -
    -    customers.each do |c|
   15      puts c.to_csv if whitelist.contains?(c.email)
    -    end
    -    mysql_connection.close
```

This code produces the following:

```
Homer,Simpson,homer@example.com
Barney,Gumble,barney_gumble@example.org
...
Ned,Flanders,nflanders@example.net
```

That's it. We could happily move to the next project. But wouldn't it be interesting to know how many customers actually convert their coupon? To do this, we have to store at least the customer IDs of all coupon recipients somewhere. Let's put them into the order database in a new table called coupon_recipients. This will let us check how many of the customers on this list placed an order after the coupon mailing.

File 20
```
create table coupon_recipients (
  customer_id int not null,
  created timestamp default sysdate
);
```

For the first time in this chapter we're going to write data into the
database. It's nearly the same as reading information, but there are
a few subtleties we have to take care of:

File 19 Line 1
```ruby
require 'oci8'

class Recipient
  def initialize(connection)
    sql = 'insert into coupon_recipients (customer_id) values(:1)'
    @insert_rec = connection.parse(sql)
  end

  def create(customer)
    @insert_rec.bind_param(1, customer.id)
    @insert_rec.exec
  end
end
```

Here, we've used another form of bind variable, numbering them rather
than naming them explicitly. It's more or less a matter of taste whether
you bind parameters by name or by number, but you have to be consistent. If you've used numbers as placeholders for the parameters in
the SQL statement, you have to bind them by number later. That's
especially important for output parameters:

File 41 Line 1
```ruby
connection = OCI8.new('maik', 'maik')
cursor = connection.parse("begin :now := sysdate; end;")
cursor.bind_param(':now', Time.mktime(1972, 9, 30), Date)
puts cursor[':now']
puts cursor[1]
cursor.exec
puts cursor[':now']
puts cursor[1]
cursor.close
connection.logoff
```

At the time of this writing, this produces:

```
1972-09-30
nil
2005-04-03
nil
```

There's something even more critical hidden in our Recipient class:

File 19 Line 1
```ruby
require 'cusfinder'
connection = OCI8.new('maik', 'maik')
connection.autocommit = true
recipients = Recipient.new(connection)
customer = Customer.new(1, 'Selma', 'Bouvier', 'selma@example.com')
recipients.create(customer)
connection.logoff
```

See that we've enabled the *autocommit* feature of the connection object *autocommit*
on line 3. This makes sure that every SQL statement gets committed
immediately, saving any changes to the database when the statement
is executed. That's what we'd normally expect to happen.

Oracle is a transactional database—you can group several SQL statements as if they were one. If any of the statements fail, all the statements will be ignored—the database content will not be changed. The
current transaction can be committed by executing the COMMIT command, or it can be rolled back by calling ROLLBACK. Setting autocommit
to **true** is like calling COMMIT after every single SQL statement. Without
it, nothing would ever get written to the database. You wouldn't even
notice it, because from the database's point of view it's not an error.

Our final version of the coupon application differs only slightly from our
original approach:

File 14

```
Line 1   require 'cusfinder'
   -     require 'whitelist'
   -     require 'recipient'
   -
   5     # Read all potential customers
   -     ora_connection = OCI8.new('maik', 'maik')
   -     ora_connection.autocommit = true
   -     recipients = Recipient.new(ora_connection)
   -     finder = CustomerFinder.new(ora_connection)
   10    customers = finder.find(180)
   -
   -     # Sort out customers not in whitelist
   -     mysql_connection = Mysql.new('localhost', '', '', 'webshop')
   -     whitelist = Whitelist.new(mysql_connection)
   15
   -     customers.each do |c|
   -       if whitelist.contains?(c.email)
   -         puts c.to_csv
   -         recipients.create(c)
   20      end
   -     end
   -
   -     ora_connection.logoff
   -     mysql_connection.close
```

The most important changes affect the Oracle connection object. We've
set its autocommit feature to true. We also defer closing the connection
until the end of the program, because it's needed during the whole
runtime.

The Fruits of Our Labor

Two weeks ago the coupons were sent to their lucky recipients. Today started like any other: you switched on your computer and went into the kitchen to get a (free) cup of coffee. As you came back to your desk to create yet more extraordinary code, one of the marketing guys was waiting for you. "You're the techie who sent out the coupons two weeks ago, aren't you?" he asks. Before you can say a word, he proceeds: "Although we worked several weeks on the functional specification of the coupon application, we somehow forgot to define some statistics requirements. Now we're afraid that we can't find out how successful our *marvelous* and *groundbreaking* coupon idea was. Is there any way you could create some statistics, anyhow?"

Mostly, you're surprised that something like a functional specification exists—it's the first you heard of it. But, when you recover, you remember the coupon_recipients table and open a SQL*Plus shell:

```
SQL> select count(*) from coupon_recipients;

  COUNT(*)
----------
      3145

SQL> select count(*) from orders where customer_id in ( \
  2    select customer_id from coupon_recipients \
  3  ) and created > sysdate - 14;

  COUNT(*)
----------
       917

SQL> select 917 * 100 / 3145 from dual;

917*100/3145
------------
  29.1573927

SQL>
```

Turning around to the marketing guy, you say, "29.16% of the coupon recipients placed an order during the last two weeks. Do you need anything else?" He is obviously impressed: "No, thank you very much! You did an awesome job, and I wouldn't be surprised if you get a corner office soon." You lean back and take a sip of your coffee. It's still hot.

Managing Database Resources

So far, our examples have been simple, and we didn't care about performance and optimization. But opening a new database connection is expensive and should not be performed unnecessarily. If you need only a single connection, databases can be represented as singleton objects. A singleton object is available everywhere in your program and can be created only once. Thanks to the Ruby standard library, it's a piece of cake to create a singleton encapsulating our OCI8 driver:

File 40

```ruby
require 'oci8'
require 'singleton'

class Database
  include Singleton

  attr_reader :connection

  def initialize
    @connection = nil
  end

  def connect(usr, pwd, dbname = nil)
    @connection = OCI8.new(usr, pwd, dbname)
    @connection.autocommit = true
    @connection
  end

  def disconnect
    if !@connection.nil?
      @connection.logoff
      @connection = nil
    end
  end
end
```

Class Database makes a connection to our database available wherever we need it, and we get access to the one and only instance by calling Database.instance(). At program start we have to call Database.instance.connect(usr,pwd) once, and from then on Database.instance.connection contains our connection.

2.2 Database Interface (DBI)

It's a bit annoying that the information we needed for our coupon application is spread across two databases—it might be a good idea to change this situation someday. Anticipating this change, it might be advantageous to make our application more independent of the underlying drivers. As we've seen in the previous sections, accessing databases using native drivers in principle differs only slightly from vendor to vendor: you have to obtain a connection, create or prepare statements, execute statements, and retrieve results eventually. Technically, though, there are many subtle (and sometimes not so subtle) differences. Countless attempts have been made to standardize this interface. For example, on the Microsoft Windows platform there is ODBC, OLE DB, and ADO.NET, to name just a few. Java has its JDBC, and dynamic languages such as Perl, Python, and Ruby use an approach called *DBI* (Database Interface).[7]

DBI

database abstraction layers

database driver

All *database abstraction layers* work in a similar fashion: they define an abstract interface to the database, and a concrete implementation, called a *database driver*, for each specific database. For the Ruby DBI library, these drivers are known as DBD modules.[8] These drivers are accessed by your program through a standard interface,[9] so you don't have to remember whether the method to get a new connection was called new(), connect(), create_connection(), or whatever. In DBI it's called connect(driver_url, user=nil, auth=nil, params=nil) for every database, and it always expects the same parameters in the same order.

Compared to other database abstraction layers, DBI is extremely simple. To use it you have to know only two classes, DatabaseHandle and StatementHandle. A database handle represents a connection to the database, while a statement handle represents an active SQL statement. To examine whether we can benefit from using DBI in our Prag-Bouquet application, we'll change the Whitelist class to use it:

File 24

```
Line 1  require 'dbi'

        DBI.connect('DBI:Mysql:webshop', '', '') do |conn|
          conn.select_all('select * from whitelist') { |row| p row }
     5  end
```

---

[7]This list proves the old adage: the good thing about standards is that there are so many to choose from.

[8]http://ruby-dbi.rubyforge.org/DBD_SPEC.html

[9]http://ruby-dbi.rubyforge.org/DBI_SPEC.html

Because of the block syntax supported by the DBI methods, our demonstration program became extremely compact. In line 3, DBI.connect() returns a database handle that gets passed into the block. When the program reaches the end of the block, the connection is closed automatically. Within the block we call select_all(), which executes a SELECT statement and calls a code block for every row that was returned. Again, we do not have to care about resource management—the statement will be released at the end of the block. The only thing left to do is to integrate the code into the Whitelist class:

File 25

```
Line 1    require 'dbi'
    -     class Whitelist
    -       def initialize(connection)
    -         @whitelist = {}
    5         connection.select_all('select email from whitelist') do |row|
    -           @whitelist[row[0]] = true
    -         end
    -       end
    -       def contains?(email) @whitelist.has_key?(email); end
    10    end
```

We did not change the interface, and only the connection object has to be instantiated differently to use the Whitelist class:

File 25

```
Line 1    connection = DBI.connect('DBI:Mysql:webshop', '', '')
    -     whitelist = Whitelist.new(connection)
    -     puts whitelist.contains?('homer@example.com')
    -     connection.disconnect
```

Should we move the whitelist table from MySQL to our Oracle database, we only have to change the string "Mysql" to "Oracle", and the program will still work.

Encouraged by our success, we'll change the Oracle stuff in our CustomerFinder class to use DBI too:

File 23

```
Line 1    class CustomerFinder
    -       def initialize(connection)
    -         @find_stmt = connection.prepare(<<-SQL)

    5     select a.id, a.name, a.surname, a.email
    -     from    customers a, orders b
    -     where   a.id = b.customer_id
    -     and     b.created < sysdate - :days
    -     and     b.created = (
    10      select max(created)
    -         from    orders
    -         where   customer_id = a.id
    -       )
    -       SQL
    15    end
```

```
         def find(days)
           @find_stmt.bind_param(':days', days)
20         @find_stmt.execute
           customers = []
           while row = @find_stmt.fetch do
             customers << Customer.new(*row)
           end
25         customers
         end
       end
```

As with the previous example, we did not have to change a lot. Instead of calling parse() on our connection object in line 3, we have to call prepare() now. Similarly, exec() becomes execute() on line 18. We have to pass a DBI connection object now:

File 23

```
Line 1   connection = DBI.connect('DBI:Oracle', 'maik', 'maik')
         finder = CustomerFinder.new(connection)
         customers = finder.find(180)
         customers.each { |c| puts c.email }
5        connection.disconnect
```

Despite all this, the benefits of a database abstraction layer aren't as big as you might think. It's convenient to work with DBI when you have to access a database product that you haven't worked with before, but you shouldn't assume that you can easily replace your existing database with a completely different one only because you're using an abstraction layer. Moving from one database to another is one of the most complicated feats in developing enterprise software.

Because there are so many proprietary additions to SQL in every vendor's implementation, writing portable statements is nearly impossible. Often such statements look quite harmless. For example, look at the statement starting on line 3 in our CustomerFinder class. It contains at least three potential problems:

- Not all databases support subselects.

- sysdate is specific to Oracle. In MySQL you'd have to use now(), and in DB2 it'd be current timestamp.

- The syntax of arithmetic expressions for dates (such as sysdate-180) differs from vendor to vendor.

Sometimes the problems aren't directly related to a SQL statement but are caused by some side effects like autogenerated identifiers that are not available in every database. To support such database-specific functions, the drivers used by DBI allow for some extensions, but if you want to write portable software, it's certainly not a good idea to use them. For example, to read the last autogenerated identifier from a MySQL database, you call the last_insert_id() method. This method is not available for Oracle databases, and it's not easy to simulate the autogeneration feature in Oracle.

A last problem with DBI could be performance: the extra layers and the need to map features can decrease performance significantly. For example, accessing MySQL using the native driver is twice as fast as using the DBI layer.

There are much more important (and tricky) issues that might prevent you from easily changing your database. Consider, for example, C/C++ programs that contain *embedded SQL*. Even if you're lucky and have *embedded SQL* access to the source code of all programs running in your environment, it still will be a lot of work to adjust them all.

So, if you know up front that you have to support multiple databases, you can gain a lot by using an abstraction layer, but you have to plan for it carefully.

2.3 Object-Relational Mappers

A lot of people working in the software development department of Prag-Bouquet have been thinking about reorganizing the current database landscape for quite a long time. The design of many databases has become a bit messy over the years, and it's a big problem that logic and data are spread across Oracle and MySQL databases. To save license costs, all the Oracle databases should be migrated to a MySQL database in the future, and all new stuff should be implemented in the MySQL database right from the beginning.

The first feature that has to be added is an automatic management system for ordering flowers. Today flowers are ordered from a big wholesaler more or less manually by the buying department. The clerks get daily order reports, and they can see how many flowers are still in stock. Then they do some simple calculations using a spreadsheet application and place new orders accordingly. It's your task now to automate this process as far as possible; i.e., you have to create a database for the flowers in stock and to remove flowers from stock whenever a new bouquet leaves PragBouquet.

Generating Unique IDs

It's really strange: humankind is talking about going to Mars, but creating artificial primary keys in databases is still a problem in the 21st century, because there's no standard.

From a design point of view, there are a lot of advantages to creating an artificial unique (numeric) primary key for every table in the database, even if a natural primary key does exist. Numeric values need only a small amount of space and can be indexed efficiently.

Although there's a need for unique IDs in every database, all vendors come up with their own ideas and concepts to generate them. It's easy to generate them to be more or less portable by creating a table containing only two columns:

```
create table sequences (
  value int default 1 not null,
  table_name varchar(64)
);
```

To create a sequence for our customers table, we insert a new row into the sequences table:

```
insert into sequences (table_name) values ('customers');
```

Generating a new sequence value is straightforward then:

```
begin
  update sequences set id = id + 1
    where table_name = 'customers';
  select id from sequences
    where table_name = 'customers';
end;
```

Unfortunately, this solution is not particularly efficient, because it has to be executed in a transaction that can slow down things a bit. Oh, and did I mention that not all databases support transactions?

Whenever your program relies upon autogenerated identifiers, you should encapsulate this process carefully to prevent bad surprises when you have to migrate to another database.

Before opening your text editor, you take a day off to think about the new database structure, and after 24 hours of thinking, you finally had this revolutionary idea: you need a table that represents flowers:

File 4

```
Line 1   create table flowers(
    -        id int unsigned not null auto_increment primary key,
    -        name varchar(64) not null,
    -        price double not null
    5    );
```

That should be sufficient for a first version: flowers have a name, a price, and an artificial primary key that is created by the database automatically. The "only" step left to do is to map the flowers table to a Flower class and map all its columns to the according attributes.

You have read Martin Fowler's *Patterns of Enterprise Application Architecture* [Fow03], and you still remember his ActiveRecord pattern and its definition:

"An object that wraps a row in a database table or view encapsulates the database access and adds domain logic on that data."

Before creating an ActiveRecord class to map the flowers table, we'll encapsulate access to the MySQL database in a singleton:

File 6

```
Line 1   require 'dbi'
    -    require 'singleton'
    -
    -    class Database
    5      include Singleton
    -      attr_reader :connection
    -
    -      def initialize() @connection = nil; end
    -
    10     def connect(usr, pwd, db)
    -        @connection = DBI.connect("DBI:Mysql:#{db}", usr, pwd)
    -      end
    -
    -      def disconnect
    15       @connection.disconnect if !@connection.nil?
    -        @connection = nil
    -      end
    -    end
```

We used DBI both for convenience and because it allows us to simulate prepared statements even though MySQL may not support them. After calling Database.instance.connect() once, we can access the database connection calling Database.instance.connection() from anywhere in the code we want. So, let's use it to create new flowers:

```
File 6    Line 1    class Flower
             -        attr_reader :id
             -        attr_accessor :name, :price
             -
             5        def Flower.create(name, price)
             -          connection = Database.instance.connection
             -          @@create_flower ||= connection.prepare(<<-SQL)
             -          insert into flowers (name, price) values(?,?)
             -          SQL
            10          @@create_flower.execute(name, price)
             -          flower_id = connection.func(:insert_id)
             -          Flower.new(flower_id, name, price)
             -        end
             -
            15        def to_s
             -          "A #{@name} (#{@id}) costs $#{@price}."
             -        end
             -
             -        private
            20
             -        def initialize(id, name, price)
             -          @id, @name, @price = id, name, price
             -        end
             -      end
```

Nothing special happens here: in line 7 we prepare our SQL statement, and in line 10 we execute it (we prepared the statement only once and stored a reference to it in the class variable @@create_flower). Prepared statements are a new feature in MySQL. They are not in widespread use today, and are not supported by the current Ruby drivers. Despite this, it makes sense to use DBI's prepared statements, because they prevent SQL injection attacks by quoting the parts of a SQL statement that are substituted in from the outside.

In line 11 we find the primary key of the newly created row by asking MySQL for the last insert ID. We use the func(func_name) method of the DBI class, which allows us to access database-specific functions.

Virtually planting a rose looks like this:

```
File 6    Line 1    Database.instance.connect('', '', 'webshop')
             -      rose = Flower.create('rose', 1.99)
             -      puts rose
```

This code produces the following:

```
A rose (1) costs $1.99.
```

The first version of the Flower class allows for creating new objects by calling create(name,price). This method inserts a new row into the database, reads the ID that has been generated by MySQL, and returns a new Flower object. To make sure that no conflicts happen in the database because of duplicate id values, we have declared the initialize() method private. Hence, only methods of the Flower class are able to create new objects.

For the sake of completeness, we add the remaining methods needed to be fully *CRUD* compliant (CRUD stands for Create, Read, Update, and Delete): *CRUD*

File 6

```
Line 1    class Flower
   -        def Flower.find(name)
   -          connection = Database.instance.connection
   -          @@find_flower ||= connection.prepare(<<-SQL)
   5          select id, name, price from flowers where name = ?
   -          SQL
   -          @@find_flower.execute(name)
   -          flower = @@find_flower.fetch
   -          return nil if flower.nil?
  10          Flower.new(*flower)
   -        end
   -
   -        def update
   -          connection = Database.instance.connection
  15          @@update_flower ||= connection.prepare(<<-SQL)
   -          update flowers set name = ?, price = ? where id = ?
   -          SQL
   -          @@update_flower.execute(@name, @price, @id)
   -        end
  20
   -        def destroy
   -          connection = Database.instance.connection
   -          @@destroy_flower ||= connection.prepare(<<-SQL)
   -          delete from flowers where id = ?
  25          SQL
   -          @@destroy_flower.execute(@id)
   -        end
   -      end
```

Now we can retrieve, update, and delete Flower objects in the database:

File 6

```
Line 1    rose = Flower.find('rose')
   -      rose.price = 2.49
   -      rose.update
   -
   5      rose = Flower.find('rose')
   -      puts rose
   -      rose.destroy
   -      puts Flower.find('rose')
   -      Database.instance.disconnect
```

> ### Object-Relational Mappers for Ruby
>
> Because of its dynamic nature, Ruby is a perfect language for creating tools like object-relational mappers: you can easily create classes and methods on the fly, and determining the structure of a database is not a big problem with most database systems either.
>
> Unsurprisingly, several projects have been initiated to implement an object-relational mapper,* but ActiveRecord is by far the most popular and most advanced. It's much more than a simple mapper; it's fast, it supports nearly every database available, and it is constantly enhanced by a big community.
>
> ---
>
> *Kansas (http://raa.ruby-lang.org/project/kansas) and Og (http://www.nitrohq.com/view/Og) are interesting, for example.

This produces the following:

```
A rose (1) costs $2.49.
nil
```

It took less than an hour to create the ActiveRecord, and it works fine, but despite all this you still think that sometimes life isn't fair: all your friends are hanging around at the beach having fun, and you're writing tons of boring SQL statements only to read and save Flower objects. Enough is enough, and hence you decide to look for a tool that will do all this tedious stuff for you.

ActiveRecord Basics

ActiveRecord is an enhanced implementation of Martin Fowler's *ActiveRecord* object-relational mapping pattern.[10] ActiveRecord was created by David Heinemeier Hansson because he needed it for the famous Ruby on Rails project.[11] ActiveRecord now supports nearly every database system currently in use (MySQL, PostgreSQL, SQLite, Microsoft SQL Server, Oracle, and DB2).

Code always trumps prose, so instead of explaining academic persistence strategies, let's start by telling ActiveRecord to connect to our database:

---

[10]http://www.martinfowler.com/eaaCatalog/activeRecord.html
[11]http://www.rubyonrails.com

```
Line 1    require 'rubygems'
   -      require 'active_record'
   -
   -      ActiveRecord::Base.establish_connection(
   5        :adapter => 'mysql',
   -        :host => '127.0.0.1',
   -        :database => 'webshop'
   -      )
```

These statements load the ActiveRecord Gem (for more details about RubyGems see Section 6.4, *RubyGems*, on page 302), and then establish a connection to the webshop database running on localhost.

Now we have to map the flowers table to a Ruby class called Flower:

```
Line 1    class Flower < ActiveRecord::Base; end
```

That's it! All we had to do was derive our class from ActiveRecord::Base. Every instance of class Flower represents a single row of the flowers table.

ActiveRecord derives the name of the database table by taking the class name, turning it into lowercase, and pluralizing it. So, Flower becomes flowers, and PragmaticProgrammer becomes pragmatic_programmers. You can also set the table name explicitly, either because the built-in pluralization rules don't work for you or because you want to map to an existing table whose name doesn't meet ActiveRecord's expectations:

```
class LegacyTable < ActiveRecord::Base
  set_table_name 'xy12aj'
end
```

All Flower objects automatically have accessors for all the columns of the flowers table, so there'll be accessors named name() and price():

```
Line 1    flower = Flower.new
   -      flower.name = 'primrose'
   -      flower.price = 0.99
```

ActiveRecord stores all columns internally in a hash called attributes, but using this knowledge is dangerous, because it links us to ActiveRecord's implementation. Instead, we should access column values using just the attributes. For example, we could add a to_s() method to our class.

```
Line 1    class Flower < ActiveRecord::Base
   -        def to_s
   -          "A #{self.name} (#{self.id}) costs $#{self.price}."
   -        end
   5      end
```

In addition, ActiveRecord creates methods for reading, updating, and deleting rows in the database. To initialize the flowers table with some lovely plants, we can do the following:

File 5

```
Line 1    [
     -        ['rose', 1.10],
     -        ['violet', 0.40],
     -        ['sunflower', 0.40],
     5        ['clove', 0.65],
     -        ['lily', 0.80]
     -    ].each do |name, price|
     -        flower = Flower.new(:name => name, :price => price)
     -        flower.save
    10    end
```

The database will then contain the following rows:

```
mysql> select * from flowers;
+----+-----------+-------+
| id | name      | price |
+----+-----------+-------+
|  1 | rose      |   1.1 |
|  2 | violet    |   0.4 |
|  3 | sunflower |   0.4 |
|  4 | clove     |  0.65 |
|  5 | lily      |   0.8 |
+----+-----------+-------+
5 rows in set (0.00 sec)
```

It's important that every table that is mapped has an id column that gets filled automatically when a new row is created (the column name is id by default, but like the table name you can change it calling set_primary_key(column_name)).[12]

For reading *all* entities belonging to a particular class, we use Active-Record's find(*args) method and pass it the :all option:

File 5

```
Line 1    Flower.find(:all).each do |f|
     -        puts "A #{f.name} costs $#{f.price}."
     -    end
```

This gives us a list of all flowers:

```
A rose costs $1.1.
A violet costs $0.4.
A sunflower costs $0.4.
A clove costs $0.65.
A lily costs $0.8.
```

---

[12]Not all databases support columns that get incremented automatically. For details, see the documentation of the ActiveRecord adapter for your database system.

As well as defining methods that perform more fine-grained searches, ActiveRecord dynamically defines *finder methods* for each column and for all combinations of columns. This example finds a flower by its name:

File 5

```
Line 1   rose = Flower.find_by_name('rose')
```

The following statement:

File 5

```
Line 1   Flower.find_all_by_price(0.4).each { |f| puts f }
```

returns a list of flowers costing $0.40 each:

```
A sunflower (48) costs $0.4
A violet (47) costs $0.4
```

Finally, we can search for flowers having a particular name and price:

File 5

```
Line 1   clove = Flower.find_by_name_and_price('clove', 0.65)
```

All the find() methods we've used previously are created automatically— there is a method_missing() handler that turns your method calls into SQL statements.

If searching for columns having certain values is not sufficient, you can use another variant of find() that accepts a list of conditions as they may appear in the WHERE clause of a SELECT statement:

File 5

```
Line 1   cheap = Flower.find(:all, :conditions => ['price < 0.8'])
    -    cheap.each { |f| puts f }
```

This prints the following values:

```
A clove (49) costs $0.65
A sunflower (48) costs $0.4
A violet (47) costs $0.4
```

To prevent SQL injection attacks in the condition string, you can use a variant of the find() method that supports placeholders. The following code produces the same result as the previous example:

File 5

```
Line 1   cheap = Flower.find(:all, :conditions => ['price < ?', 0.8])
    -    cheap.each { |f| puts f }
```

You don't like sunflowers? Destroy 'em:

File 5

```
Line 1   sunflower = Flower.find_by_name('sunflower')
    -    sunflower.destroy
```

ActiveRecord gives us the CRUD methods (Create, Read, Update, and Delete) for free—this alone is a great benefit. But ActiveRecord does a lot more. In the next section we'll see how it helps us express the relationships between tables.

Cultivating Relationships with Flowers

Now that we have so many flowers, we should try to make some wonderful bouquets out of them. We'll need another table to represent them. Because we know that we will access it with ActiveRecord, we'll call it bouquets. Bouquets have a name and a base price (which covers wrapping paper, florist work, and so on):

File 4

```
create table bouquets(
    id int unsigned not null auto_increment primary key,
    name varchar(64) not null,
    base_price double not null
);
```

The relationship between bouquets and flowers is simple: bouquets have many flowers, and flowers may belong to several different bouquets. (Obviously what we mean here is that roses may appear in many bouquets, not that a particular rose is in many direct bouquets. The latter could lead to some interesting problems on Valentine's Day.) SQL pros call this a *many-to-many relationship*. To implement it, they usually introduce a *join table* (see Figure 2.2, on the next page), which maps rows from one table to the other, and vice versa:

many-to-many relationship

join table

File 4

```
create table bouquets_flowers(
    bouquet_id int not null,
    flower_id int not null
);
alter table bouquets_flowers add constraint fk1_bouquet
  foreign key (bouquet_id) references bouquets(id);
alter table bouquets_flowers add constraint fk2_flower
  foreign key (flower_id) references flowers(id);
```

The table name is no coincidence. We want to implement the relationship between the bouquets table and the flowers table. By default, ActiveRecord searches for a table that is named after the tables to be joined. Concatenate the table names in lexical order and separate them by an underscore, and you have the name of your join table. In addition, the join columns follow a naming scheme, too. You have to append _id; to the class name in lowercase letters (camel case is turned into underscores).

When you adhere to the naming rules, ActiveRecord makes it easy to express the relationship between flowers and bouquets using special macros:

File 7

```
class Bouquet < ActiveRecord::Base
  has_and_belongs_to_many :flowers
end
```

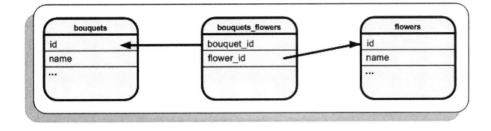

Figure 2.2: Join Table for Bouquets and Flowers

```
class Flower < ActiveRecord::Base
  has_and_belongs_to_many :bouquets
end
```

Many-to-many relationships are symmetrical, so we have to use the has_and_belongs_to_many() macro in both the Flower and Bouquet classes.

The following code snippet creates a new bouquet and stores it in the database:

```
Line 1   rose = Flower.find_by_name('rose')
   -     bouquet = Bouquet.new
   -     bouquet.name = 'Red Dream'
   -     bouquet.base_price = 2.49;
   5     bouquet.save
   -     6.times { bouquet.flowers << rose }
   -     bouquet.flowers << Flower.find_by_name('sunflower')
```

In line 6, we add six roses to our bouquet. In the following line we add a single sunflower. The flowers member of the Bouquet class was created automatically after we called has_and_belongs_to_many(). It acts as an array, except that whenever we add a flower to it, it creates a new entry in the join table.

After storing the bouquet, the database content looks as follows:

```
mysql> select * from flowers where name in ('rose', 'sunflower');
+----+-----------+-------+
| id | name      | price |
+----+-----------+-------+
|  1 | rose      |   1.1 |
|  3 | sunflower |   0.4 |
+----+-----------+-------+
2 rows in set (0.02 sec)
```

File 7

```
mysql> select * from bouquets;
+----+-----------+------------+
| id | name      | base_price |
+----+-----------+------------+
|  1 | Red Dream |       2.49 |
+----+-----------+------------+
1 row in set (0.00 sec)

mysql> select * from bouquets_flowers;
+------------+-----------+
| bouquet_id | flower_id |
+------------+-----------+
|          1 |         1 |
|          1 |         1 |
|          1 |         1 |
|          1 |         1 |
|          1 |         1 |
|          1 |         1 |
|          1 |         3 |
+------------+-----------+
7 rows in set (0.00 sec)
```

As expected, the bouquets_flowers table contains seven rows describing the content of the "Red Dream" bouquet. Six of them refer to the rose entry in the flowers table, and one refers to the sunflower. To read all components with SQL we'd need a select statement with a join clause. ActiveRecord does this dirty work transparently:

File 7

```
b = Bouquet.find_by_name('Red Dream')
puts "'#{b.name}' contains #{b.flowers.size} flowers:"
b.flowers.each { |f| puts f.name }
```

These statements disassemble our bunch of flowers:

```
'Red Dream' contains 7 flowers:
sunflower
rose
rose
rose
rose
rose
rose
```

This is nice and easy, but it's also a bit messy. Instead of storing every rose in a single row, it would be better to store the information that there are six roses in this bouquet. To do this, we'll add another piece of information to the relationship between flowers and bouquets:

File 1

```
alter table bouquets_flowers add (quantity int not null);
```

The join table bouquets_flowers now also stores the quantity of a particular flower that belongs to a bouquet. To populate this column, we use the push_with_attributes() method:

File 8

```
Line 1   rose = Flower.find_by_name('rose')
   -     sunflower = Flower.find_by_name('sunflower')
   -     bouquet = Bouquet.new
   -     bouquet.name = 'Honeybunch'
   5     bouquet.base_price = 1.37;
   -     bouquet.save
   -     bouquet.flowers.push_with_attributes(rose, :quantity => 1)
   -     bouquet.flowers.push_with_attributes(sunflower, :quantity => 6)
```

We can read the information back from the database (remember, we're still working with a database):

File 8

```
Line 1   b = Bouquet.find_by_name('Honeybunch')
   -     puts "'#{b.name}' contains #{b.flowers.size} different flowers:"
   -     b.flowers.each { |f| puts "#{f.name} (#{f.quantity})" }
```

This prints a compact recipe for the "Honeybunch" bouquet:

```
'Honeybunch' contains 2 different flowers:
sunflower (6)
rose (1)
```

The join table looks like this:

```
mysql> select * from bouquets_flowers;
+------------+-----------+----------+
| bouquet_id | flower_id | quantity |
+------------+-----------+----------+
|          2 |         3 |        6 |
|          2 |         1 |        1 |
+------------+-----------+----------+
2 rows in set (0.00 sec)
```

It's easy to add more logic to our domain classes, such as a method that calculates the price of a bouquet:

File 8

```
Line 1   class Bouquet
   -       def price
   -         flowers.inject(self.base_price) { |total, f|
   -           total += f.price * f.quantity.to_i
   5         }
   -       end
   -     end
   -     b = Bouquet.find_by_name('Honeybunch')
   -     puts "'#{b.name}' costs $#{b.price}."
```

For our "Honeybunch" bouquet, the following prints:

```
'Honeybunch' costs $4.87.
```

Let's summarize what we've done so far: we created three database tables that represent flowers, bouquets, and their many-to-many relationship. The table names and the names of their columns conformed to a fairly natural convention, one that you may have used anyway. To map them to a Ruby class hierarchy that lets us manipulate them in every imaginable way, we needed six lines of code:

File 8

```
Line 1    class Bouquet < ActiveRecord::Base
   -        has_and_belongs_to_many :flowers
   -      end

   5      class Flower < ActiveRecord::Base
   -        has_and_belongs_to_many :bouquets
   -      end
```

What Do We Have in Stock?

We shouldn't forget that we originally wanted to automate the ordering process for flowers. We still have to implement the concept of stock:

File 4

```
create table stock_items(
    id int unsigned not null auto_increment primary key,
    quantity int not null
);
```

Each row of the stock_items table represents the quantity of a particular flower that we currently have in stock—there is a stock item for every *one-to-one relationship* flower, and vice versa.[13] This is a classic *one-to-one relationship*, which can be modeled in the database like this:

File 2

```
alter table flowers add (stock_item_id int not null);
alter table flowers add constraint fk1_flowers
    foreign key (stock_item_id) references stock_items(id);
```

Here's the Ruby model:

File 11

```
Line 1    class Bouquet < ActiveRecord::Base
   -        has_and_belongs_to_many :flowers
   -      end
   -      class Flower < ActiveRecord::Base
   5        has_and_belongs_to_many :bouquets
   -        belongs_to :stock_item
   -      end
   -      class StockItem < ActiveRecord::Base
   -        has_one :flower
  10      end
```

---

[13]We could have added the quantity column to the flowers table, but in the future we will stock more than flowers.

It reads a bit like the notes you typically scribble on a piece of paper when thinking about a new database, doesn't it? Despite that, it's actual code that runs. In line 6 we declare that every flower belongs in stock, and line 9 makes every stock item a flower.

Like has_and_belongs_to_many(), the has_one() and belongs_to() macros automatically create some methods for the classes that use them. Let's fill our stock with some flowers:

File 11

```
Line 1    [
    -        ['rose', 1.10, 1000],
    -        ['violet', 0.40, 2000],
    -        ['sunflower', 0.40, 500],
    5        ['clove', 0.65, 2000],
    -        ['lily', 0.80, 1500]
    -    ].each do |name, price, quantity|
    -        si = StockItem.new(:quantity => quantity)
    -        si.save
    10       Flower.new(
    -            :stock_item => si,
    -            :name => name,
    -            :price => price
    -        ).save
    15   end
```

Note that in line 11 we have connected a particular flower with the current stock item by setting its stock_item attribute.

We can print a stock report like this:

File 11

```
Line 1    puts "Stock items:"
    -    StockItem.find(:all).each { |si|
    -        puts "#{si.flower.name}: #{si.quantity} in stock."
    -    }
```

This produces the following values:

```
Stock items:
rose: 1000 in stock.
violet: 2000 in stock.
sunflower: 500 in stock.
clove: 2000 in stock.
lily: 1500 in stock.
```

This time the magic is hidden in line 3. Obviously, ActiveRecord has added a flower member to the StockItem class that contains the Flower object that belongs to a certain instance.

Now for the real thing: the ultimate stock management system! First of all, we map all database tables to Ruby classes and add bits of business logic where necessary:

```
File 3     Line 1    class Bouquet < ActiveRecord::Base
              -        has_and_belongs_to_many :flowers
              -
              -        def price
              5          flowers.inject(self.base_price) do |total, f|
              -            total += f.price * f.quantity.to_i
              -          end
              -        end
              -
              10       def add(flower, quantity)
              -          self.flowers.push_with_attributes(
              -            flower,
              -            :quantity => quantity
              -          )
              15       end
              -      end
              -
              -      class Flower < ActiveRecord::Base
              -        has_and_belongs_to_many :bouquets
              20       belongs_to :stock_item
              -      end
              -
              -      class StockItem < ActiveRecord::Base
              -        has_one :flower
              25     end
```

No big surprises here. The only new method is the add(flower,quantity) method in Bouquet, and it was added only for convenience. More interesting is the Stock class:

```
File 3     Line 1    class Stock
              -        def add_flower(name, price, quantity)
              -          si = StockItem.new(:quantity => quantity)
              -          si.save
              5          si.create_flower(
              -            :name => name,
              -            :price => price
              -          )
              -        end
              10       def remove(bouquet)
              -          Bouquet.transaction do
              -            bouquet.flowers.each do |f|
              -              si = StockItem.find(f.stock_item_id)
              -              if si.quantity < f.quantity.to_i
              15               raise 'Not enough flowers left!'
              -              end
              -              si.quantity -= f.quantity.to_i
              -              si.save
              -            end
              20         end
              -        end
```

```
     -      def print_report
     -        StockItem.find(:all).each do |si|
    25          puts "#{si.flower.name}: #{si.quantity} in stock."
     -        end
     -      end
     -    end
```

It has everything we'd normally expect a Stock class to have: we can add a certain number of flowers having a certain price just by calling add_flower(name, price, quantity). The remove(bouquet) method will remove all flowers belonging to a bouquet from stock, and print_report() will print something nice for the clerks.

In line 11 we used another valuable ActiveRecord feature: transactions. When removing a bouquet from the database, we want to remove it completely—all the flowers go, or none go. The transaction() method executes a code block and performs a rollback if an exception was raised in the block.

Let's fill our stock and print a first report:

File 3
```
Line 1  stock = Stock.new
     -    [
     -      ['rose', 1.10, 1000],
     -      ['violet', 0.40, 2000],
    5      ['sunflower', 0.40, 6]
     -    ].each do |name, price, quantity|
     -      stock.add_flower(name, price, quantity)
     -    end
     -    stock.print_report
```

This produces the following values:

```
rose: 1000 in stock.
violet: 2000 in stock.
sunflower: 500 in stock.
```

Then we create a new bouquet:

File 3
```
Line 1  bouquet = Bouquet.new(
     -      :name => 'Honeybunch',
     -      :base_price => 1.37
     -    )
    5    bouquet.save
     -    bouquet.add(Flower.find_by_name('rose'), 1)
     -    bouquet.add(Flower.find_by_name('sunflower'), 6)
     -    puts "'#{bouquet.name}' costs $#{bouquet.price}."
```

and print its price:

```
'Honeybunch' costs $4.87.
```

Where to Put Constraints?

Putting constraints on columns and on the relationships between tables is a two-edged sword. On the one hand, you have constraints that apply globally and can be checked only by the database system itself. It does not make sense—and often is impossible—to implement primary keys, foreign keys, or unique constraints in your application.

On the other hand, you have issues such as column value constraints like "prices should not be negative." To assert that a numerical column value always is in a certain range can be easily achieved in both the database and the application. ActiveRecord supports this with its validation mechanism.

When you know for sure that a database will be used exclusively by your application, you may put the constraints on your data into the database. In all other cases, try to put as much of your business logic into your application, because it can be found more easily (you don't have to look into the database *and* the application), and you won't affect other (future) applications that might have different or additional constraints on some columns.

No matter which way you choose, don't forget the DRY principle—Don't Repeat Yourself.* Define every constraint just once, either in the application or in the database.

---

*http://www.artima.com/intv/dry.html

Finally, we remove all flowers belonging to the bouquet from stock:

File 3

```
Line 1    stock.remove(bouquet)
    -     stock.print_report
```

and print another report:

```
rose: 999 in stock.
violet: 2000 in stock.
sunflower: 494 in stock.
```

It's almost unbelievable: the only SQL statements we had to write were the table definitions (if you want to avoid writing table definitions, too, refer to Section 2.3, *Migrating Database Schemas*, on page 48). ActiveRecord let us implement PragBouquet's new stock management system in less than 80 lines of Ruby code that reads like a specification.

Validation

As we all know, the most difficult tasks in software development are usually more or less unrelated to the actual problem being solved. The biggest problems are caused by error conditions: users enter invalid data, networks break down, hard disks crash, and so on.

This is also true in database programming. The most important technique for preventing errors in relational databases is to impose constraints on columns so that they contain only valid values. As a special case of this, we need to maintain referential integrity—to make sure that foreign keys always refer to existing table rows in the other table.

All relational database systems allow you to put constraints on columns and tables somehow, but there are huge differences between their capabilities (many versions of MySQL, for example, allow you to define foreign key constraints, but they do not actually check them). To overcome these incompatibilities, ActiveRecord lets you define validations for your database objects in Ruby code.

For our Flower and Bouquet object, the rules are simple:

```
class Bouquet < ActiveRecord::Base
  has_and_belongs_to_many :flowers

  def validate
    errors.add_on_empty %w(name base_price)
    unless base_price >= 0.0
      errors.add('base_price', 'is negative')
    end
    errors.add('flowers', 'must exist') unless flowers.size > 0
  end
end

class Flower < ActiveRecord::Base
  has_and_belongs_to_many :bouquets

  def validate
    errors.add_on_empty %w(name price)
    errors.add(:price, 'is negative') unless price >= 0.0
  end
end
```

Every ActiveRecord object has a member called errors which is of type ActiveRecord::Errors. Before writing an object to the database using the save() method, ActiveRecord calls the validate() method of the object. After validate() returns, ActiveRecord checks to see whether any error has been written to the errors object. If any error occurred, the database will not be updated, and save() returns false (you can also use the save!() variant that will raise a validation exception rather than returning false).

The rules for our domain objects are simple: the name and base price of a bouquet may not be empty, the base price has to be non-negative, and every bouquet must have at least one flower. Flowers must have a name and a price, too, and their price has to be greater than or equal to zero. The validation for this is shown in the following snippet:

File 12

```
Line 1   print 'Trying to save nameless flower: '
     -   puts Flower.new(:name => nil, :price => 0).save
     -   print 'Trying to save really cheap flower: '
     -   puts Flower.new(:name => 'cheap', :price => -1).save
     5   print 'Trying to save a valid flower: '
     -   puts Flower.new(:name => 'daisy', :price => 0.02).save
```

This produces the following:

```
Trying to save nameless flower: false
Trying to save really cheap flower: false
Trying to save a valid flower: true
```

Now we can prevent ourselves from storing imaginary bouquets:

File 12

```
Line 1   rose = Flower.find_by_name('rose')
     -   sunflower = Flower.find_by_name('sunflower')
     -   bouquet = Bouquet.new
     -   bouquet.name = 'Honeybunch'
     5   bouquet.base_price = 1.37
     -   print 'Trying to save bouquet without flowers: '
     -   puts bouquet.save
     -   bouquet.flowers.push_with_attributes(rose, :quantity => 1)
     -   bouquet.flowers.push_with_attributes(sunflower, :quantity => 6)
    10   print 'Trying to save valid bouquet: '
     -   puts bouquet.save
```

This produces the following:

```
Trying to save bouquet without flowers: false
Trying to save valid bouquet: true
```

Migrating Database Schemas

One of the biggest problems with relational databases is maintaining their schemas and content. For example, in the development phase you often have to rename, drop, or add a column to a table. On your local machine this is not a big deal—you can mess with your private database installation however you want. However, when you check your code in, your fellow developers might be surprised to see that a new column is used in your Ruby code that is not present in their database.

ActiveRecord migration addresses this problem in a pragmatic way. The Migration class[14] defines methods for manipulating database schemas without writing a single DDL (Data Definition Language) statement. You can create and drop tables and indices, and you can add, rename, or drop columns, without knowing anything about the nitty-gritty details of the CREATE TABLE and ALTER TABLE statements of the database system you're using. Migration handles all this for you. This has significant advantages:

- All changes to your database schema are documented in Ruby code.

- The application can be easily migrated to every database system that is supported by Migration. (At the time of this writing, it works on MySQL, PostgreSQL, Microsoft SQL Server, and Oracle. Support for DB2 is in the works.)

To make the automatic flower ordering process even more intelligent, let's add a new column containing the average lifetime of a flower to the flowers table. When we have a lot of roses in stock and know that they survive only a few days in the cold store, it could make sense to make bouquets containing roses a bit cheaper in the shop.

Let's call our new column life_time. Using migrations, we'll add it like this:

File 9

```
Line 1  class AddLifeTime < ActiveRecord::Migration
   -       def self.up
   -          add_column :flowers, :life_time, :integer, :default => 5
   -       end
   5
   -       def self.down
   -          remove_column :flowers, :life_time
   -       end
   -    end
```

Every migration step is encapsulated in a class (AddLifeTime in our case) that is derived from ActiveRecord::Migration. The migration class has to implement the up() and down() methods for upgrading and downgrading the database schema. In these methods you can use methods such as create_table(), drop_table(), add_column(), rename_column(), remove_column(), add_index(), and remove_index() to modify your schema in any way you'd like. In addition, you can call execute(sql) to run arbitrary SQL statements.

---

[14]http://api.rubyonrails.com/classes/ActiveRecord/Migration.html

Let's test our migration class:

```
Line 1    AddLifeTime.up
   -      Flower.reset_column_information
   -      [
   -        ['rose', 1.10, 4],
   5        ['sunflower', 0.40, 10],
   -        ['lily', 0.80, 5]
   -      ].each do |name, price, life_time|
   -        flower = Flower.new(
   -          :name => name,
  10          :price => price,
   -          :life_time => life_time
   -        )
   -        flower.save!
   -      end
  15
   -      Flower.find(:all).each do |f|
   -        puts "A #{f.name} costs $#{f.price} and lives " +
   -          "for #{f.life_time} days."
   -      end
```

This produces the following:

```
A rose costs $1.1 and lives for 4 days.
A sunflower costs $0.4 and lives for 10 days.
A lily costs $0.8 and lives for 5 days.
```

After calling the up() method of class AddLifeTime, we can use the life_time attribute like any other attribute. The only important step to remember is to call reset_column_information() (as we did in line 2) after changing a database schema. This will clear all cached column information. This is necessary only in this test case, because the program changes the schema while it is running.

Now the flowers table looks as follows:

```
mysql> describe flowers;
+-----------+------------------+------+-----+---------+----------------+
| Field     | Type             | Null | Key | Default | Extra          |
+-----------+------------------+------+-----+---------+----------------+
| id        | int(10) unsigned |      | PRI | NULL    | auto_increment |
| name      | varchar(64)      |      |     |         |                |
| price     | double           |      |     | 0       |                |
| life_time | int(11)          | YES  |     | 5       |                |
+-----------+------------------+------+-----+---------+----------------+
4 rows in set (0.00 sec)
```

As expected, Migration has added a new life_time column behind the scenes that we could remove just as easily by calling AddLifeTime.down.

The default lifetime value is five days. What if we wanted to set it to another value for existing rows right after we have added the new column? Simple answer: set it to whatever value you like in the up() method:

File 10

```
Line 1    class AddLifeTime < ActiveRecord::Migration
    -        def self.up
    -          add_column :flowers, :life_time, :integer, :default => 5
    -          Flower.reset_column_information
    5          Flower.find(:all).each do |f|
    -            f.life_time = 3
    -            f.save!
    -          end
    -        end
    10
    -        def self.down
    -          remove_column :flowers, :life_time
    -        end
    -      end
```

Right after adding the new column, we call reset_column_information() in line 4 to activate it. Then, in line 5, we use the ordinary find(*args) method to iterate over all flowers and set their lifetime to three days.

To implement a real migration strategy, you'd need to write support scripts that work out which of your migrations to apply, but ActiveRecord::Migration will simplify this task significantly.[15]

Conclusion

ActiveRecord can seem pretty magical, shielding you from the low-level SQL needed to perform CRUD operations and joins between tables. And, for much of the time, that's good enough. But ActiveRecord can't do everything. SQL is still a very important technology. The examples in this chapter were chosen to demonstrate ActiveRecord's strengths. If you cannot develop a complete database from scratch and instead have to integrate with a legacy schema, things can get much more complicated. ActiveRecord relies upon a lot of conventions, and modeling complicated relationships between tables that have primary keys spanning several columns can be tricky to impossible.[16]

---

[15]The Ruby on Rails project has a sophisticated solution for migrating database schemas. You should have a look at it.

[16]Read what the pros have to say: http://blogs.pragprog.com/cgi-bin/pragdave.cgi/Tech/Ruby/IsRailsReadyForPrimeTime.html.

In any case you should study the ActiveRecord documentation carefully (or look at *Agile Web Development with Rails* [TH05]), because it has many useful features (such as table inheritance) that we did not cover here. Additionally, its capabilities differ from database system, to database system so, for example, not all the features that are available with MySQL are also available if you use DB2.

2.4 Lightweight Directory Access Protocol (LDAP)

We use directories in the real world all the time: telephone books, lists of network accounts, address books, the domain name service (DNS), and so on. Typically, directories are organized hierarchically—as trees—and their entries are often read and rarely modified.

Implementing directories with relational database systems can be a bit complicated. Even though many database vendors added tools for hierarchical queries to their products, using them is still far from being convenient. (Some vendors, including Oracle, even ship a separate directory service that is based on their relational database product.)

Because of this, a standard for accessing directories was created as part of the *X.500 directory specification*. It was called *Directory Access Protocol* (DAP). Unfortunately, it was both complex and complicated, and no one implemented it completely.

X.500 directory specification

Directory Access Protocol

As a consequence, an easier standard was defined: the Lightweight Directory Access Protocol (LDAP).[17] This is the most widespread directory service in use today.

I'll give a short introduction to LDAP in the rest of this section. If you're already familiar with LDAP you can safely skip it and go directly to Section 2.4, *An Address Book for PragBouquet Customers*, on page 56.

Simply put, LDAP is to directories what SQL is to relational databases. It helps you to model real-world entities as *directory entries* (not as tables) that have different attributes. Attributes have a name, a type, and a multidimensional value; i.e., attributes can have a list of values. Every directory entry (from now on we call them *entries* for short) has at least one attribute called objectclass that determines which attributes the entry has.

directory entries

---

[17]http://www.faqs.org/rfcs/rfc2251.html

In LDAP you put all object classes and their according attribute type definitions belonging to a particular problem domain into a *schema*. *schema* The core schema, for example, contains the definition of the residential-Person object class:

```
objectclass (
  2.5.6.10
  NAME 'residentialPerson'
  DESC 'RFC2256: an residential person'
  SUP person
  STRUCTURAL
  MUST l
  MAY (
    businessCategory $ x121Address $ registeredAddress $
    destinationIndicator $ preferredDeliveryMethod $
    telexNumber $ teletexTerminalIdentifier $ telephoneNumber $
    internationaliSDNNumber $ facsimileTelephoneNumber $
    preferredDeliveryMethod $ street $ postOfficeBox $
    postalCode $ postalAddress $ physicalDeliveryOfficeName $
    st $ l
  )
)
```

This looks similar to SQL's create table statement, doesn't it? The biggest difference is that the type of the attributes (SQL calls them *columns*) are defined separately. The meaning of the different declarations and keywords is as follows:

- In LDAP, every definition begins with an *object identifier* (OID) that *object identifier* uniquely identifies the object class or attribute type worldwide. OIDs are numbers separated by periods and have to be registered at the *Internet Assigned Numbers Authority* (IANA).[18] Private OIDs always start with 1.3.6.1.4.

- Object classes have a name that is defined with the NAME keyword. To prevent name clashes, you should add a unique prefix or postfix to your own object class and attribute type names.

- DESC lets you give a human-readable description of the object class.

- The SUP keyword points to the superclass of an object class. LDAP is object oriented, and an object class can inherit the attributes of another class. Every class has at least one superclass called top.

---

[18]http://www.iana.org/cgi-bin/enterprise.pl

- An LDAP class can be a STRUCTURAL, AUXILIARY, or ABSTRACT class. Abstract classes are classes that are meant only to be base classes (such as top). Classes meant to define completely new object hierarchies are declared as STRUCTURAL. AUXILIARY classes let you "mixin" attributes into existing structural classes.

- MUST expects a dollar-separated list which contains the classes' mandatory attributes.

- MAY expects a dollar-separated list containing the classes' optional attributes.

Attribute types, such as the telephoneNumber attribute we have used in the residentialPerson object class, are defined as follows:

```
attributetype (
  2.5.4.20
  NAME 'telephoneNumber'
  DESC 'RFC2256: Telephone Number'
  EQUALITY telephoneNumberMatch
  SUBSTR telephoneNumberSubstringsMatch
  SYNTAX 1.3.6.1.4.1.1466.115.121.1.50{32}
)
```

Like an object class, the attribute type definition starts with an OID. NAME and DESC have the same meaning as in the object class definition. The remaining keywords have the following meaning:[19]

- EQUALITY specifies which algorithm should be used to test whether two telephoneNumber attributes are equal. This is a little bit more sophisticated than a simple string comparison, because telephone numbers often contain characters only for better readability. For example, "0049 (0) 1234 / 56 78" and "004912345678" are completely different strings, but they represent the same telephone number. The LDAP standard defines a lot of equality algorithms.

- SUBSTR lets you define which algorithm should be used to check whether a particular telephoneNumber number attribute contains a particular substring.

- The SYNTAX element refers to the OID of the attributes' syntax. LDAP defines a syntax for many types that are used often such as integers, strings, timestamps, and even JPEG files.

---

[19]To learn about attribute types, you have to read RFC 2252: http://www.faqs.org/rfcs/rfc2252.html.

It's not difficult to build your own object classes and attribute types, but it's certainly a good idea first to check whether the object class you need has not already be defined. LDAP specifies dozens of base classes for all the elements you typically find in directories: person, residentialPerson, organizationalPerson, and so on. Often it's sufficient to derive a new class from an existing one, adding just a few attributes. For example, if you need to store address data containing the geographical position of the address, you can derive a new geoPerson class from residentialPerson, adding longitude and latitude attributes.

That's all not too different from what you do with relational databases (except for the inheritance features), and you could use LDAP to store nonhierarchical data. But usually LDAP repositories represent hierarchical trees of entries belonging to one or more object classes.

Each entry has a unique name, the *distinguished name* (DN). The DN consists of several *relative distinguished names* (RDN). An RDN is a list of attribute name/value pairs that are separated by a comma or a semi-colon. For example, telephoneNumber=004912345678 could be an RDN with the attribute name telephoneNumber and the value 004912345678. A more precise RDN could be

distinguished name

relative distinguished names

```
cn=Maik Schmidt,telephoneNumber=004912345678
```

This additionally specifies the cn ("common name") attribute of a person object.

As we all know, a picture is worth approximately 2^{10} words, so let's have a look at Figure 2.3, on page 60. The *root entry* of the directory in this figure has a DN consisting of two RDNs: dc=pragbouquet,dc=com.[20] It automatically becomes an RDN for all entries in the tree. The deeper you go down the hierarchy, the longer the DNs and RDNs get. For example, the distinguished names of all entries on the left side contain the relative distinguished name uid=4711,dc=pragbouquet,dc=com. Simply put, DNs specify leaves, and RDNs specify subtrees.

root entry

LDAP allows you to read, modify, and delete subtrees and single nodes of your directories. In relational databases you specify particular rows with a WHERE clause in your SQL statements. In LDAP you use RDNs and DNs to do so.

---

[20]dc stands for *domain component*. dc is a mandatory attribute for entries belonging to the organization object class.

We mentioned before that directory entries are often read and rarely updated. Hence, the LDAP standard defined a technology that makes an initial import of directory entries easy: the *LDAP Data Interchange Format* (LDIF).[21] It's a simple textual file format for describing directory entries. Here's an LDIF representation of the root entry and one of its descendants of our sample directory:

LDAP Data Interchange Format

```
# First (root) entry: the PragBouquet organization.
dn: dc=pragbouquet,dc=com
objectclass: dcObject
objectclass: organization
o: PragBouquet
dc: pragbouquet

# Second entry: an address book for customer 4711.
dn:uid=4711,dc=pragbouquet,dc=com
objectclass: top
objectclass: person
objectclass: uidObject
uid: 4711
cn: John Jackson
sn: Jackson
description: Address book of John Jackson.
```

LDIF is line oriented. Comment lines start with a # character. All the other lines represent an attribute and its corresponding value, separated by a colon. If an attribute has more than one value, it may appear several times. Every LDAP server comes with a bunch of utilities for modifying an existing repository and for importing .ldif files.

Although a lot of directory services work more or less invisibly, touched only by your system administrators, chances are good that you'll have to integrate with one someday, because LDAP is gaining popularity among application developers, too. In the following sections we'll show how to manipulate a directory service based on OpenLDAP with Ruby.

An Address Book for PragBouquet Customers

The marketing department made yet another astonishing observation: there are people who celebrate their birthdays every year! Wouldn't it be great if PragBouquet customers could easily send them a bouquet on those birthdays? And wouldn't it be nice if PragBouquet customers could be spared the extra work of entering the same address data for the recipients, over and over again?

---

[21]http://www.faqs.org/rfcs/rfc2849.html

So, marketing came up with an ingenious idea. All PragBouquet customers should have their own address book where they can store the addresses of the people they've ever sent a bunch of flowers.

The web shop team said that it's not a big deal to create a user interface for the address book, but they asked you to create the corresponding backend services. Fortunately, they want to give Ruby on Rails[22] a try, so you can use Ruby for implementing the address book logic.

When thinking about things like address books, LDAP immediately comes to mind, so you decide to implement the address book as a directory service using the OpenLDAP[23] system. It has everything you need, it's available for free, it works on top of several database systems, and it ships with several utilities for reading and manipulating data.

For the development phase we install an OpenLDAP server on our local machine and configure it using this configuration file:

File 39

```
Line 1   include /sw/etc/openldap/schema/core.schema

     -   database bdb
     -   suffix "dc=pragbouquet,dc=com"
     5   rootdn "cn=root,dc=pragbouquet,dc=com"
     -   rootpw secret
     -   directory /sw/var/openldap-data
     -   index objectclass eq
```

That is really all we need to get our address book application up and running. We have to include the core schema, because we'll need some of its definitions (person, residentialPerson, and uidObject). In addition, we have to define the database we want to use (the LDAP standard does not define how the directory is to be stored). It's a Berkeley DB (bdb)[24] with all data files stored in directory /sw/var/openldap-data. The distinguished name of our root node (needed for administrative purposes only) is cn=root,dc=pragbouquet,dc=com. We have to authenticate ourselves using the nearly unbreakable plain-text password *secret* whenever we want to write to the database.

LDAP allows you to create a sophisticated directory layout for address books comprising lots of organizational units or even define your own object classes, but we will use a more modern and simpler approach.

---

[22]http://www.rubyonrails.com
[23]http://www.openldap.org
[24]http://sleepycat.com

We will organize our directory in a flat way using domain components and uid attributes.[25]

Before diving into Ruby code, let's take a closer look at the directory structure and then initialize our repository with some sample data stored in init.ldif:

File 34

```
Line 1   # Create the PragBouquet organization.
    -    dn: dc=pragbouquet,dc=com
    -    objectclass: dcObject
    -    objectclass: organization
    5    o: PragBouquet
    -    dc: pragbouquet

    -    # Create an address book for customer 4711.
    -    dn:uid=4711,dc=pragbouquet,dc=com
   10    objectclass: top
    -    objectclass: person
    -    objectclass: uidObject
    -    uid: 4711
    -    cn: John Jackson
   15    sn: Jackson
    -    description: Address book of John Jackson.

    -    # Create the first address book entry for customer 4711.
    -    dn:cn=Marge Jackson,uid=4711,dc=pragbouquet,dc=com
   20    objectclass: top
    -    objectclass: residentialPerson
    -    cn: Marge Jackson
    -    sn: Jackson
    -    l: Springfield
   25    st: IL
    -    street: Evergreen Terrace 42
    -    postalCode: 62701
    -    description: Don't forget our wedding anniversary!

   30    # Create the second address book entry for customer 4711.
    -    dn:cn=P.H. Beans,uid=4711,dc=pragbouquet,dc=com
    -    objectclass: top
    -    objectclass: residentialPerson
    -    cn: P.H. Beans
   35    sn: Beans
    -    l: Springfield
    -    st: MO
    -    street: Nuclear Powerplant Road 1
    -    postalCode: 65801
   40    description: My boss.
    -
```

---

[25]http://www.faqs.org/rfcs/rfc2377.html

```
     -   # Create an address book for customer 0815.
     -   dn:uid=0815,dc=pragbouquet,dc=com
     -   objectclass: top
    45   objectclass: person
     -   objectclass: uidObject
     -   uid: 0815
     -   cn: Max Mustermann
     -   sn: Mustermann
    50   description: Address book of Max Mustermann.
     -
     -   # Create the first address book entry for customer 0815.
     -   dn:cn=Jane Doe,uid=0815,dc=pragbouquet,dc=com
     -   objectclass: top
    55   objectclass: residentialPerson
     -   cn: Jane Doe
     -   sn: Doe
     -   street: 125 N. Arbitrary Street
     -   st: DC
    60   l: Washington
     -   postalCode: 20500
     -   description: My Sweetheart!
```

The previous LDIF file should be nearly self-explanatory (comment lines start with a # character). Every entry has a *distinguished name* (DN). All its other attributes are listed as "key: value" pairs. All attributes are potentially multidimensional, so they may appear several times.

distinguished name

Note that we use the attribute uid to structure our address books. Every web shop user is identified by a particular identifier (it might be a customer ID, an e-mail address, or something similar). Whenever a customer creates a completely new address book (not an address book entry), a new directory entry for her user ID will be added. The directory belonging to our init.ldif file looks like Figure 2.3, on the next page (we have left out most attributes for brevity).

Let's start our server and load the initial data using the ldapadd command:

```
mschmidt:~/ldap> sudo slapd
Password:
mschmidt:~/ldap> ldapadd -c -x -D "cn=root,dc=pragbouquet,dc=com" \
> -W -f init.ldif
Enter LDAP Password:
adding new entry "dc=pragbouquet,dc=com"

adding new entry "uid=4711,dc=pragbouquet,dc=com"

adding new entry "cn=Marge Jackson,uid=4711,dc=pragbouquet,dc=com"
```

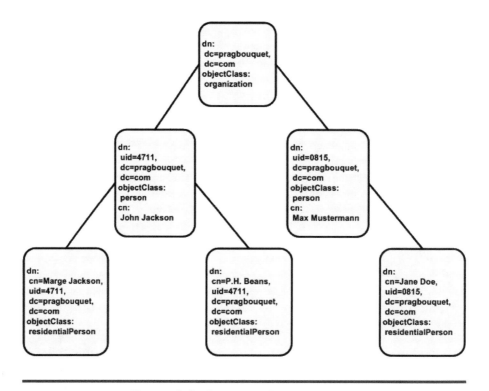

Figure 2.3: ADDRESS BOOK LAYOUT

```
adding new entry "cn=P.H. Beans,uid=4711,dc=pragbouquet,dc=com"

adding new entry "uid=0815,dc=pragbouquet,dc=com"

adding new entry "cn=Jane Doe,uid=0815,dc=pragbouquet,dc=com"
```

Our .ldif file didn't contain any errors, and six new entries have been created.

OpenLDAP's ldapsearch command allows us to query the repository. It prints its results in LDIF. To become a bit more familiar with our directory, let's print the address book of the user identified by uid 4711:

```
mschmidt:~/ldap> ldapsearch -x -s one \
> -b 'uid=4711,dc=pragbouquet,dc=com' \
> '(objectclass=*)'
# extended LDIF
#
# LDAPv3
# base <uid=4711,dc=pragbouquet,dc=com> with scope one
# filter: (objectclass=*)
```

```
# requesting: ALL
#

# Marge Jackson, 4711, pragbouquet.com
dn: cn=Marge Jackson,uid=4711,dc=pragbouquet,dc=com
objectClass: top
objectClass: residentialPerson
cn: Marge Jackson
sn: Jackson
l: Springfield
st: IL
street: Evergreen Terrace 42
postalCode: 62701
description: Don't forget our wedding anniversary!

# P.H. Beans, 4711, pragbouquet.com
dn: cn=P.H. Beans,uid=4711,dc=pragbouquet,dc=com
objectClass: top
objectClass: residentialPerson
cn: P.H. Beans
sn: Beans
l: Springfield
st: MO
street: Nuclear Powerplant Road 1
postalCode: 65801
description: My boss.

# search result
search: 2
result: 0 Success

# numResponses: 3
# numEntries: 2
```

Obviously, everything is up and running. Our query returned the two address book entries that belong to the customer identified by user ID 4711. But what are those options we passed to the command?

- -x uses the simple authentication mechanism. In our case the communication is unencrypted, and no password is needed.

- -s one searches the directory "one level beyond base," so it returns all entries below our search base, but not the base itself. -s base would have returned the base object only, and -s sub would have returned the base object and all its descendants.

- -b 'uid=4711,dc=pragbouquet,dc=com' sets the search base to the distinguished name uid=4711,dc=pragbouquet,dc=com, so that all entries of the subtree belonging to this DN will be returned.

- (objectclass=*) specifies a filter for the entries to be returned. The (objectclass=*) filter is comparable to SQL's SELECT * statement and selects all entries no matter what attributes they have. If we were interested in entries from Illinois only, we could have set the filter to (st=IL).

In the following sections we'll see how to manipulate our repository with Ruby.

Ruby/LDAP

The Ruby/LDAP[26] library was initially created by Takaaki Tateishi and is currently maintained by Ian Macdonald. It supports all LDAP clients that comply with the LDAP Application Program Interface.[27] You can use Ruby/LDAP to interface with OpenLDAP, Netscape, and ActiveDirectory, among others.

As a first exercise we'll try to read John Jackson's address book. It should not be too surprising that accessing a directory service looks similar to accessing a relational database system:

File 33

```
Line 1  require 'pp'
        require 'ldap'
        include LDAP

5       begin
          connection = Conn.new('127.0.0.1', LDAP_PORT)
          connection.set_option(LDAP_OPT_PROTOCOL_VERSION, 3)
          connection.bind do
            base_dn = 'uid=4711,dc=pragbouquet,dc=com'
10          scope = LDAP_SCOPE_ONELEVEL
            filter = '(objectClass=*)'
            connection.search(base_dn, scope, filter) do |entry|
              pp entry.to_hash
            end
15        end
        rescue Exception => ex
          puts ex
        end
```

This prints the following:

```
{"cn"=>["Marge Jackson"],
 "st"=>["IL"],
 "l"=>["Springfield"],
 "sn"=>["Jackson"],
```

---

[26]http://ruby-ldap.sourceforge.net
[27]http://www.faqs.org/rfcs/rfc1823.html

```
"description"=>["Don' t forget our wedding anniversary!"],
"postalCode"=>["62701"],
"street"=>["Evergreen Terrace 42"],
"objectClass"=>["top",  "residentialPerson"],
"dn"=>["cn=Marge Jackson,uid=4711,dc=pragbouquet,dc=com"]}
{"cn"=>["P.H. Beans"],
 "st"=>["MO"],
 "l"=>["Springfield"],
 "sn"=>["Beans"],
 "description"=>["My boss."],
 "postalCode"=>["65801"],
 "street"=>["Nuclear Powerplant Road 1"],
 "objectClass"=>["top",  "residentialPerson"],
 "dn"=>["cn=P.H. Beans,uid=4711,dc=pragbouquet,dc=com"]}
```

First, we create a new connection to the LDAP service by calling the
method LDAP::Conn.new(host='localhost', port=LDAP_PORT). We then set the
LDAP_OPT_PROTOCOL_VERSION option, because we've set up an LDAPv3
service (it's OpenLDAP's default).

In line 8 we bind our connection object to the server. The real work
is performed in the code block we pass to the bind(dn=nil, password=nil,
method=LDAP_AUTH_SIMPLE) method. The heart of our "program logic" is
the search() method. It expects the following parameters:

1. base_dn contains the base DN of the subtree to search in.

2. scope defines the search scope; one of: LDAP_SCOPE_ONELEVEL,
   LDAP_SCOPE_SUBTREE, or LDAP_SCOPE_BASE.

   In our example we have used LDAP_SCOPE_ONELEVEL, which means
   "one level beyond base." We are not interested in the base object
   (the address book owner) itself.

   If we had set the scope to LDAP_SCOPE_SUBTREE the program would
   have printed the entry for the address book owner, too:

```
{"cn"=>["John Jackson"],
 "sn"=>["Jackson"],
 "uid"=>["4711"],
 "description"=>["Address book of John Jackson."],
 "objectClass"=>["top",  "person",  "uidObject"],
 "dn"=>["uid=4711,dc=pragbouquet,dc=com"]}
 ...
```

   LDAP_SCOPE_BASE returns only the base object (the address book
   owner in our case).

3. filter contains the LDAP search filter to be used.

4. The attributes array contains the name of the attributes which will be returned. If it is empty or nil (the default), all attributes are returned.

5. The attributes_only flag indicates whether only the names of the attributes should be returned (true). When it is set to false (the default), it returns both names and values.

6. seconds specifies the seconds portion of the search timeout. It defaults to 0. If either this parameter or the useconds parameter is greater than 0, the timeout mechanism will be activated.

7. useconds specifies the microseconds portion of the search timeout. It defaults to 0. If this parameter or the seconds parameter is greater than 0, the timeout mechanism will be activated. To set a timeout of 2.5 seconds, set seconds to 2 and useconds to 500.

8. sort_attribute specifies the attribute by which to sort the search result entries. If no sort attribute is specified (the default), the order of the result entries is unpredictable.

9. sort_proc may contain a code block that is used for sorting the entries returned by the server. It defaults to nil, so the order of the result entries is unpredictable.

search() is an iterator. It expects a code block that gets passed the current entry as an LDAP::Entry object. In line 13 we turn these objects into hashes and print them, nicely formatted.

Reading LDAP entries seems to be fairly easy. Let's try to create new ones now. First let's add an empty address book for Jane Doe (she is already a member of Max Mustermann's address book, but that doesn't matter, because for us they are two different customers):

File 32

```
Line 1   User = Struct.new(:uid, :forename, :surname)
    -    class AddressBook
    -      BASE_DC = 'dc=pragbouquet,dc=com'
    -
    5      attr_reader :user
    -
    -      def initialize(connection, user)
    -        @connection, @user = connection, user
    -      end
   10
    -      def AddressBook.create(connection, user)
    -        cn = user.forename + ' ' + user.surname
    -        adr_book = []
    -
```

```
15      [
          ['objectclass', %w(top person uidObject)],
          ['uid', [user.uid]],
          ['cn', [cn]],
          ['sn', [user.surname]],
20        ['description', ['Address book of ' + cn]]
        ].each do |attr, values|
          adr_book << LDAP.mod(LDAP_MOD_ADD, attr, values)
        end

25      connection.add(
          'uid=' + user.uid + ',' + BASE_DC,
          adr_book
        )
        AddressBook.new(connection, user)
30    end
    end
```

On line 1 we declare a User class that contains all the attributes we need to manage an address book for a web shop user: a user ID (typically something like a customer ID or an e-mail address), a first name, and a surname.

New address books are created using create(connection,user). Objects returned by initialize(connection,user) refer to address books that have to exist already. This time we did not make our connection object available as a singleton. If we decide to do so later, we can easily change our class.

The interesting stuff happens in the create(connection,user) method. We have to iterate over an array of two-dimensional arrays. Because LDAP attributes can often appear multiple times, each entry contains the name of an attribute to be added and an array of values.

LDAP::Mod objects represent modifications to a single attribute. These modifications can be of type LDAP_MOD_ADD, LDAP_MOD_REPLACE, or LDAP_MOD_DELETE (some LDAP servers define extension types).[28] In line 22 we create LDAP::Mod objects for adding attributes by calling the LDAP.mod(mod_type,attr,values) method and append them to the adr_book array. The result is an array that contains "add modifications" for all the attributes we're storing for a new address book.

Finally, in line 25, we send our modifications list to the server and can create a new AddressBook object:

---

[28] If you want to add binary values, you have to logically **or** the modification type with LDAP_MOD_BVALUES, so to add a binary value you'd use LDAP_MOD_ADD | LDAP_MOD_BVALUES.

File 32

```
Line 1   connection = Conn.new
    -    connection.set_option(LDAP_OPT_PROTOCOL_VERSION, 3)
    -    connection.bind('cn=root,dc=pragbouquet,dc=com', 'secret')
    -
    5    user = User.new('23', 'Jane', 'Doe')
    -    address_book = AddressBook.create(connection, user)
```

We had to use a variant of the bind() method in line 3. Because we want to use our connection for writing, we have to authenticate ourselves, passing the root DN and the corresponding password.

Now that we've seen how to add entries to an LDAP database in principle, let's define a method for adding bouquet recipients to an existing address book:

File 32

```
Line 1   Recipient = Struct.new(
    -        :forename, :surname, :street, :postal_code,
    -        :city, :state, :description
    -    )
    5
    -    class AddressBook
    -      def udn
    -        'uid=' + @user.uid + ',' + BASE_DC
    -      end
   10
    -      def add(recipient)
    -        cn = recipient.forename + ' ' + recipient.surname
    -        entry = {
    -          'objectclass' => %w(top residentialPerson),
   15          'cn' => [cn],
    -          'sn' => [recipient.surname],
    -          'l' => [recipient.city],
    -          'street' => [recipient.street],
    -          'postalCode' => [recipient.postal_code],
   20          'st' => [recipient.state || ''],
    -          'description' => [recipient.description || '']
    -        }
    -        @connection.add('cn=' + cn + ',' + udn(), entry)
    -      end
   25    end
```

There is not much to say here.

We declared a Recipient class that represents the happy recipients of a bouquet, and an add(recipient) method that adds a Recipient object to the address book of a particular user. This time we did not create an array of LDAP::Mod objects.

Instead we used a hash containing all the attributes (and their corresponding values) for the new recipient. LDAP::Conn.add(dn, entry) can handle a hash object, too. For convenience we defined the udn() method that returns the distinguished name for a directory entry belonging to a particular user ID. So, let's add a new entry to Jane Doe's address book:

File 31

```
Line 1   user = User.new('23', 'Jane', 'Doe')
    -    address_book = AddressBook.new(connection, user)
    -    recipient = Recipient.new(
    -      'Jose', 'Rodriguez',
    5      'Casanova Street 6', '77002',
    -      'Houston', 'TX',
    -      'Rrrrrrr!'
    -    )
    -    address_book.add(recipient)
```

Hmmm, did it work? We'd better implement a method to print the whole address book:

File 32

```
Line 1   class AddressBook
    -      def each
    -        @connection.search(
    -          udn,
    5          LDAP_SCOPE_ONELEVEL,
    -          '(objectClass=residentialPerson)',
    -          nil, false, 0, 0,
    -          'sn'
    -        ) do |recipient|
    10          yield recipient
    -        end
    -      end
    -
    -      def each_recipient
    15        each do |entry|
    -          rec_data = entry.to_hash
    -          sn = rec_data['sn'][0]
    -          cn = rec_data['cn'][0]
    -          cn.sub!(Regexp.new(' ' + sn + '$'), '')
    20          yield Recipient.new(
    -            cn,
    -            sn,
    -            rec_data['street'][0],
    -            rec_data['postalCode'][0],
    25            rec_data['l'][0],
    -            rec_data['st'][0],
    -            rec_data['description'][0]
    -          )
    -        end
    30      end
    -    end
```

Yeah, that's Ruby code!

Why Isn't AddressBook#each Private?

Back in the dark and ancient days of object-oriented programming, a lot of people were obsessed with declaring everything private whenever possible (not when it made sense!).

Of course, purists may say that the each() method of the AddressBook class should be declared private, because it passes LDAP::Entry objects to its code block and reveals some of its innards. What if you change your address book backend? Or use a relational database instead of an LDAP repository?

They are right—in a way—but at the moment it's more important to create an API that's easy to use and—more important—easy to test. It's more difficult to test a private each() method. The users of your AddressBook class won't care about method visibility, but they will care about bugs that could have been prevented by simple unit tests...

As a rule of thumb, you should care only about the visibility of your methods when programming libraries that will be used by a large number of programmers. When writing code for applications, it's usually more important to think about issues such as testability.

Starting on line 2, we define an iterator that passes every recipient to a code block. In line 6 we define an object filter for the first time—we are interested only in objects of class residentialPerson—and in line 8 we set the sort attribute to sn,; so the results are sorted by the recipient's surname attribute. In the preceding line we had to explicitly pass the default values for all remaining parameters. We hope named parameters will be introduced in Ruby 2.0....

The each_recipient() method is a piece of cake. In line 16 we turn each LDAP::Entry object into a hash and use its entries to initialize a new Recipient object. Line 19 is a bit more interesting: here we extract the recipient's first name from the entries' common name.

Now let's print the address book of Jane Doe:

```
Line 1   user = User.new('23', 'Jane', 'Doe')
   -     address_book = AddressBook.new(connection, user)
   -     address_book.each_recipient { |r| pp r}
```

File 36

This produces the following:

```
#<struct Recipient
 forename="Jose",
 surname="Rodriguez",
 street="Casanova Street 6",
 postal_code="77002",
 city="Houston",
 state="TX",
 description="Rrrrrrr!">
```

That's correct, and Jose Rodriguez's entry was the one we expected.
But the formatting needs some adjustments:

File 32

```
Line 1    require 'ldap/ldif'
   -      class AddressBook
   -         include Enumerable
   -
   5         def to_ldif
   -            inject('') { |ldif,e| ldif << e.to_ldif }
   -         end
   -      end
```

That's a perfect example for idiomatic Ruby: because we have defined
an each() method, we can include the Enumerable module. Because we
called include Enumerable, we can use the inject(initial) method to create
an LDIF representation of the whole address book with a single line of
code (note that we had to require 'ldap/ldif', too).

So, let's do it:

File 37

```
Line 1    user = User.new('23', 'Jane', 'Doe')
   -      address_book = AddressBook.new(connection, user)
   -      puts address_book.to_ldif
```

Here's the corresponding LDIF output:

```
dn: cn=Jose Rodriguez,uid=23,dc=pragbouquet,dc=com
cn: Jose Rodriguez
st: TX
l: Houston
objectClass: top
objectClass: residentialPerson
sn: Rodriguez
description: Rrrrrrr!
postalCode: 77002
street: Casanova Street 6
```

That sure looks like something that could be imported by any modern
address book application, doesn't it?

Jane just realized that Jose did not get the last present she sent (the
biggest bouquet that has ever been produced by PragBouquet) because

Jane got the wrong house number: it's 8 not 6. We need to change the entry:

File 32

```
Line 1   class AddressBook
     -       def modify(recipient)
     -         cn = recipient.forename + ' ' + recipient.surname
     -         entry = {
     5           'l' => [recipient.city],
     -           'street' => [recipient.street],
     -           'postalCode' => [recipient.postal_code],
     -           'st' => [recipient.state],
     -           'description' => [recipient.description]
    10         }
     -         @connection.modify('cn=' + cn + ',' + udn(), entry)
     -       end
     -   end
```

LDAP::Conn.modify(dn,attributes) modifies the object identified by the distinguished name dn, setting its attributes to the content of the attributes parameter. This parameter can be a hash or an array of LDAP::Mod objects. The following snippet corrects Jose's address:

File 35

```
Line 1   user = User.new('23', 'Jane', 'Doe')
     -   address_book = AddressBook.new(connection, user)
     -   recipient = Recipient.new(
     -     'Jose', 'Rodriguez',
     5     'Casanova Street 8', '77002',
     -     'Houston', 'TX',
     -     'Rrrrrrr!'
     -   )
     -   address_book.modify(recipient)
```

Although Jose definitely got Jane's present this time, he was not as enthusiastic as Jane would have liked, so she decides to remove him from her address book. Fortunately, we have defined an appropriate method already:

File 32

```
Line 1   class AddressBook
     -       def remove(recipient)
     -         cn = recipient.forename + ' ' + recipient.surname
     -         @connection.delete('cn=' + cn + ',' + udn())
     5       end
     -   end
```

The only new thing is the delete(dn) call we used in line 4. Now removing Jose is easy:

File 38

```
Line 1   user = User.new('23', 'Jane', 'Doe')
     -   address_book = AddressBook.new(connection, user)
     -   recipient = Recipient.new('Jose', 'Rodriguez')
     -   address_book.remove(recipient)
```

Two weeks later Jane met a guy called Ron, and now she doesn't need her PragBouquet address book any longer:

File 32

```
Line 1    class AddressBook
   -          def delete() @connection.delete(udn); end
   -      end
```

ActiveLDAP

After reading the preceding sections about databases, ActiveRecord, and LDAP, you might be thinking that it would be a good idea to develop an ActiveRecord equivalent for LDAP. What would you call it? Active-LDAP, perhaps? I've got good news for you: Will Drewry had the same idea. He has released a small library called ActiveLDAP that maps LDAP repository structures to Ruby classes, and vice versa.[29] Under the hood, it is based on Ian Macdonald's Ruby/LDAP library.

Let's use ActiveLDAP to clean up our customer account data. Users of PragBouquet's web shop have to enter their e-mail address and a password to create an account. These two values are stored in an LDAP repository. Later, they can be used to log into the web shop, allowing them to place new orders or look at current orders.

People who have an account do not necessarily have to be customers. Unless someone actually ordered something from the shop, PragBouquet will not ask for address data, and so on. As a result, there are nominal accounts that have been created but never have been used for shopping. The marketing department wants to know how many there are, and it wants the e-mail addresses belonging to these accounts. (Maybe they can find out why these people never bought anything.)

PragBouquet runs an OpenLDAP server that manages the account data of all customers and of all employees. The server has been configured like this:

File 30

```
Line 1    include /sw/etc/openldap/schema/core.schema
   -      include /sw/etc/openldap/schema/cosine.schema
   -      include /sw/etc/openldap/schema/nis.schema
   -
   5      database bdb
   -      suffix "dc=pragbouquet,dc=com"
   -      rootdn "cn=root,dc=pragbouquet,dc=com"
   -      rootpw secret
   -      directory /sw/var/openldap-data
  10      index objectclass eq
```

---

[29]http://ruby-activeldap.rubyforge.org

Because we store account data that depends on the posixGroup and posixAccount object classes, we have to include the nis schema. This schema in turn depends on the cosine schema, so we include that, too.

Sample data in the repository looks like this:

File 27

```
Line 1    # Create the PragBouquet organization.
   -      dn: dc=pragbouquet,dc=com
   -      objectclass: dcObject
   -      objectclass: organization
   5      o: PragBouquet
   -      dc: pragbouquet
   -
   -      # Create a container for all groups.
   -      dn:ou=Groups,dc=pragbouquet,dc=com
  10      objectclass: organizationalUnit
   -      ou: Groups
   -
   -      # Create a group for employee accounts.
   -      dn:cn=employees,ou=Groups,dc=pragbouquet,dc=com
  15      objectclass: top
   -      objectclass: posixGroup
   -      cn: employees
   -      gidNumber: 42
   -
  20      # Create a group for customer accounts.
   -      dn:cn=customers,ou=Groups,dc=pragbouquet,dc=com
   -      objectclass: top
   -      objectclass: posixGroup
   -      cn: customers
  25      gidNumber: 23
   -
   -      # Create an account for employee Maik Schmidt.
   -      dn:uid=mschmidt,cn=employees,ou=Groups,dc=pragbouquet,dc=com
   -      objectclass: top
  30      objectclass: account
   -      objectclass: posixAccount
   -      cn: Maik Schmidt
   -      uid: mschmidt
   -      uidNumber: 1000
  35      gidNumber: 42
   -      userPassword: {SSHA}wFH8hVlIQKttNK2+334mh2K3PHBRv9Lt
   -      homeDirectory: /home/mschmidt
   -
   -      # Create an account for employee Carl Coder.
  40      dn:uid=ccoder,cn=employees,ou=Groups,dc=pragbouquet,dc=com
   -      objectclass: top
   -      objectclass: account
   -      objectclass: posixAccount
   -      cn: Carl Coder
  45      uid: ccoder
```

```
       uidNumber: 1001
       gidNumber: 42
       userPassword: {SSHA}ytRSx9Sc8v3RmitArARTfPRdQRCGZRs9
       homeDirectory: /home/ccoder
50
       # Create an account for Homer Simpson.
       dn:uid=homer@example.com,cn=customers,ou=Groups,dc=pragbouquet,dc=com
       objectclass: top
       objectclass: account
55     objectclass: posixAccount
       cn: Homer Simpson
       uid: homer@example.com
       uidNumber: 2000
       gidNumber: 23
60     userPassword: {SSHA}DFTpR8b5R+x+p5E9fj1NZwrQQLRgfeBn
       homeDirectory: /tmp


       # Create an account for Jane Doe.
       dn:uid=jane_doe@example.net,cn=customers,ou=Groups,dc=pragbouquet,dc=com
65     objectclass: top
       objectclass: account
       objectclass: posixAccount
       cn: Jane Doe
       uid: jane_doe@example.net
70     uidNumber: 2001
       gidNumber: 23
       userPassword: {SSHA}lc7hXzhDP9T8qS51TUSE/89oLfq4EWti
       homeDirectory: /tmp
```

There are two groups, called "customers" and "employees." Each has two entries: Carl Coder and Maik Schmidt belong to the employees group, and Homer Simpson and Jane Doe to the customers group.

In Ruby, we'll represent these groups using classes Group and Customer. Our hope is that (just as ActiveRecord does for database tables) Active-LDAP will create them automatically for us.

But before we can use ActiveLDAP, we have to initialize it:

File 26

```
Line 1    require 'rubygems'
          require 'activeldap'

          ActiveLDAP::Base.connect(
5           :base => 'dc=pragbouquet,dc=com',
            :bind_format => 'cn=root,dc=pragbouquet,dc=com',
            :password_block => Proc.new { 'secret' },
            :allow_anonymous => false
          )
```

After loading the ActiveLDAP Gem, call ActiveLDAP::Base.connect(options), passing it the following options:

- base defines the search base that will be appended to all distinguished name attributes.
- bind_format contains the distinguished name to be used for binding to the server. Usually, this is the rootdn defined in the OpenLDAP server configuration.
- password_block points to a code block that returns a password. Defaults to nil.
- If allow_anonymous is true, it is possible to bind to the server anonymously after all other bind methods fail. Otherwise it is not. Defaults to true.

The connect() method supports many more options, but we don't need them here. If you don't want to modify data in your LDAP repository and your server allows anonymous binding, you don't have to call connect() at all—ActiveLDAP will do it for you automatically:

File 26

```
Line 1    class Group < ActiveLDAP::Base
   -          ldap_mapping :dnattr => 'cn', :prefix => 'ou=Groups'
   -      end

   5      customers = Group.new('customers')
   -      puts "The 'customers' group has the following attributes:"
   -      customers.attributes.each { |a| puts "  #{a}" }

   -      puts "\nIts group id is #{customers.gidNumber}."
  10
   -      puts "\nWe have the following groups:"
   -      Group.find_all('*').each { |g| puts "  #{g}" }
```

This produces the following:

```
The 'customers' group has the following attributes:
  gidNumber
  cn
  memberUid
  commonName
  description
  userPassword
  objectClass

Its group id is 23.

We have the following groups:
  employees
  customers
```

Although the example is short, there's a lot to be explained. In line 1 we derive our Group class from ActiveLDAP::Base. That would be sufficient if we were mapping a relational database using ActiveRecord, but for LDAP we have to call ldap_mapping() in line 2. It accepts the following parameters:

- prefix is the static (more or less) part of the distinguished name that will always be prepended to the base defined in the connect() call. It defaults to `ou=class name` (`ou=Group` in our case).

- dnattr contains the variable part of the distinguished name of an object. It defaults to `cn`, so we could have left it out this time.

- classes contains an array of all object classes whose attributes should be mapped to the ActiveLDAP object. Its default value is [`top`].

When we create the ActiveLDAP object in line 5, it references the LDAP object with the DN cn=customers,ou=Groups,dc=pragbouquet,dc=com.

In line 7 we use the reflective features of ActiveLDAP for the first time and print a list of all attributes belonging to a Group object. ActiveLDAP gives you accessors for all these attributes for free.

Then, in line 12, we read some real data from our repository with the find_all() method. ActiveLDAP objects can use the following class methods to search for entries in a repository:

- find(config={}) returns the dnattr of the first entry that matches a certain query. config can be a String or a Hash object. If it is a String, it will be matched against dnattr. For example, Group.find(`e*`) returns the common name attribute of the first group entry whose cn attribute starts with e. In our case, it returns `employees`.

  If config is a hash, it may contain the keys:attribute,:value, and :objects. The :attribute and :value parameters can be used to search for objects where a particular attribute has a particular value. To find the common name of the group having the group ID 23, run the following statement:

  ```
  Group.find(:attribute => 'gidNumber', :value => '23')
  ```

  Usually, you are not interested only in the dnattr of an object but in the object itself. To get back complete objects, pass :objects => true:

  ```
  Group.find(
    :attribute => 'gidNumber',
    :value => '23',
    :objects => true)
  ```

- find_all(config={}) works like the find() method but returns *all* the entries matching a certain query.

- search(config={}) gives you more or less direct access to the search() method of the underlying Ruby/LDAP library. It implements the :attrs, :base, :filter, and :scope parameters, corresponding to the attributes, base_dn, filter, and scope parameters of the Ruby/LDAP search() method described on page 62. The return value has the same format, too:

```
Group.search(:filter => '(cn=cus*)')
```

This returns the following:

```
[
  {
    "gidNumber" => ["23"],
    "cn" => ["customers"],
    "objectClass" => ["posixGroup"],
    "dn" => ["cn=customers,ou=Groups,dc=pragbouquet,dc=com"]
  }
]
```

The following code segment separates the customer account data from the employee account data:

File 26

```
Line 1    class Customer < ActiveLDAP::Base
   -        ldap_mapping :dnattr => 'uid',
   -                     :prefix => 'cn=customers,ou=Groups'
   -        end
   5
   -        puts "Our customers are:"
   -        Customer.find_all('*').each { |c| puts "  #{c}" }
   -        h = Customer.new('homer@example.com')
   -        puts "\nCommon name attribute:"
  10        p h.cn
   -        p h.cn(true)
```

This produces the following:

```
Our customers are:
  homer@example.com
  jane_doe@example.net

Common name attribute:
  ["Homer Simpson"]
   "Homer Simpson"
```

The definition of the Customer class does not differ much from the Group class—we just set the dnattr and prefix attributes differently. In lines 10 and 11, we print the common name attribute of a Customer object.

Usually, all attribute values will be returned as an array, as every LDAP attribute is potentially multidimensional. If you want to get back an attribute value as a String object, pass true to the accessor.

We have everything at hand now to solve our little problem. The following method expects an array containing the e-mail addresses of all customers who have ever bought something in our web shop. It returns a list of e-mail addresses of all people who have created an account but have never used it to send some flowers:

File 26
```ruby
Line 1   def get_unused_accounts(used_accounts)
    -        unused_accounts = []
    -        Customer.find_all('*').each do |email|
    -          unused_accounts << email if !used_accounts.include?(email)
    5        end
    -        unused_accounts
    -      end

    -      puts get_unused_accounts(['homer@example.com'])
```

Our original job is done, but since we have a test system up and running anyway, wouldn't it be fun to see what other interesting features ActiveLDAP has to offer?

Perhaps you want to delete the unused accounts?

File 26
```ruby
Line 1   def delete_unused_accounts(used_accounts)
    -        Customer.find_all('*').each do |cn|
    -          Customer.new(cn).delete if !used_accounts.include?(cn)
    -        end
    5      end
```

Or perhaps you want to tag them with a special note in their description attribute?

File 26
```ruby
Line 1   def mark_unused_accounts(used_accounts)
    -
    -        Customer.find_all('*').each do |cn|
    -          if !used_accounts.include?(cn)
    5            c = Customer.new(cn)
    -            c.description = 'unused'
    -            c.write
    -          end
    -        end
    10     end
```

ActiveLDAP gives us all the CRUD methods for free. This feature alone makes it a valuable tool. But it gives us even more, allowing us to define relationships between objects as if we were working with a relational database:

```
File 28   Line 1   class Customer < ActiveLDAP::Base
            -          ldap_mapping :dnattr => 'uid',
            -                       :prefix => 'cn=customers,ou=Groups'
            -
            5          belongs_to :groups,
            -                     :class_name => 'Group',
            -                     :foreign_key => 'gidNumber',
            -                     :local_key => 'gidNumber'
            -          end
           10
            -          h = Customer.new('homer@example.com')
            -          h.groups.each { |g| puts g.cn }
```

This prints the following:

```
customers
```

Great, isn't it? In line 5 we declare that every customer belongs to a group, with the relationship defined by the gidNumber attribute in both the Group and Customer classes. The first parameter of the belongs_to() method is the name of the new member variable to be created in the Customer class. The second parameter is a hash that contains up to three parameters: :class_name points to the class to which your current class belongs. :foreign_key determines which attribute of the "foreign" class should be used to build the relationship, and :local_key determines which attribute of the local class will be considered.

The newly created groups method accepts an optional boolean argument. If you pass true, it returns an array of Group objects. If you pass false, you'll get back an array of strings containing the dnattr of every group to which our customer belongs.

If you know ActiveRecord, you'll know that if you have a method called belongs_to(), there's likely to be a method called has_many(), too:

```
File 29   Line 1   class Group < ActiveLDAP::Base
            -          ldap_mapping :dnattr => 'cn', :prefix => 'ou=Groups'
            -          has_many :members,
            -                   :class_name => 'Employee',
            5                   :local_key => 'gidNumber',
            -                   :foreign_key => 'gidNumber'
            -          end
            -
            -          class Employee < ActiveLDAP::Base
           10          ldap_mapping :dnattr => 'uid',
            -                       :prefix => 'cn=employees,ou=Groups'
            -          end
            -
            -          employees = Group.new('employees')
           15          employees.members.each { |e| puts e.cn }
```

This outputs the following list:

```
Maik Schmidt
Carl Coder
```

There is really not much to say here: has_many(member,options) works
exactly like belongs_to(member,options).

Conclusion

ActiveLDAP is in an early stage of development, and it will certainly
take some time until all the details are settled. Despite this, it's an
amazingly useful tool and makes working with LDAP a breeze.

Chapter 3

Processing XML

Exchanging data between processes, components, and companies has always been a vital part of enterprise software. Many attempts have been made to create a universal format for data exchange, but they all have failed for various technical and political reasons.

It's hard to believe it took several decades before something like a standard for a platform-independent data representation was both created *and* accepted. The *eXtensible Markup Language* (XML) has, over the years, evolved into such an industry standard for portable data. That's because it has some useful characteristics:

eXtensible Markup Language

- It is plain text.

- It has been standardized by the W3C.[1]

- It is machine independent (so low-level details such as byte ordering do not matter).

- It is easy to use.

- It supports international character sets.

XML is supported by all modern programming languages. The current Ruby distribution comes with good XML support, but compared to languages such as Java and C#, there is still a lot to be done. On the one hand, it is easy to create and parse XML documents in Ruby. On the other hand, Ruby lacks support for some important technologies such as Document Type Definitions (DTDs), schema validation, and XSLT.

---

[1]http://www.w3.org/XML

REXML: What's the Difference?

Although several XML parsers exist for Ruby (for example, NQXML* or xmlparser[†]), the most popular is Sean Russel's REXML.

The majority of XML parsers are based on either the SAX2 or DOM APIs. These have been standardized and hence look the same in all programming languages. That's certainly a good thing, because if you're familiar with DOM programming in Java, you do not have to learn a lot to do DOM programming in C++ or Ruby.

The downside is that general approaches such as DOM are a compromise and tend not to be tailored to exploit the strengths of a particular language. Sean Russel felt so too, and while looking for better alternatives he found the Electric XML library for Java (created by a company called The Mind Electric).[‡] REXML is a pure Ruby implementation of the original Electric XML API.

REXML is not a copy of the Java API but a genuine Ruby port. All classes and methods have been renamed to follow Ruby conventions, and special Ruby features (such as iterators) have been used wherever it was possible and advantageous. In addition, REXML comes with a lot of features that were not part of the original Electric XML interface. There is support for SAX2, a proprietary stream parsing API, an experimental pull parser, and an experimental RELAX NG validator.

---

*`http://nqxml.sourceforge.net`
[†]This is a binding for James Clark's expat XML parser. It can be found under `http://www.yoshidam.net/Ruby.html#xmlparser`.
[‡]The company is called Webmethods today, and the Electric XML library is now integrated into their products. It's no longer available as a stand-alone product.

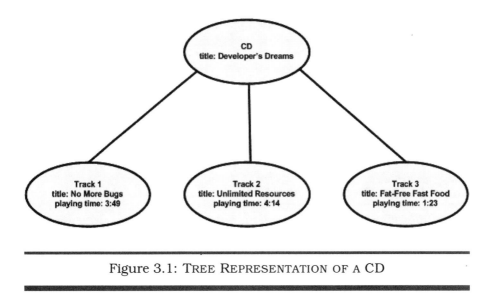

Figure 3.1: TREE REPRESENTATION OF A CD

It's unlikely that you can find a single company in this world that does not use XML in some capacity and a lot of enterprise data is no longer only stored in tables but between angle brackets. Hence, you better know how to extract it and in the following sections we'll cover the most important XML-processing requirements: we'll show you how to create XML documents, how to parse them, and how to validate them.

3.1 A Short XML Reminder

XML is a subset of the more flexible and more liberal *Standard Generalized Markup Language* (SGML). It allows you to define your own markup languages for describing data organized hierarchically in a tree structure. For example, Figure 3.1 shows a possible tree representation of an audio CD. Its XML representation might look like this:

Standard Generalized Markup Language

```xml
<?xml version='1.0' encoding='ISO-8859-1'?>

<!-- Comments look like this! -->
<cd title="Developer's Dreams">
  <track id='1' title='No More Bugs' playing-time='3:49'/>
  <track id='2' title='Unlimited Resources' playing-time='4:14'/>
  <track id='3' title='Fat-Free Fast Food' playing-time='1:23'/>
</cd>
```

All XML documents must be well-formed, which roughly means the following:

- The document must have a single top-level element.

- All elements have to be closed explicitly, and they have to be nested properly; i.e., `<a><b></a></b>` is not allowed, because element `<b>` must be closed before element `<a>`.

- Attributes always have a value, and this value has to be set in single or double quotes. HTML attributes such as NOWRAP or colspan=5 are not allowed in XML documents.

Should I Use Elements or Attributes?

Sometimes it's just a matter of taste, but more often it's a decision that should be made carefully.

The following cases force us to use elements:

- The information you want to describe can potentially occur more than once or can potentially have child elements. It's important to plan for such cases up front—if you are not sure, use an element.

- Whitespace characters are significant.

In other cases, we prefer attributes over elements:

- You do not have to worry about whitespace characters. Using attributes, it's clear that hello differs from ⌞hello⌟.

- Attributes often produce less noise and are more readable. For example, compare this:

```
<person>
  <name>Homer</name>
  <middle-name>Jay</middle-name>
  <surname>Simpson</surname>
</person>
```

to this:

```
<person name="Homer" middle-name="Jay" surname="Simpson"/>
```

- Attributes are slightly faster, because they usually need less space than elements, and therefore less text has to be processed by the XML parser (this is especially true for documents with long tag names for elements that get opened and closed over and over again). In addition, they increase parsing speed because of the inner structure of most XML parsers. Many XML parsers are event driven and use the SAX2 API. They search for the start tag of elements, and whenever they find one, they call the startElement()

method, transmitting the element name and a list of all attributes belonging to the current element.

If you have a document fragment looking like this:

```
<book>
  <title>Pragmatic Project Automation</title>
  <isbn>0974514039</isbn>
  <publisher>Pragmatic Bookshelf</publisher>
</book>
```

startElement( ) is called four times (for each of the elements *<book>*, *<title>*, *<isbn>*, and *<publisher>*), and calling methods in programming languages supporting polymorphism is expensive. If we use attributes instead of elements, our document will look like this:

```
<book title='Pragmatic Project Automation' isbn='0974514039'
      publisher='Pragmatic Bookshelf' />
```

Now startElement( ) is called only once for every *<book>* element. You might not consider this a big performance boost, but if you're Amazon.com and have to parse several hundred thousand books having dozens of elements, it certainly will matter.

3.2 Generating XML Documents

Generating XML documents is often necessary for communicating with other systems. If you are using technologies such as SOAP or XML-RPC, you do not have to worry about the XML generation yourself, because it will be done under the hood by supporting libraries. But there are still many applications today expecting XML documents that you have to create "manually."

In this section we'll show you various techniques for generating XML documents. You'll see how to create documents using rather naive approaches (such as writing raw strings). We'll then look at more sophisticated technologies, such as the REXML API.

To Score Well

From the beginning, customers using PragBouquet's web shop could freely choose from various payment methods: prepaid, invoice, or credit card. But after some months you came to realize that there were actually customers who cheated you. They ordered flowers but never paid for them. Therefore, the company decided to buy a so-called e-score

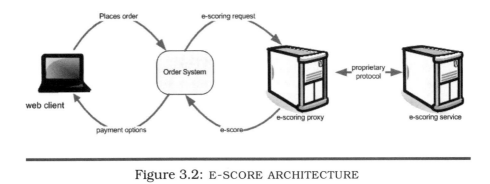

Figure 3.2: E-SCORE ARCHITECTURE

application. This assigns a risk score to each of your new customers. A customer with a low e-score will be allowed to order only if he or she pays up front.

The e-score provider uses a proprietary protocol but gives you a proxy application that hides all that stuff behind an XML/HTTP layer. It expects an XML file containing a list of customers and returns a similar document where every customer is assigned a risk score. You can see the architecture in Figure 3.2.

It's your task to convert a customer address into an XML document acceptable to the e-scoring application. Based on the response, you'll then decide which payment options will be offered to the customer.

The input documents are simple: they consist of a list of *<person>* elements. Of course, the e-scoring company—like every company employing more than two people—defined its own XML markup, looking like this:

File 169

```
<persons>
  <person name='Max' surname='Mustermann'>
    <address>
      <street>Musterstr. 42</street>
      <city>Berlin</city>
      <postal-code>11011</postal-code>
    </address>
  </person>
</persons>
```

Generating XML Documents Using Raw Strings

Because XML documents are nothing but text, it's tempting to generate them using strings. So, let's start with a simple helper function that tags a certain value:

```
Line 1   def tag(tag_name, value, attrs ={})
    -        tmp = "<#{tag_name}"
    -        if attrs
    -          attrs.each { |k,v| tmp += " #{k}='#{v}' " }
    5        end
    -        tmp + ">#{value}</#{tag_name}>\n"
    -      end
    -
    -      puts tag('hello', 'world')
    10     puts tag('a', 'b', { 'c' => 'd' })
```

This produces the following:

```
<hello>world</hello>
<a c='d'>b</a>
```

For generating our *<person>* elements, we'll take the object-oriented road—we'll create classes for both addresses and persons. Because they are only storage classes, we use Struct to create them automatically then add to_xml() methods to turn them into XML documents:

```
Line 1   Address = Struct.new(:street, :city, :postal_code)
    -
    -      class Address
    -        def to_xml
    5          tag('address',
    -            tag('street', self.street) +
    -            tag('city', self.city) +
    -            tag('postal-code', self.postal_code)
    -          )
    10       end
    -      end
```

One of the things that makes working with Ruby so much fun is reopening classes. After Struct created an Address class for us, we reopened its definition and added our to_xml() method. It works the same way for the Person class:

```
Line 1   Person = Struct.new(:name, :surname, :address)
    -
    -      class Person
    -        def to_xml
    5          tag('person',
    -            self.address.to_xml, {
    -              'name' => self.name,
    -              'surname' => self.surname
    -            }
    10         )
    -        end
    -      end
```

Finally, we check whether it all works together:

```
Line 1    address = Address.new(
   -         'Musterstr. 42',
   -         'Berlin',
   -         '11011'
   5      )
   -      max_m = Person.new('Max', 'Mustermann', address)
   -      puts max_m.to_xml
```

This produces the following:

```
<person name='Max' surname='Mustermann'><address>
    <street>Musterstr. 42</street>
<city>Berlin</city>
<postal-code>11011</postal-code>
</address>
</person>
```

Although everything looks fine, you should follow this approach only in the simplest cases, because it has some serious disadvantages. For example, you cannot move around and refine document fragments. This is a pity, because XML is such a flexible format and it happens often that new elements or attributes get added to existing document structures. If you've worked exclusively with strings, you have to either parse or manipulate them directly to add the new stuff.

Let's assume we have access to one of those new localization services that determine the geographic coordinates of an address, and you want to add this information to the XML representation of the Address objects without both adding a position attribute and changing to_xml().

Accessing the localization service is easy: you give it the street, the postal code, and the city, and it returns a pair of coordinates:

```
address = Address.new(
  'Musterstr. 42',
  '11011',
  'Berlin'
)
coordinates = LocalizationService.locate(address)
puts coordinates.latitude    # -> 51.5245
puts coordinates.longitude   # -> 6.75
```

Representing the coordinates in XML would probably look like this:

```
<position latitude='51.5245' longitude='6.75' />
```

How can you add this to an existing XML file containing <address> elements? You can try using regular expressions and all the fancy methods of the String class, but think about it for a moment: did you consider all special cases? What about comments or CDATA sections? What

Character	XML Entity	Character	XML Entity
'	'	"	"
<	<	>	>
&	&		

Figure 3.3: XML STANDARD ENTITIES

---

about *<address>* elements that don't belong to *<person>* elements? Or *<address>* elements that already have a *<position>* element?

You have to admit that it can get complicated. Sometimes it's nearly impossible to perform this kind of manipulation without parsing the document fragment, adding the new stuff using conventional DOM manipulation methods, and finally creating a new XML string again.

Believe it or not, we still have some disadvantages left. For example, if you work with raw strings, chances are good that you forget to mark up elements correctly as we did in our tag() function previously. What if a person's address is Main Street 7 & 8? The resulting *<street>* element would be as follows:

```
<street>Main Street 7 & 8</street>
```

Every standards-compliant XML parser will reject this, complaining that your document isn't well-formed—blanks are not allowed after an ampersand. Whenever the parser sees an ampersand, it assumes it introduces an entity reference, which has to have an alphanumeric name, ends with a semicolon, and has been defined in a Document Type Definition (DTD). Similar things will happen whenever you use one of XML's special characters. If you really want to use strings for generating your documents, you'll have to replace these characters with their standard entities shown in Figure 3.3.

Adding such a mechanism to our tag() method is easy:

```ruby
def encode_markup(text)
  return '' if text.nil? or text == ''
  text.gsub!('&', '&amp;')
  text.gsub!("'", '&apos;')
  text.gsub!('"', '&quot;')
  text.gsub!('<', '&lt;')
  text.gsub!('>', '&gt;')
end
```

```
def tag(tag_name, value, attrs = nil)
  tmp = "<#{tag_name}"
  if attrs
    attrs.each { |k,v| tmp += " #{k}='#{encode_markup(v)}' " }
  end
  tmp + ">#{encode_markup(value)}</#{tag_name}>\n"
end

puts tag('favorite', 'Starsky & Hutch')
```

This produces the following:

```
<favorite>Starsky &amp; Hutch</favorite>
```

You'll face more subtle problems if you ignore character set issues (as we did in the tag() method). An XML document that does not explicitly specify a character set encoding in its header automatically is supposed to contain only UTF-8 characters. For ASCII texts this is perfect, but what if you have a customer from Germany with the popular surname Müller? In UTF-8 the German umlaut, ü, is represented as a two-byte sequence (0xc2, 0x81), but it's a single byte (0xfc) in the character set ISO-8859-1 (see Section 6.1, *Internationalization and Localization*, on page 243, for more details).

Whenever you get text data from an external source, from a database, from a file, or from an HTTP server, for example, you have to determine what character set encoding has been used.

If the specified encoding and the document's content do not match, your XML parser will reject it or—even worse—will misinterpret some characters. Before reading on, you should have a look at Joel Spolsky's awesome essay *The Absolute Minimum Every Software Developer Absolutely, Positively Must Know About Unicode and Character Sets (No Excuses!).*[2]

Iconv

For our documents we now have two choices: we can set the encoding attribute in the XML header correctly, or we can convert our final document into UTF-8. To convert texts between different character sets in Ruby, you can use the *Iconv* library. Its interface is simple: a single line of code converts text encoded in the ISO-8859-1 character set into the UTF-8 character set:

```
Iconv.conv('utf-8', 'iso-8859-1', 'Müller')
```

---

[2]http://www.joelonsoftware.com/articles/Unicode.html

Our final version of method tag() will use this, assuming that all element and attribute values are encoded in ISO-8859-1:

e 172

```ruby
Line 1    require 'iconv'
    -
    -     def empty?(text) text.nil? or text == ''; end
    -
    5     def encode_markup(text)
    -         return '' if empty?(text)
    -         text.gsub!('&', '&amp;')
    -         text.gsub!("'", '&apos;')
    -         text.gsub!('"', '&quot;')
    10        text.gsub!('<', '&lt;')
    -         text.gsub!('>', '&gt;')
    -     end
    -
    -     def to_utf8(text)
    15        Iconv.conv('utf-8', 'iso-8859-1', text)
    -     end
    -
    -     def encode(value)
    -         encode_markup(to_utf8(value))
    20    end
    -
    -     def tag(tag_name, value, attrs ={})
    -         tmp = "<#{tag_name}"
    -         if !attrs.nil? and !attrs.empty?
    25            attrs.each { |k,v| tmp += " #{k}='#{encode(v)}' " }
    -         end
    -         if !empty?(value)
    -             tmp += ">#{encode(value)}</#{tag_name}>\n"
    -         else
    30            tmp += "/>\n"
    -         end
    -     end
    -     end
```

This version is much better than our first one, but it's also much longer,
and it still has some flaws that cannot be solved easily. For example, it
does not check whether element and attribute names are valid according to the XML standard (be honest: do you know the rules?). Additionally, you cannot reformat the generated document—you do not have
much control over indentation, line breaks, etc. Obviously, generating
well-formed XML documents is not as simple as it seems.

Generating XML Documents with REXML

Although REXML does not implement the original DOM interface, it
offers an API based on trees. Using this API you can convert an XML
document into trees and create trees that represent XML documents.

Everything starts with a document. With REXML you create it like this:

```
require 'rexml/document'
doc = REXML::Document.new
```

An empty document is as useful as an empty bottle of beer. Let's add an element to it:

```
root = REXML::Element.new('my-root')
doc.add_element(root)
puts doc.to_s
```

This produces the following:

```
<my-root/>
```

Creating attributes makes our toolbox complete:

```
root.add_attribute('an-attribute', 'a-value')
puts doc.to_s
```

This results in the following:

```
<my-root an-attribute='a-value'/>
```

Now we can turn our Address object into XML the right way.

File 174

```
Line 1    class Address
   -        def to_xml
   -          adr = REXML::Element.new('address')
   -          adr.add_element('street').add_text(self.street)
   5          adr.add_element('city').add_text(self.city)
   -          adr.add_element('postal-code').add_text(self.postal_code)
   -          adr
   -        end
   -      end
  10
   -      address.to_xml.write($stdout, 0)
```

This produces the following:

```
<address>
  <street>Musterstr. 42</street>
  <city>Berlin</city>
  <postal-code>11011</postal-code>
</address>
```

That's how it should look: every element is created explicitly, and the to_xml() method no longer returns a simple string but a document fragment. In addition, we can now use the write() method. This allows us to control the string representation of an XML document. It expects an object derived from IO and the level of indentation to be used.

The result of the to_xml() method can be processed further by other methods now. Adding coordinates to an Address object, for example, can be done like this:

e 174

```
Line 1   adr = address.to_xml
     -   pos = REXML::Element.new('position')
     -   pos.add_attribute('longitude', '12.345')
     -   pos.add_attribute('latitude', '56.789')
     5   adr.add_element(pos)
     -   adr.write($stdout, 0)
```

This produces the following:

```
<address>
  <street>Musterstr. 42</street>
  <city>Berlin</city>
  <postal-code>11011</postal-code>
  <position latitude='56.789' longitude='12.345' />
</address>
```

REXML correctly encodes markup characters, but you still can't ignore character set encoding issues. REXML internally uses the UTF-8 character set, so you have to encode all strings before inserting them into a REXML document, and you have to decode them accordingly when reading them back.

We already saw how to achieve this using the Iconv library in Section 3.2, *Generating XML Documents Using Raw Strings*, on page 86. You can also use Ruby's unpack() and pack() methods.

"hello".unpack("C*").pack("U*") turns a string into UTF-8. To do the opposite, call "hello".unpack("U*").pack("C*").

Builder

As we've seen, building well-formed XML documents is not a trivial task. So people constantly try to simplify it. One of those people is Jim Weirich, who produced the Builder library for Ruby.[3] Its core class is Builder::XmlMarkup, which provides everything you need to generate well-formed XML documents. For example:

le 158

```
Line 1   require 'rubygems'
     -   require 'builder'
     -
     -   doc = Builder::XmlMarkup.new
     5   doc.person(:name => 'Max', :surname => 'Mustermann')
     -   puts doc.target!
```

---

[3]http://builder.rubyforge.org

This prints the following little document:

```
<person surname="Mustermann" name="Max"/>
```

The technique is probably familiar to Ruby fans: Builder defines a special handler named method_missing() that catches calls to unknown methods and turns them into XML tags with the same name as the method that was called originally. In addition, a hash of parameters is turned into attributes of the newly created element.

The resulting document can be obtained by calling target!() as we did in line 6.

To build hierarchical documents, XmlMarkup has a nice syntax: if you pass a code block to one of those "unknown" methods, it gets passed the current element automatically:

File 158

```
Line 1    xml = ''
    -     doc = Builder::XmlMarkup.new(:target => xml)
    -     doc.person(:name => 'Max', :surname => 'Mustermann') { |person|
    -       person.address { |address|
    5         address.street('Hauptstr. 42')
    -       }
    -     }
    -     puts xml
```

This produces the following:

```
<person surname="Mustermann" name="Max"><address>
   <street>Hauptstr. 42</street></address></person>
```

Intuitive, isn't it? Note that in line 2 we have specified the target option and set it explicitly to a String object. Hence, Builder fills up the xml variable with our document. The target option accepts any object that responds to the <<(text) operator.

That's all very nice, but the formatting of the result document is, let's say, suboptimal. Fortunately, there is the indent option:

File 158

```
Line 1    xml = ''
    -     doc = Builder::XmlMarkup.new(:target => xml, :indent => 2)
    -     doc.person(:name => 'Max', :surname => 'Mustermann') { |person|
    -       person.address { |address|
    5         address.street('Hauptstr. 42')
    -         address.tag!('postal-code', '12345')
    -         address.city('Musterstadt')
    -       }
    -     }
    10    puts xml
```

This prints this beautiful XML document:

```
<person surname="Mustermann" name="Max">
  <address>
    <street>Hauptstr. 42</street>
    <postal-code>12345</postal-code>
    <city>Musterstadt</city>
  </address>
</person>
```

There's also a margin option, which specifies the indentation offset, so you can format your XML documents in any way you like.

Did you notice the little trick with the postal code in line 6? postal-code() is not a valid method name in Ruby, but <postal-code> is a perfectly valid XML tag. To get around this, Builder lets you explicitly insert tags using the tag!(sym,*args,&block) method.

To make sure that we do not get into trouble when XML documents without an explicit encoding get prohibited by federal law, we better add another line of code:

```
Line 1   xml = ''
   -     doc = Builder::XmlMarkup.new(:target => xml, :indent => 2)
   -     doc.instruct!
   -
   5     doc.person(:name => 'Max', :surname => 'Mustermann') { |person|
   -       person.address { |address|
   -         address.street('Hauptstr. 42')
   -         address.tag!('postal-code', '12345')
   -         address.city('Musterstadt')
   10      }
   -
   -       person.position(:longitude => '12.345', :latitude => '56.789')
   -     }
   -
   15    puts xml
```

This produces this perfect XML document:

```
<?xml version="1.0" encoding="UTF-8"?>
<person surname="Mustermann" name="Max">
  <address>
    <street>Hauptstr. 42</street>
    <postal-code>12345</postal-code>
    <city>Musterstadt</city>
  </address>
  <position longitude="12.345" latitude="56.789"/>
</person>
```

That's nearly all you have to know to create XML documents with Builder, but for some special cases you'd might need to use some of the following methods as well:

text!(text)

Allows you to create elements with mixed content:

File 158

```
doc = Builder::XmlMarkup.new(:indent => 2)
doc.foo { |f|
  f.bar
  f.text! "I live outside the bar!\n"
}
puts doc.target!
```

This prints the following:

```
<foo>
  <bar/>
I live outside the bar!
</foo>
```

cdata!(data)

Inserts a CDATA section into an XML document:

File 158

```
doc = Builder::XmlMarkup.new
doc.cdata!('Do not run with scissors!')
puts doc.target!
```

This prints the following:

```
<![CDATA[Do not run with scissors!]]>
```

comment!(text)

Inserts a comment into an XML document:

File 158

```
doc = Builder::XmlMarkup.new
doc.comment!('Some comments are totally useless!')
puts doc.target!
```

This prints the following:

```
<!-- Some comments are totally useless! -->
```

declare!(instruction,*args,&block)

Allows you to insert DTD declarations into your document:

File 158

```
doc = Builder::XmlMarkup.new
doc.declare!(:ENTITY, :pp, 'Pragmatic Programmers')
puts doc.target!
```

This prints the following:

```
<!ENTITY pp "Pragmatic Programmers">
```

Conclusion

It should be clear by now that creating XML documents is by no means as simple as it seems. Because of this, you've probably already received or created documents that were not well-formed or that contained characters that did not match the document's encoding.

Although it is tempting to use a raw string approach, it does not scale very well and has a lot of drawbacks. Compared to using REXML or Builder, it's even more complex and results in more code (and ugly code). From a pragmatic point of view it is certainly beneficial to do it correctly from the beginning. In *Refactoring to Patterns* [Ker04], you will even find patterns that help you to refactor "I absolutely wanted to create XML myself" code.

3.3 Processing XML Documents

Imagine you've sent a bunch of flowers to a person you like. Wouldn't it be interesting to know whether he or she got the flowers on time, or even whether the person refused the flowers? Fortunately, all big parcel services offer their customers the opportunity to check the status of a parcel using the Internet.

PragBouquet works together with several parcel services. Although we could simply give our customers the tracking numbers assigned by the particular service to their order, that means they would then need to visit the shipping service's site and enter that number to track their flowers. That isn't great customer service on our part.

A better solution is to periodically track the status of all undelivered orders in our system and inform our customers about all important events in the life of a delivery via e-mail or SMS messages. To do this, we'll have to take a closer look at the parcel service's web services.

A typical parcel tracking result looks like this:

ile 177

```
<tracking-result>
  <parcel-history tracking-no='2X42'>
    <event timestamp='2005-05-02T04:05:00'
        state='picked-up' />
    <event timestamp='2005-05-02T08:30:00'
        state='first-delivery-attempt' />
    <event timestamp='2005-05-03T09:05:00'
        state='second-delivery-attempt' />
    <event timestamp='2005-05-04T10:15:00'
        state='refused-damaged'>
      <consignee>Mrs. Smith</consignee>
    </event>
    <event timestamp='2005-05-04T19:07:00' state='returns-to-sender' />
  </parcel-history>
```

```
<parcel-history tracking-no='2X43'>
  <event timestamp='2005-05-02T04:25:00' state='picked-up'/>
  <event timestamp='2005-05-02T09:15:00' state='delivered'>
    <consignee>Mr. Gumble</consignee>
  </event>
</parcel-history>

<parcel-history tracking-no='2X44'>
  <event timestamp='2005-05-02T03:55:00' state='picked-up'/>
</parcel-history>
</tracking-result>
```

Here we have the history of three different parcels, each identified by a unique tracking number:

- Parcel 2X42 was picked up by the parcel service at the production site at 4:05 a.m. on May 2nd. They tried to deliver it on the same day and later on May 3rd without success. On May 4th the driver finally met Mrs. Smith, but she refused to accept the parcel because it was damaged. Now it's on its way back home.

- Parcel 2X43 is a textbook example: Picked up, delivered.

- Parcel 2X44 was picked up but has not yet been delivered.

In the following sections we'll demonstrate how to parse a document such as this using different approaches.

XML Processing with REXML

One of the key problems when dealing with XML documents is parsing them and representing the result in our programs. Currently, there are two major parsing schemes: tree parsing and stream parsing. A tree parser reads an XML document as a whole and represents it as a tree in memory. Stream parsers expect you to provide a so-called listener that is invoked whenever the parser finds a new element. Hence, *all* elements get processed in the order of their start tags, and the listener is responsible for handling them.

Both approaches have their advantages and disadvantages. Tree-style parsers are significantly slower and consume much more memory. On the upside, they give you convenient access to the tree's nodes. On the other hand, stream parsers are fast and do not consume much memory, but they force you to organize the elements yourself. Choosing the right way to parse your documents depends to a large extent on your performance needs and on how you want to process the document. If you want to process every node, a stream parser is what you need. If you often have to access different node sets, a tree parser might be a better choice.

There are standard APIs for both tree and stream parsing: DOM and SAX2, respectively. DOM has been standardized by the W3C, and SAX2 is an open standard maintained by David Megginson.[4] Because it's so simple, there's not much discussion about the usefulness of the SAX2 API. DOM, though, has always been something of an *enfant terrible*. Its inventors wanted the DOM API to work in as many environments and programming languages as possible. Even COBOL programmers should have their DOM parser. This requirement turned DOM into the beast it is today. Ironically, nearly every programming platform now has an additional convenience API for tree parsing. Java, for example, has JDOM[5] and XOM.[6]

REXML is no exception to this rule and supports both tree and stream parsing. For reasons explained in the preceding paragraphs, the only standard API it supports is SAX2. Its tree parsing API is completely proprietary but meets the needs of a Ruby programmer much better than DOM.

Tree Parsing

Easy things should be easy. Turning an XML document into a tree could not be much easier than this:

File 168

```
Line 1    require 'rexml/document'
    -     include REXML
    -
    -     doc = Document.new("<sample>Our first example.</sample>")
    5     print doc.root.name, ": ", doc.root.text, "\n"
```

This produces the following:

```
sample: Our first example.
```

The first two lines load the REXML module and include its namespace into our code, so we don't have to prefix all its class names with REXML:: over and over again (from now on we're going to omit these lines). By calling Document.new() with our little example document in line 4, we

---

[4]http://www.saxproject.org
[5]http://www.jdom.org
[6]http://www.xom.nu

turn a string into an instance of class Document. The new() method accepts parameters of different types:

- Instances of class REXML::Document will get copied.
- Strings containing XML documents will be parsed and turned into instances of class REXML::Document.
- Instances of class IO will be read and then parsed. For example, to parse a file called example.xml, you'd call this:
  ```
  Document.new(File.new(' example.xml' ))
  ```

Finally, the last line of our example program prints the name and the content of our document's root element, which is an instance of class REXML::Element. Not surprisingly, the root element can be accessed using a document's root() method.

Our first successful parsing attempts should give us enough confidence to tackle our original problem: processing parcel-tracking results. Let's load and parse our document and play around a bit with its elements and attributes:

File 184

```
Line 1   doc = Document.new(File.new(' packages.xml' ))
         tracking_results = doc.root
         first_parcel = tracking_results.elements[1]
         tracking_no = first_parcel.attributes[' tracking-no' ] # -> 2X42
```

All REXML elements (including the root element) have an accessor called elements containing an array of the element's children. This array is indexed starting at 1, not 0, so to get the first child of the root element you have to call doc.root.elements[1] instead of doc.root.elements[0]. As a shortcut, you can index the element directly to access its children: doc.root[0]. In this case, the index starts at 0, and you get the element's *children* (which are not necessarily elements; they could, for example, be text nodes).

Every element also has an attributes accessor that contains all that element's attributes. It can be used as a hash, so the attribute tracking-no= of our first <*parcel-history*> element can be found by using the expression doc.root.elements[1].attributes['tracking-no'].

It's nice that accessing elements and attributes is easy with REXML, but it's not exactly what we need, because we do not know up front how many parcel histories we will get from our provider. It would be nice to be able to iterate over a set of elements matching certain criteria. For example, we might want to get at all the children of an element with a certain name. each_element() comes to the rescue:

File 184

```
doc.root.each_element('parcel-history') do |ph|
  puts ph.attributes['tracking-no']
end
```

This produces the following:

```
2X42
2X43
2X44
```

It seems that each_element() allows you to iterate over all children having a particular name, but that's only half the story. each_element() expects an *XPath* expression. XPath can be used for describing nearly arbitrary node sets. We'll talk more about XPath in Section 3.3, *XPath*, on page 117, but for now we'll try to get by with what we have already:

XPath

File 178

```
Line 1   require 'time'
    -    require 'rexml/document'
    -    include REXML
    -
    5    Event = Struct.new(:timestamp, :state, :consignee)
    -
    -    class Event
    -      def to_s
    -        self.timestamp.strftime('%Y-%m-%d %H:%M') + ": " + self.state
    10       end
    -    end
    -
    -    class ParcelHistory
    -      attr_reader :tracking_no, :events
    15     def initialize(tracking_no)
    -        @tracking_no = tracking_no
    -        @events = []
    -      end
    -      def add_event(event) @events << event; end
    20   end
    -
    -    class ParcelHistoryParser
    -      def initialize(source)
    -        @doc = Document.new(source)
    25     end
    -      def each_parcel
    -        @doc.root.each_element('parcel-history') do |ph|
    -          history = ParcelHistory.new(ph.attributes['tracking-no'])
    -          ph.each_element("event") do |event_element|
    30           history.add_event(to_event(event_element))
    -          end
    -          yield history
    -        end
    -      end
    35
```

```
      -          private
      -
      -          def to_event(element)
      -            timestamp = Time::xmlschema(element.attributes['timestamp'])
     40            state = element.attributes['state']
      -            consignee = nil
      -            if !element.elements['consignee'].nil?
      -              element.elements['consignee'].text
      -            end
     45            Event.new(timestamp, state, consignee)
      -          end
      -        end
      -
      -        parser = ParcelHistoryParser.new(File.new('packages.xml'))
     50        parser.each_parcel do |history|
      -          puts history.tracking_no + ":"
      -          history.events.each { |e| puts "  " + e.to_s }
      -        end
```

This produces the following:

```
2X42:
  2005-05-02 04:05: picked-up
  2005-05-02 08:30: first-delivery-attempt
  2005-05-03 09:05: second-delivery-attempt
  2005-05-04 10:15: refused-damaged
  2005-05-04 19:07: returns-to-sender
2X43:
  2005-05-02 04:25: picked-up
  2005-05-02 09:15: delivered
2X44:
  2005-05-02 03:55: picked-up
```

Admittedly, for Ruby this is a really big example, but we will dissect it class by class. Classes Event and ParcelHistory are only for storage purposes. Event encapsulates all attributes describing an event in the lifetime of a parcel and ParcelHistory accumulates a list of such events.

Event is pretty trivial, so we let class Struct create it for us automatically. In lines 8 to 10 we reopen it to add our own to_s() method. Because ParcelHistory contains an array (events), which has to be managed "manually," we could not use Struct to create it. Struct should be used only for the simplest cases, such as when you have a list of atomic attributes that do not depend on each other and do not demand any logic while initializing, setting, and getting them.

The real fun begins on line 13. Class ParcelHistoryParser provides all the functionality that turns a parcel history document from all sources supported by the REXML parser into a list of ParcelHistory objects.

Mixed Content

In line 43 of our parcel parser example we determine the name of a consignee by calling text() on an instance of Element. In our case this is perfect, because we expect any <*consignee*> element to have exactly one child node of type text. What would happen if it had more than one? The answer is simple: text() returns only the first child node of type text. You have to be careful when dealing with so-called mixed content—elements that have child nodes of different types. Given the following document:

File 175

```
doc = Document.new(<<-XML)
<root>
  <a>
    First!
    <b>xyz</b>
    Second!
    <b>abc</b>
    Third!
  </a>
</root>
XML
```

the following code:

```
puts doc.elements['root/a'].text
```

produces this:

```
First!
```

If we use the texts() method, with code like this:

```
puts doc.elements['root/a'].texts
```

we'll instead see the following:

```
First!

Second!

Third!
```

Sometimes you don't parse an XML document yourself, but get it as a REXML::Document object from another method. In these cases be prepared to get elements that do not contain mixed content but instead contain more than one text node. Depending on how the elements were built, it happens easily:

File 167

```
e = Element.new('example')
e.add_text('foo')
e.add_text(Text.new('bar'))
puts e.texts.size # -> 2
```

Right at the beginning of our code, in initialize(source), you can see one of the biggest advantages of dynamic languages such as Ruby: we initialize the attribute doc with our parsed document without caring where the document came from originally. As we explained previously, REXML accepts an XML string, an object derived from IO, or another REXML::Document instance. Automatically, our initialize(source) method behaves in the same liberal fashion. For unit testing we can feed our parser with constant strings or files, and in production it will probably get a Socket object or something similar without changing a single line of code.

Our next method is each_parcel(). It's a Ruby *iterator*. Iterators invoke a block of code for every member of a collection. Within each_parcel() we iterate over all <*parcel-history*> elements, and for each of these elements we iterate over all <*event*> elements. Every <*event*> element is converted into an Event object by calling to_event(element), and all the Event objects are added to their corresponding ParcelHistory object. The yield() call in line 32 invokes the code block that is associated with each_parcel(), passing it the current ParcelHistory object.

At the end of our program, we finally use our ParcelHistoryParser to write the content of our example document to the console. Note that we have solved only the mechanical, part of our problem—we have parsed the tracking results and represented them in our own class hierarchy. Academics call this process *deserialization* or *XML data binding*. Because it really is mechanical there are tools out there that will do it automatically for you. We'll look at such a tool in Section 3.3, *XML Processing with XmlSimple*, on page 126.

For the final solution the results still have to be interpreted—we need a class that determines the actual state of each package, stores it in a database, and sends e-mails or SMS messages but that has nothing to do with XML. In this section we wanted to show you how you can process an XML document using the basic functions of REXML.

REXML Stream Parsing

Last Valentine's Day was chaotic: PragBouquet's parcel-tracking system nearly broke down under the heavy load. Mother's Day is looming, so you did some performance tests and found that one of the biggest bottlenecks was the XML processing. Obviously, loading several thousand tracking results into memory was not a good idea, particularly because you then process all the tracking results serially anyway.

It would be much better if you could parse the XML documents serially, element by element. Fortunately, REXML's stream-parsing API allows you to do just that. Stream parsers always work the same way: they process an XML document character by character and invoke methods on a so-called listener class whenever an interesting event occurs: when a start tag was found, text was found, a comment was found, and so on.

Calling REXML::Document.parse_stream(source,listener) invokes the REXML stream parser, where source is an XML source and listener is your listener class. Let's see what happens if we pass an empty listener:

File 180

```
class ParcelHistoryListener; end

Document.parse_stream(
   File.new('packages.xml'),
   ParcelHistoryListener.new
)
```

This produces the following:

```
c:/ruby/lib/ruby/1.8/rexml/parsers/streamparser.rb:37:in 'send':
undefined method 'xmldecl' for #<ParcelHistoryListener:0x2ad5620>
   (NoMethodError)
   from c:/ruby/lib/ruby/1.8/rexml/parsers/streamparser.rb:37:in 'parse'
   from c:/ruby/lib/ruby/1.8/rexml/document.rb:171:in 'parse_stream'
   from sp_empty_listener.rb:8
```

Not surprisingly, the stream parser complains that it could not find the xmldecl() method in our ParcelHistoryListener class. Obviously, this method is invoked when the stream parser finds an XML declaration, and that's the first thing in our tracking results document.

Let's do some more reverse engineering (that's more exciting than reading API docs, isn't it?) by adding method_missing(method_id,*args) to our listener class. This is a Ruby-standard method that's called whenever an undefined method is called in an object. method_id is the name of the method called (as a symbol), and args is any arguments that were passed to it:

File 181

```
class ParcelHistoryListener
   def method_missing(method_id, *args)
      puts "Method '#{method_id.id2name}' was called."
   end
end
```

```
Document.parse_stream(
    File.new('packages.xml'),
    ParcelHistoryListener.new
)
```

This produces the following:

```
Method 'xmldecl' was called.
Method 'comment' was called.
Method 'tag_start' was called.
Method 'text' was called.
Method 'tag_start' was called.
Method 'text' was called.
Method 'tag_start' was called.
Method 'tag_end' was called.
Method 'text' was called.
Method 'tag_start' was called.
...
Method 'tag_end' was called.
Method 'text' was called.
Method 'comment' was called.
Method 'text' was called.
Method 'comment' was called.
Method 'text' was called.
```

At the very least, the stream parser expects us to implement methods called xmldecl(), comment(),tag_start(),text(), and tag_end(). We stop playing detective now and have a look at the complete list of possible events:

xmldecl(version, encoding, standalone)

> Called when the parser encounters an XML declaration. xmldecl will be called with parameters that directly reflect an XML declaration's attributes, so for the following declaration:

> ```
> <?xml version='1.0' encoding='iso-8859-1'?>
> ```

> the parser would invoke xmldecl(version='1.0', encoding='iso-8859-1', standalone=nil). Note that the default value for encoding and standalone is nil, which is different from the XML standard's default values (utf-8 and no).

tag_start(name, attrs)

> Called when the beginning of an element is found. name contains the element's name, and attrs is an array containing the element's attributes, where every list item is a two-element array consisting of the attribute's name and its value. If the element has no attributes, attrs is an empty array. Given the following element:

> ```
> <person name='Homer' age='45' />
> ```

the parser invokes the following:

```
tag_start('person', [['name', 'Homer'], ['age', '45']])
```

tag_end(name)

Called when the end of element <*name*> was found.

text(text)

Called when text is encountered in the document. For nicely formatted documents, this method is invoked more often than you might think, because by default whitespace in your document is significant. The actual text is passed as the parameter.

cdata(content)

Called when a CDATA section has been found. Parameter content contains the CDATA section including all whitespace characters.

comment(text)

Called when a comment has been found. The comment text is passed in text without the <!-- and --> sequences.

instruction(target, instruction)

Processing instructions were introduced in XML for passing information to particular applications reading a document. They have the following format:

```
<?target [instructions depending on application]?>
```

Common targets are xml-stylesheet and php. Whenever the stream parser detects a processing instruction, it calls instruction(), setting target and instruction accordingly. The processing instruction:

```
<?xml-stylesheet href='sitestyle.css' type='text/css'?>
```

would call:

```
instruction("xml-stylesheet", "href='sitestyle.css' type='text/css' ")
```

doctype(root_name, pub_sys, long_name, uri)

Documents may be associated with a DTD that can be used for validating the document's content. DTDs come in different flavors:

- `<!DOCTYPE root SYSTEM "http://path/to/dtd">`
- `<!DOCTYPE rss PUBLIC`
  `"-//Netscape Communications//DTD RSS 0.91//EN"`
  `"http://my.netscape.com/publish/formats/rss-0.91.dtd">`
- `<!DOCTYPE books [`
  `<!ELEMENT books (book*)>`
  `<!ATTLIST book title CDATA #IMPLIED isbn CDATA #IMPLIED>`
  `]>`

If a document contains a document type declaration (there is only one allowed), the stream parser calls the doctype() method, setting all parameters accordingly. All attributes that have not been declared in the document type declaration will be set to nil.

elementdecl(declaration)

Called when an element declaration like <!ELEMENT books (book*)> was found in a document type definition.

attlistdecl(element_name, attributes, raw_content)

Called for every attribute list declaration in a DTD. Parameter element_name contains the name of the element the attribute list has been defined for, attributes is a hash containing all the attributes and raw_content contains the original declaration from the DTD. For example, the following declaration:

```
<!ATTLIST book title CDATA #IMPLIED isbn CDATA #IMPLIED>
```

would result in the following method call:

```
attlistdecl(
  'book',
  { 'title' => '', 'isbn' => '' },
  '<!ATTLIST book title CDATA #IMPLIED isbn CDATA #IMPLIED>'
)
```

entity(entity_name)

Called when an entity reference (such as %shortcut;) is found in a document type declaration.

entitydecl(declaration)

Called when an entity declaration (e.g., <!ENTITY ms Maik Schmidt>) is found in a document type definition.

notationdecl(content)

If you want to embed non-XML content (such as images or audio files) in your document, you can describe it in more detail using *notations* in a DTD. The stream parser calls notationdecl() when it finds a notation type attribute in a DTD. For the following:

```
<!NOTATION gif SYSTEM 'image/gif'>
```

the parser would invoke:

```
notationdecl(['gif', 'SYSTEM', 'image/gif'])
```

This attribute type is rarely used in practice.

That's a lot of methods, but we already knew that XML is a fairly complex beast. For building our own listener classes it seems that we have only a few options: we could implement all of the previous methods, leaving some of them empty, or we could implement only the methods we definitely need and define method_missing() to suppress the rest. Because this is such a common scenario, REXML has a predefined solution for it, namely, REXML::StreamListener.

REXML::StreamListener is a template module that can be used when building your own listeners. It provides an empty implementation for all methods that can potentially be invoked by the stream parser. You include it in your listener class:

`File 182`

```
Line 1    require 'rexml/streamlistener'

          class ParcelHistoryListener
            include StreamListener
5
            def tag_start(tag_name, attrs)
              puts tag_name
            end
          end
10
          Document.parse_stream(
            File.new('packages.xml'),
            ParcelHistoryListener.new
          )
```

This produces the following:

```
tracking-result
parcel-history
event
event
event
event
consignee
event
parcel-history
event
event
consignee
parcel-history
event
```

That's highly convenient, especially because many of the stream parser events are related to DTDs, which aren't used often nowadays.

We should not forget that we still have a problem to solve: the tree-parsing approach was too slow, and we wanted to enhance it using a stream parser. Our listener class might look like this:

```
Line 1    class ParcelHistoryListener
            include StreamListener

            def initialize
5             @in_consignee = false
            end

            def tag_start(tag_name, attrs)
              if tag_name == 'parcel-history'
10                @parcel_history = ParcelHistory.new(attrs['tracking-no'])
              elsif tag_name == 'event'
                timestamp = Time::xmlschema(attrs['timestamp'])
                state = attrs['state']
                @event = Event.new(timestamp, state, nil)
15              elsif tag_name == 'consignee'
                @in_consignee = true
              end
            end

20          def tag_end(tag_name)
              if tag_name == 'parcel-history'
                puts @parcel_history.tracking_no + ":"
                @parcel_history.events.each { |e| puts '  ' + e.to_s }
              elsif tag_name == 'event'
25                @parcel_history.add_event(@event)
              elsif tag_name == 'consignee'
                @in_consignee = false
              end
            end
30
            def text(value)
              if @in_consignee
                @event.consignee = '' unless @event.consignee
                @event.consignee << value
35              end
            end
          end

          Document.parse_stream(
40            File.new('packages.xml'),
            ParcelHistoryListener.new
          )
```

This produces the following:

```
2X42:
  2005-05-02 04:05: picked-up
  2005-05-02 08:30: first-delivery-attempt
  2005-05-03 09:05: second-delivery-attempt
  2005-05-04 10:15: refused-damaged
  2005-05-04 19:07: returns-to-sender
2X43:
```

```
    2005-05-02 04:25: picked-up
    2005-05-02 09:15: delivered
2X44:
    2005-05-02 03:55: picked-up
```

Here we have a classical stream-parsing example. We had to only implement three StreamListener methods: tag_start(), tag_end(), and text(). The single biggest difference between tree parsing and stream parsing is that stream parsers force you to maintain state yourself. For example, as you can see in lines 32 to 35, we are interested in text nodes only if we are currently in a *<consignee>* element. Therefore, we store this state in the boolean instance variable @in_consignee.

Method tag_start() is responsible for creating new elements. Whenever we encounter a new *<parcel-history>* or *<event>* element, we create a corresponding ParcelHistory or Event object and store it in an instance variable. The only exceptions to this are *<consignee>* elements.

But It's Not Standard

Long before XML became more popular among software developers than caffeine, there were no standards except the XML standard itself. If you wanted to process XML documents, you were forced to write your own parser or to use one of countless proprietary solutions. To overcome this awkward situation, a group of developers collaboratively developed an API on the XML-DEV mailing list and called it Simple API for XML (SAX). This happened in 1998, and SAX version 1.0 quickly became the de facto industry standard for XML stream parsing. The current version is called SAX2 and was released in 2002. Since then, nothing has changed in the API.

Because of the nature of stream parsing, both the proprietary REXML approach and the SAX2 API are similar. You have to define a listener whose methods are invoked by the parser, whenever it encounters an interesting event.

For the sake of completeness we'll show you the REXML::SAX2Listener class in its entirety, but we'll often refer to REXML::StreamListener to avoid redundancy.

start_document()
> Called at the beginning of a document.

end_document()
> Called at the end of a document.

start_element(uri, localname, qname, attributes)

> Called when the beginning of a new element is encountered. uri contains the namespace URI of the element (an empty string when the element is not associated with a namespace). If the element is associated with a namespace, localname contains the element's name without the namespace prefix, and otherwise it is empty. qname contains the element's qualified name—the name as it originally appeared in the XML document. It might be empty for elements associated with a namespace URI. attributes contains all the element's attributes.

end_element(uri, localname, qname)

> Called when the end of an element is encountered.

cdata(content)

> See the description in Section 3.3, *REXML Stream Parsing*, on page 104.

characters(text)

> See the description of text() in Section 3.3, *REXML Stream Parsing*, on page 104.

comment(comment)

> See Section 3.3, *REXML Stream Parsing*, on page 104.

start_prefix_mapping(prefix, uri)

> Called at the beginning of a namespace declaration. prefix is the namespace prefix, and uri the namespace URI.

end_prefix_mapping(prefix)

> Called at the end of a namespace declaration when the current namespace goes out of scope.

processing_instruction(target, data)

> See the description of instruction() in Section 3.3, *REXML Stream Parsing*, on page 104.

doctype(name, pub_sys, long_name, uri)

> See the description in Section 3.3, *REXML Stream Parsing*, on page 104.

elementdecl(content)

> See the description in Section 3.3, *REXML Stream Parsing*, on page 104.

attlistdecl(element, pairs, contents)

> See the description in Section 3.3, *REXML Stream Parsing*, on page 104.

entitydecl(content)

> See the description in Section 3.3, *REXML Stream Parsing*, on page 104.

notationdecl(content)

> See the description in Section 3.3, *REXML Stream Parsing*, on page 104.

Let's rewrite our ParcelHistoryListener using the SAX2 parser:

```
Line 1   require 'time'
   -     require 'rexml/parsers/sax2parser'
   -     require 'rexml/sax2listener'
   -
   5     class ParcelHistoryListener
   -       include REXML::SAX2Listener
   -
   -       def initialize
   -         @in_consignee = false
  10       end
   -
   -       def start_element(uri, localname, tag_name, attrs)
   -         if tag_name == 'parcel-history'
   -           @parcel_history = ParcelHistory.new(attrs['tracking-no'])
  15         elsif tag_name == 'event'
   -           timestamp = Time::xmlschema(attrs['timestamp'])
   -           state = attrs['state']
   -           @event = Event.new(timestamp, state, nil)
   -         elsif tag_name == 'consignee'
  20           @in_consignee = true
   -         end
   -       end
   -
   -       def end_element(uri, localname, tag_name)
  25         if tag_name == 'parcel-history'
   -           puts @parcel_history.tracking_no + ":"
   -           @parcel_history.events.each { |e| puts '  ' + e.to_s }
   -         elsif tag_name == 'event'
   -           @parcel_history.add_event(@event)
  30         elsif tag_name == 'consignee'
   -           @in_consignee = false
   -         end
   -       end
   -
  35
   -
```

File 179

```
    -       def characters(value)
    -         if @in_consignee
    -           @event.consignee = '' unless @event.consignee
   40           @event.consignee << value
    -         end
    -       end
    -     end
    -
   45   parser = REXML::Parsers::SAX2Parser.new(File.new('packages.xml'))
    -   parser.listen(ParcelHistoryListener.new)
    -   parser.parse
```

We already knew that both APIs were similar, but isn't it surprising how similar they really are? In the ParcelHistoryListener class itself we had to change only the names and the signature of some methods. tag_start(tag_name, attrs) became start_element(uri, localname, tag_name, attrs), tag_end(tag_name) became end_element(uri, localname, tag_name), and text(value) became characters(value). Instead of StreamListener we had to include SAX2Listener, but not a single line of business logic had to be changed.

Because it's not part of the REXML::Document class, invoking the parser is a bit different. Additional parsers can be found in the rexml/parsers directory and reside in the REXML::Parsers namespace. In the last three lines of our program, we create the REXML::Parsers::SAX2Parser, pass it our implementation of a REXML::SAX2Listener, and eventually start the parsing process.

SAX was originally defined to make XML processing easier for Java, so its design reflects the typical shortcomings of a more or less static programming language. Sean Russel realized this and added some sugar to REXML that makes it more, let's say, Rubyesque.

For example, if you are interested only in a small subset of your document's nodes, you don't have to implement a complete listener class. It's possible to associate SAX2 events with a code block. To extract all text nodes from the following document:

File 176

```
<?xml version="1.0" encoding="iso-8859-1"?>

<todo-list>
  <to-do>Write a book.</to-do>
  <to-do>Learn a new programming language.</to-do>
  <to-do>Don&apos;t Repeat Yourself</to-do>
</todo-list>
```

We could do the following:

```
Line 1   require 'rexml/parsers/sax2parser'
   -
   -     todo_list = File.new('todo.xml')
   -     parser = REXML::Parsers::SAX2Parser.new(todo_list)
   5     parser.listen(:characters) { |text| puts "* #{text}" }
   -     parser.parse
```

and it produces this:

```
Line 1   *
   -
   -     * Write a book.
   -     *
   5
   -     * Learn a new programming language.
   -     *
   -
   -     * Don&apos;t Repeat Yourself
  10     *
   -     *
```

Hmm, that's not exactly what we expected, is it? The standard entity ' has not been resolved, and obviously our code block was called for *all* text nodes, even for those containing only whitespace characters.

REXML's handling of all things related to DTDs is rudimentary, and you have to do a lot of tasks yourself that other parsers won't expect you to do. It's a bit annoying, but at least for the XML standard entities we have to perform only simple text substitutions.

To solve our whitespace problem, we could check whether the text that is passed to the code block is empty. But wouldn't it be much nicer if we could tell the parser to call our code block only for *<to-do>* elements? Here we go:

```
Line 1   def decode_markup(text)
   -       text.gsub!(/&lt;/, '<')
   -       text.gsub!(/&gt;/, '>')
   -       text.gsub!(/&apos;/, "'")
   5       text.gsub!(/&quot;/, '"')
   -       text.gsub!(/&amp;/, '&')
   -       text
   -     end
   -
  10     todo_list = File.new('todo.xml')
   -     parser = REXML::Parsers::SAX2Parser.new(todo_list)
   -     parser.listen(:characters, ['to-do']) { |text|
   -       puts "* #{decode_markup(text)}"
   -     }
  15     parser.parse
```

This produces the following:

```
* Write a book.
* Learn a new programming language.
* Don't Repeat Yourself
```

As well as taking the event to listen for, the listen() method can take a list of element names. It's even possible to pass regular expressions that describe the element names to be matched against.

In the following descriptions of the variants of the listen() method, the parameters have the following meaning:

- symbol can be one of :start_element, :end_element, :characters, :cdata, :start_prefix_mapping, :end_prefix_mapping, :processing_instruction, :doctype, :attlistdecl, :elementdecl, :entitydecl, :notationdecl, :xmldecl, or :comment.

- array contains regular expressions or strings that will be matched against fully qualified element names.

- listener implements all methods of the REXML::SAX2Listener class.

- block will be passed the same arguments as the corresponding REXML::SAX2Listener method would get. The method name is the same as the matched symbol.

You can invoke listen() as follows:

listen(symbol, array, &block)

Listens to the symbol event for all elements in array. For example, the following:

```
parser.listen(:characters, %w(name surname)) do |text|
    puts text
end
```

prints the text of all <*name*> and <*surname*> elements.

listen(symbol, &block)

Calls block whenever the symbol event occurs. For example, the following:

```
parser.listen(:comment) { |text| puts text }
```

prints all comments in a document.

listen(array, listener)

Invokes methods of listener only for elements whose names are in array. For example, the following:

```
class MyListener
  include REXML::SAX2Listener
  ...
end

parser.listen(%w(to-do), MyListener.new)
```

invokes listener methods only for *<to-do>* elements.

listen(array, &block)

> block is called when the :start_element event occurs and the name of the current element is in array. For example, the following:
>
> ```
> parser.listen(%w(order person)) do |uri, localname, qname, attr|
>   attr.each { |k, v| puts "#{k}=#{v}" }
> end
> ```
>
> prints all attributes of all *<order>* and *<person>* elements.

listen(listener)

> Listens to all events and invokes the according methods of the listener.
>
> ```
> class MyListener
>   include REXML::SAX2Listener
>   ...
> end
>
> parser.listen(MyListener.new)
> ```
>
> That's the standard way of SAX2 parsing.

XPath

In Section 3.3, *Tree Parsing*, on page 99, we saw that the each_element() method of class REXML::Element accepts an element name or a so-called XPath expression. According to the official specification,[7] "XPath is a language for addressing parts of an XML document, designed to be used by both XSLT and XPointer." And that's exactly how it is: with XPath you can extract single nodes and node sets matching certain criteria from an XML document. Simply put, XPath is for XML documents what regular expressions are for strings.

XPath expressions are not XML documents or document fragments themselves: they have their own syntax. We will not fully cover XPath and all its nitty-gritty details, but we will at least show you enough of

---

[7]http://www.w3.org/TR/xpath

its syntax to move conveniently through typical XML documents using REXML (for a complete reference see *XPath and XPointer* [Sim02]).

Besides XPath support in the Element class, REXML has a class called XPath. This class contains three methods that allow you to select arbitrary node sets from a certain element:[8]

each(element,xpath=nil,namespaces={})

> Iterates over all nodes matching xpath in the context of element. xpath defaults to '*'. The namespaces hash may contain a namespace mapping.

first(element,xpath=nil,namespaces={})

> Returns the first node matching xpath in the context of element. xpath defaults to *. Iterates over all nodes matching xpath in the context of element.

match(element,xpath=nil,namespaces={})

> Returns all nodes matching xpath in the context of element. xpath defaults to *.

In the following shortened version of our tracking history document from Section 3.3, *Processing XML Documents*, on page 97, we use these methods to demonstrate how REXML's XPath support works:

File 190

```xml
<tracking-result>
  <parcel-history tracking-no='2X42'>
    <event timestamp='2005-05-02T04:05:00'
        state='picked-up' />
    <event timestamp='2005-05-02T08:30:00'
        state='first-delivery-attempt' />
    <event timestamp='2005-05-04T10:15:00'
        state='refused-damaged'>
      <consignee>Mrs. Smith</consignee>
    </event>
    <event timestamp='2005-05-04T19:07:00' state='returns-to-sender' />
  </parcel-history>

  <parcel-history tracking-no='2X43'>
    <event timestamp='2005-05-02T04:25:00' state='picked-up' />
    <event timestamp='2005-05-02T09:15:00' state='delivered'>
      <consignee>Mr. Gumble</consignee>
    </event>
  </parcel-history>
</tracking-result>
```

---

[8]These methods potentially deal with objects of different classes. For example, match() may return objects of class Element, Attribute, etc.

We assume that the doc variable has been initialized like this:

▸191
```
doc = Document.new(File.new('packages.xml'))
```

Let's start with some simple examples:

▸191
```
puts XPath.match(doc, '/tracking-result/parcel-history')[1]
```

This produces the following:

```
<parcel-history tracking-no='2X43'>
   <event timestamp='2005-05-02T04:25:00' state='picked-up'/>
   <event timestamp='2005-05-02T09:15:00' state='delivered'>
      <consignee>Mr. Gumble</consignee>
   </event>
</parcel-history>
```

XPath expressions are made up of *location paths* and *location steps*. In the previous example, the location path is /tracking-result/package-history. It consists of two location steps: /tracking-result and package-history.

location paths

location steps

As you might have guessed, location steps are separated by a slash, but the leading slash in the first location step is not a delimiter—it identifies the document root. So the first location step identifies the *<tracking-result>* child of the document root—the root element. The second location step identifies all *<parcel-history>* children of the preceding element (the *<tracking-result>* element). Because there are three of them, match() returns them all as an array. We select the second one.

We can achieve the same result a bit differently by using XPath's index features. Node sets can be treated as arrays and can be indexed using square brackets:

▸191
```
puts XPath.first(doc, '/tracking-result/parcel-history[2]')
```

Did you notice that we used the index 2? It's true: XPath indices start at 1, not 0! That's why the indexing of the elements array of class REXML::Element starts at 1, too.

It's also possible to define relative paths: they do not start with a slash. A more or less obscure way to get all the consignees belonging to delivered packages could look like this:

▸191
```
events = XPath.match(
  doc,
  '/tracking-result/parcel-history/event[@state="delivered"]'
)
events.each do |event|
  puts XPath.match(event, 'consignee')
end
```

It produces the following:

```
<consignee>Mr. Gumble</consignee>
```

XPath expressions are similar to file and directory paths under Unix, but this analogy cannot be stretched too far. Even in our small example we have encountered the first big difference: every element may have an arbitrary number of children having the same name. For example, a *<tracking-result>* element may have more than one *<package-history>* child element (which is impossible in file systems). The next big difference is that we can recursively select nodes. For example, the following statement:

File 191

```
puts XPath.match(doc, '//consignee')
```

Produces the following:

```
<consignee>Mrs. Smith</consignee>
<consignee>Mr. Gumble</consignee>
```

descendant-or-self axis

//consignee selects all *<consignee>* nodes in the document. The expression // is an abbreviation for the *descendant-or-self axis*. This contains all descendant nodes (not only direct children) belonging to a particular node, along with the node itself. At the beginning of a location path, // means "select all nodes in the document," and we refine that by adding the consignee location step.

The concepts of context and axes are important when working with XPath, because XPath interpreters see XML documents as trees where every node has a type and lives in a particular context that defines a relationship to all other nodes in the tree. For example, our tracking result document looks to an XPath interpreter like Figure 3.4, on the next page.

It is a tree consisting of 30 nodes (actually, it has many more because of all the whitespace text nodes belonging to nearly every element, but we left them out for brevity). Twelve of them are element nodes, sixteen are attribute nodes, and two are text nodes.

Given a particular node, you can easily define node sets that are somehow related to this node. For an element node, for example, you can create a set consisting of all its children, all its attributes, all its descendants, all its siblings, and so on. XPath defines some standard ways to create node sets from a given context node and calls them *axes* (you can see them in Figure 3.5, on page 123). To make things more complicated, all axes can not only select nodes by their position but also by their type. For example, the descendant-or-self axis we used previously

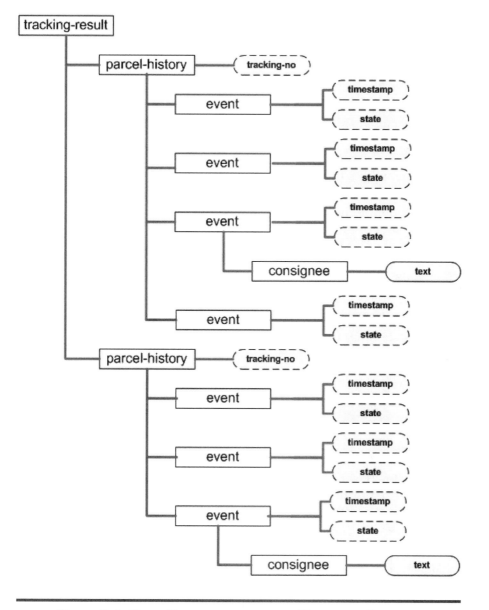

Figure 3.4: TREE REPRESENTATION OF TRACKING RESULTS

selects all nodes below the current context node, but only if they are not attribute nodes or namespace nodes.

We could have selected all consignees more verbosely without using the // abbreviation:

File 191

```
puts XPath.match(doc, 'descendant-or-self::consignee')
```

It works the same with all other axes. For example, the following two statements select all tracking numbers:

File 191

```
puts XPath.match(doc, '//parcel-history/@tracking-no')
```

File 191

```
puts XPath.match(doc, '//parcel-history/attribute::tracking-no')
```

Now we know how to access each node and some particular interesting neighbors of each of them. XPath is concise and elegant in many respects, but we could have achieved this using iterators and loops, too.

predicates

But XPath can do more for us; i.e., it allows us to use conditions—XPath calls them *predicates*—that refine node sets even further. For example, the following statement locates all events belonging to package 2X43:

File 191

```
puts XPath.match(doc, '//parcel-history[@tracking-no="2X43"]/*')
```

and produces the following:

```
<event timestamp='2005-05-02T04:25:00' state='picked-up' />
<event timestamp='2005-05-02T09:15:00' state='delivered'>
    <consignee>Mr. Gumble</consignee>
</event>
```

We've selected nodes anonymously—without knowing their names—by using the asterisk (*). It stands for "select every node you can find." Predicates are put in square brackets and can occur after any location step. They are boolean expressions. Whenever a predicate evaluates to true, the corresponding node becomes part of the result node set. XPath boolean expressions are usually of the form lvalue op rvalue, where op is one of the operators shown in Figure 3.6, on page 124.

Predicates can be stacked by chaining them together (with no separator). For example, the following statement selects all <event> elements that have been delivered on 2005-05-02:

File 191

```
puts XPath.match(
  doc,
  '//event[starts-with(@timestamp, "2005-05-02")][@state="delivered"]'
)
```

child

> All immediate children of the context node.
>
> Selects: element, processing instruction, comment, text

descendant

> All descendants of the context node; i.e., all children, grandchildren, and so on.
>
> Selects: element, processing instruction, comment, text

parent

> All nodes immediately above the context node. It may include the root node. Abbreviation: ..
>
> Selects: element

ancestor

> All ancestors of the context node; i.e., its parents, grandparents, and so one. Includes the root node.
>
> Selects: element

preceding-sibling/following-sibling

> All siblings preceding (or following) the context node having the same parent. Empty for attribute and namespace nodes. Never includes the root node.
>
> Selects: Any except attribute and namespace

preceding/following

> All nodes preceding (or following) the context node excluding any ancestors (or descendants) and excluding attribute nodes and namespace nodes. Never includes the root node.
>
> Selects: Any except attribute and namespace

attribute

> All attribute nodes of the context node. Abbreviation: @

namespace

> All namespace nodes of the context node.

self

> The context node itself. Abbreviation: .

descendant-or-self

> The context node and all its descendants. Abbreviation: //
>
> Selects: Any except attribute and namespace

ancestor-or-self

> The context node and all its ancestors. Includes the root node.
>
> Selects: element

Figure 3.5: XPath Axes

Operator	Meaning
=	Equal to
!=	Not equal to
>	Greater than
>=	Greater than or equal
<	Less than
<=	Less than or equal

Figure 3.6: XPATH BOOLEAN OPERATORS

This produces the following:

```
<event timestamp='2005-05-02T09:15:00' state='delivered'>
   <consignee>Mr. Gumble</consignee>
</event>
```

But wait, what about that first predicate? Apparently, it's a boolean expression, but it does not contain an operator. As you might have guessed already, XPath defines functions, too, and starts-with(string, substring) is one of them. If string actually starts with substring, this method returns true, and otherwise it returns false.

XPath functions are divided into four groups:[9]

- *Node set functions* let you perform operations on node sets. For example, the count(node-set) function returns the number of nodes in the argument node-set.

- *String functions* manipulate and compare strings. For instance, the normalize-space(string) function returns a normalized representation of the argument string (it defaults to the current context node). It removes leading and trailing whitespace characters and

---

[9]http://www.w3.org/TR/xpath#corelib contains a description of all functions.

replaces sequences of multiple whitespace characters by a single space.

- *Boolean functions* implement common predicates. For example, not(expr) returns true, if expr is false. Otherwise, it returns false.

- *Number functions* help you work with numeric expressions. The sum(node-set) function, for example, converts the string values of all nodes belonging to node-set into numbers and returns their overall sum.

REXML::Element has one more interesting method, xpath(). It returns one XPath belonging to a particular element (there's a nearly infinite number of XPaths leading to every XML document node). For example, the following statement

191

```
event = XPath.first(
  doc,
  '/tracking-result/parcel-history/event[@state="delivered"]'
)
puts event.xpath
```

produces the following:

```
/tracking-result/parcel-history[2]/event[2]
```

REXML's XPath support is comparatively good, but its implementation of the standard functions and some of the more complex features of the XPath specification is still a work in progress. So, before depending on a particular function, you'd better test REXML's support for it.

For example, the union operator does not work as expected. In XPath it's possible to join node sets using the | operator. The following expression should return all state= and all tracking-no= attributes:

191

```
puts XPath.match(doc, '//event/@state | //parcel-history/@tracking-no')
puts XPath.match(
  doc,
  '//event[@state="delivered"]|//event[@state="picked-up"]'
)
```

Currently, REXML returns the node set only on the left side of the | operator. The previous code prints the following:

```
picked-up
first-delivery-attempt
refused-damaged
returns-to-sender
picked-up
delivered
```

As with stored procedures in databases, it's usually not a good idea to put too much of your business logic into XPath expressions (even simple length constraints can make up a vital part of your business logic). On the other hand, XPath is probably the most convenient way to access content of XML documents, and the REXML way of life will certainly change the way you approach your next parsing problem.

XML Processing with XmlSimple

The attentive reader (and that's all of you, isn't it?) might have noticed that processing XML is often a tedious job, involving mapping elements to classes and attributes to member variables. Usually, the classes have the same names as their corresponding XML elements, and the member variables have the same names as their attribute counterparts. This calls for automation. Fortunately, a lot of tools exist to free you from this type of repetitive work.

Depending on the programming environment you're working in, you can choose from a variety of tools today ranging from small helper libraries that support your own serialization strategy to sophisticated solutions that automatically create complete class hierarchies and serializer classes based on XmlSchema files. Java and .NET certainly have the most mature support for these kind of things, but there are some useful libraries for Ruby, too.

Grant McLean got fed up writing the same code over and over again and came up with a clever solution. His Perl module XML::Simple[10] converts an XML document into a structure of hashes and arrays according to some simple rules and conventions. I often used this model back in the old days when Ruby was nearly unknown, so it seemed natural to port it across when I started using Ruby. The Ruby version, named *XmlSimple*,[11] implements nearly 100% of the original's functionality and fixes some of its major flaws.

Less talk, more examples! Here we have a configuration file called app-config.xml, as found in countless projects the world over:

File 189

```
<?xml version="1.0" encoding="iso-8859-1"?>

<app-config>
```

---

[10]http://www.cpan.org/modules/by-module/XML/XML-Simple-2.14.readme

[11]It is available as a Gem called xml-simple or from http://raa.ruby-lang.org/project/xml-simple.

```
<database env='test'>
  <usr>developer</usr>
  <pwd>foo</pwd>
</database>

<database env='production'>
  <usr>admin</usr>
  <pwd>secret</pwd>
</database>

<http-proxy>
  <host>my.proxy.host</host>
  <port>8080</port>
</http-proxy>
</app-config>
```

Configuration files like this are often read when the application starts. Their content is then made available globally using a singleton class or something similar. It would be a complete overkill to deserialize its content manually and to create a corresponding class hierarchy. A hash containing all configuration parameters would be sufficient. To achieve this with XmlSimple, do something like the following:

e 188

```
require 'xmlsimple'

cfg = XmlSimple::xml_in('appconfig.xml')
p cfg
```

This produces the following:

```
{
  "http-proxy" => [
    {
      "port" => ["8080"],
      "host" => ["my.proxy.host"]
    }
  ],
  "database" => [
    {
      "env" => "test",
      "pwd" => ["foo"],
      "usr" => ["developer"]
    },
    {
      "env" => "production",
      "pwd" => ["secret"],
      "usr" => ["admin"]
    }
  ]
}
```

XmlSimple turns the XML document into a structure consisting of hashes and arrays, where every element and attribute name becomes a hash key pointing to its associated content. Because elements can potentially occur more than once, their values are stored in arrays by default, while attribute values are not.

Our first result looks promising, but it's far from optimal. To find the password of our production database, for example, we have to search for an entry in the array cfg['database'], where the value associated with the key env is production.

To adjust the output's structure, xml_in() accepts an optional hash containing name => value option pairs. The option key_attr controls which elements should be used as the basis for the array folding. We'll set it to env:

File 188

```
cfg = XmlSimple::xml_in('appconfig.xml', 'key_attr' => 'env')
p cfg
```

Now we get the following:

```
{
  "http-proxy" => [
    {
      "port" => ["8080"],
      "host" => ["my.proxy.host"]
    }
  ],
  "database" => {                    # -> No longer an Array.
    "production" => {
      "pwd" => ["secret"],
      "usr" => ["admin"]
    },
    "test" => {
      "pwd" => ["foo"],
      "usr" => ["developer"]
    }
  }
}
```

That's much better. Now we can access the production database's password using the following:

```
cfg['database']['production']['pwd'][0]
```

The arrays containing a single element are still a bit annoying, but we can get rid of them by setting the parameter force_array to false:

File 188

```
p XmlSimple::xml_in(nil, 'key_attr' => 'env', 'force_array' => false)
```

The output is simpler:

```
{
  "http-proxy" => {
    "port" => "8080",
    "host" => "my.proxy.host"
  },
  "database" => {
    "production" => {
      "pwd" => "secret",
      "usr" => "admin"
    },
    "test" => {
      "pwd" => "foo",
      "usr" => "developer"
    }
  }
}
```

cfg['database']['production']['pwd'] now contains the database password.

As we saw, xml_in() expects some kind of XML source and a parameter hash. The XML source can be the following:

- *A filename*, as in

  ```
  cfg = XmlSimple.xml_in('appconfig.xml')
  ```

- nil

  If there is no XML source, xml_in() will check the source program's directory for a file with the same name as the script but with the extension .xml. If you want to specify options, you must specify the value nil:

  ```
  cfg = XmlSimple.xml_in(nil, 'force_array' => false)
  ```

- *A string containing XML* (recognized by the presence of < and > characters) will be parsed directly. For example:

  ```
  cfg = XmlSimple.xml_in('<cfg env="test" password="foo" />')
  ```

- *An IO object* will be read and its contents parsed. For example:

  ```
  cfg = XmlSimple.xml_in(File.new('appconfig.xml'))
  ```

XmlSimple is not a full-blown XML data-binding tool, but it does just what you need surprisingly often.

3.4   Validating XML Documents

Because you have to pay for every request to the e-scoring application even when it's syntactically invalid, you decide to validate all XML documents you're going to send before actually transmitting them (all documents we create using REXML are well-formed, but they do not have to be valid necessarily). In general, you could choose from various validation technologies, using DTDs (Document Type Definitions), XmlSchema, and RELAX NG. (Regular Language for XML, New Generation)[12] Fortunately, the decision with Ruby is easy, because REXML supports only RELAX NG. That's good news, because RELAX NG is the most powerful and most convenient of the three. The bad news is that REXML's support for RELAX NG is highly experimental, and a lot of important features do not work at all.

RELAX NG does not allow you to control the lexical appearance of a document, so you can't use it to control what kind of quotes you've used for attributes or the comments or processing instructions that can be used.

RELAX NG comes in two different syntax styles: XML syntax and compact syntax. Both have their pros and cons, but again the choice is made easy for Ruby programmers, because REXML does not support the compact syntax style. To be honest, at the current stage of development, REXML's support for RELAX NG is barely useful, but it's still possible to perform some basic validation, if you obey some simple rules.

Before diving into the details of RELAX NG, let's revisit our example document from Section 3.2, *Generating XML Documents*, on page 85.

File 169

```
<persons>
  <person name='Max' surname='Mustermann'>
    <address>
      <street>Musterstr. 42</street>
      <city>Berlin</city>
      <postal-code>11011</postal-code>
    </address>
  </person>
</persons>
```

Considering only a document's structure and not its content, a valid document fulfills the following requirements:

- There's exactly one root element called *<persons>*.

- The *<persons>* element may have one or more *<person>* children.

- A *<person>* element has exactly two attributes called name and surname.

---

[12]http://www.oasis-open.org/committees/relax-ng.

- A *<person>* element has one *<address>* child.

- Every *<address>* element has a *<street>*, a *<city>*, and *<postal-code>* child.

- The *<street>*, *<city>*, and *<postal-code>* elements may contain text.

RELAX NG allows us to translate these requirements easily into the XML syntax:

ile 185

```xml
<?xml version='1.0'?>

<element xmlns='http://relaxng.org/ns/structure/1.0' name='persons'>
  <oneOrMore>
    <element name='person'>
      <attribute name='name'/>
      <attribute name='surname'/>
      <element name='address'>
        <element name='street'><text/></element>
        <element name='city'><text/></element>
        <element name='postal-code'><text/></element>
      </element>
    </element>
  </oneOrMore>
</element>
```

To validate our example document against this schema, we do the following:

ile 186

```ruby
Line 1   require 'rexml/document'
    -    require 'rexml/validation/relaxng'
    -    include REXML
    -
    5    def read_doc(filename)
    -      doc = IO.readlines(filename).to_s
    -      doc.gsub!(/\s+</, '<')
    -      doc.gsub!(/\s+$/, '')
    -      doc
    10   end
    -
    -    begin
    -      schema = File.new('person_schema.xml')
    -      validator = Validation::RelaxNG.new(schema)
    15     parser = Parsers::TreeParser.new(read_doc('persons.xml'))
    -      parser.add_listener(validator.reset)
    -      parser.parse
    -    rescue Validation::ValidationException => e
    -      puts "An error occurred during validation: #{e}"
    20   rescue Exception => e
    -      puts "An exception occurred: #{e}"
    -    end
```

Because we don't need to process the document any further, it doesn't matter which parser we use for our validation purposes, so we arbitrarily chose the TreeParser. Most of the code should be self-explanatory: in lines 14 to 17 we initialize a validator with our schema and pass it to the parser. If anything goes wrong while validating the document, a ValidationException exception will be thrown.

But what the heck does read_doc() do? As mentioned earlier, REXML's support for RELAX NG validation is full of flaws. One of them is the incorrect handling of whitespace. Whitespace handling has always been a complicated issue in XML. When validating documents, whitespace becomes an even bigger problem. In a formatted XML document, the indentation before tags automatically is converted into text nodes. So, even if your element does not allow for text, it actually has some, if you format your document. The corresponding schema must support it too.

RELAX NG usually works pragmatically with this issue, because it considers whitespace and empty content equal—you do not have to clutter your schema document with <text> elements only because you want to format your source with whitespace. REXML currently does not implement this behavior, so instead of adding countless <text> elements, read_doc() eliminates all whitespace before < characters. Yet another annoying bug is REXML's comment handling. There's no way in RELAX NG to restrict comments in any way, but if you have a comment in an XML document you're trying to validate with REXML, it will fail miserably, because REXML complains about the unexpected comment node. Finally, REXML does not support the XML header.

xmllint

If you definitely need to validate XML documents against a particular schema, you can use xmllint.[13] xmllint is a command-line tool that is available for nearly all operating systems. It checks that a given set of XML files are well-formed and whether they are in compliance with a certain schema. The following class encapsulates access to the xmllint program. If there is native schema support someday in Ruby, you'll be able to replace the system() call easily:

File 187

```
Line 1    class Validator
              class << self
```

---

[13]http://xmlsoft.org/xmllint

```
-      def validate(document, schema)
-         option = case schema
5           when /\.dtd$/ then '-valid'
-           when /\.xml$/ then '-relaxng'
-           when /\.xsd$/ then '-schema'
-         end
-         exec_xmllint(document, schema, option)
10     end

-      private

-      def exec_xmllint(file, schema, option)
15        rc = system("xmllint -noout #{option} #{schema} #{file}")
-         status = $?.exitstatus
-         return true if rc && status == 0
-         raise 'ValidationError' if [3, 4].include?(status)
-         raise 'UnexpectedError' unless rc
20     end
-    end
-  end
```

This solution isn't particularly efficient, but it's good enough in many
cases. xmllint's validation support is excellent. From line 4 to 8 we
determine which options have to be passed to xmllint. In line 15 we
call xmllint and evaluate its return status. First we check whether the
system() call succeeded—whether it returned true or false (it will return
false, for example, if xmllint could not be found). Then we determine
xmllint's return code. xmllint returns 0 if it could parse and validate a
document successfully. If a validation error occurred, it returns 3 or 4.
All other return codes indicate errors.

To validate our sample document, you have to do this:

```
Line 1  begin
-         Validator.validate('persons.xml', 'person_schema.xml')
-       rescue => ex
-         puts ex
5       end
```

Conclusion

Validating XML documents using any kind of schema is not as useful as
it might initially seem; as a careful and defensive programmer you will
check the restrictions defined in the schema in your program anyway.
Validation makes sense only when you generate the code completely
from a schema or when you generate documents that are going to be
consumed by other applications.

Ruby's support for any kind of XML schema language is currently weak. If you are in need of high-performance XML validation, you will have to look for alternatives or—even better—implement a libxml2 binding for Ruby.

3.5 Are There Alternatives to XML?

Data representation is one of the most important things in our business; you shouldn't take it lightly. Sometimes you do not have a choice. If you have to deal with legacy data, you usually have to eat what has been served.

Although XML is a comparatively young technology, for some people it seems hard to remember the dark and ancient times without XML. Today nearly every program offers functions for importing or exporting XML or can be configured by editing one or more XML files.

Many developers do not think about alternative file formats anymore. "XML is a standard and I get a parser for free, so why should I use something else or even invent something new?" they say. Certainly this is true under some circumstances, but more often than not you're better off if you think about alternatives.

As a rule of thumb you should try to avoid XML when you know that human beings have to read or edit the documents. It's OK for machines to do it, because that's what they were built for, but you do not want your customers to learn the secrets of well-formedness. Even if your customers are programmers, they will be deeply grateful if you offer them the most convenient way to achieve their goals.

You should not use XML only because you get a parser for free. James Duncan Davidson did this when he created the Java build tool Ant, and today he publicly regrets having done it,[14] because looking back, XML wasn't an adequate choice. It does not fit the needs of a build tool, and we'll see a much better approach in Section 6.5, *Project Automation with Rake*, on page 306.

XML is quite a misnomer, because it is not a language itself but a set of rules for describing markup languages. You should never consider

---

[14]http://web.archive.org/web/20040602210721/x180.net/Articles/Java/AntAndXML.html

using XML for the description of a programming language. Probably the most obvious example of this kind of misuse is the eXtensible Stylesheet Language (XSL).[15]

Despite all this, XML should be part of every modern developer's toolbox, because it is widespread and can be handy under certain circumstances, but you should always keep this in mind: there's no such thing as "cool technology." There are only tools that help you to get your job done, and there are tools that don't.

Comma-Separated Values (CSV)

Although there is no official standard, the *Comma-Separated Values* (CSV) format may well be the most popular data exchange format ever, because countless spreadsheet and database applications use it for importing and exporting data.[16]

Comma-Separated Values

Simply put, a CSV file is a plain-text file containing tabular data where every line represents a table row and where all columns (fields) are separated by a delimiter. The lines themselves are usually separated by a carriage return. If a column contains the delimiting character or a carriage return, quotes will be put before and after its value. If the value contains quotes too, the quotes will be doubled. Optionally the first line of the file may contain the column names (separated by the delimiter, too).

Here we have a CSV representation of some bunches of flowers:

File 160

```
id,name,price,description
1,Red Dream,79.99,"Lots of red roses saying ""Come back, please!"""
2,Blue Velvet,29.99,Your Mom will love it.
```

Because the description of the "Red Dream" data set contains a comma, we had to set it in quotes. Consequently, we had to double all the quotes in the description, too.

The name Comma-Separated Values is a bit of a misnomer, because today it's used for all kind of formats where a set of attributes is separated by special characters. For every file you have to be consistent about the delimiter; i.e., all attributes in every line have to be separated by the same character. Frequently used delimiters include the

---

[15]http://www.w3.org/Style/XSL
[16]Under http://en.wikipedia.org/wiki/Comma-separated_values you'll find a lot of interesting background information.

characters ;, :, |, blanks, and tabulators. Hence, pedantic people call the format *Character-Separated Values* nowadays.

You might be tempted to create and read CSV files using strings and regular expressions, but beware: it's not as easy as it seems, and there are a lot of pitfalls lurking. In addition, Hiroshi Nakamura's excellent CSV library in the meantime became part of the standard distribution and makes both reading and writing CSV data a breeze.

Generating Comma-Separated Values

For generating CSV data we use the generate(stream,fs=',',rs=nil, &block) method of class CSV::Writer. Parameter stream is an object supporting the <<(string) operator, fs is the field separator to be used (a comma by default), rs is the record separator to be used (carriage return by default), and block is a code block to be called for every line to be generated. The code block will be called with a single parameter of class CSV::BasicWriter.

To generate our list of flowers using a semicolon as delimiter, we have to do the following:

File 162

```
Line 1   require 'csv'
    -    CSV::Writer.generate(STDOUT, ';') do |csv|
    -      csv << [1, 'Red Dream', 'Red roses saying "Come back, please!"']
    -      csv << [2, 'Blue Velvet', 'Your Mom will love it.']
    5    end
```

This produces the following:

```
1;Red Dream;"Red roses saying ""Come back, please!"""
2;Blue Velvet;Your Mom will love it.
```

Did you notice that CSV::Writer enclosed our "Red Dream" description in quotes, although it does not contain the delimiter? Always keep this in mind: there is no CSV standard, and whenever you have to create or process CSV files, you should talk to the sender or recipient of the files up front. Maybe Hiroshi's library does not emit what your counterpart expects, or vice versa.

Processing Comma-Separated Values

You already guessed it: the CSV library contains a CSV::Reader class for reading CSV files. The following program produces a price list of our flavorsome products:

File 161

```
Line 1   require 'csv'
    -    CSV::Reader.parse(File.open('products.csv', 'r')) do |row|
    -      puts "#{row[1]}: #{row[2]}"
    -    end
```

This produces the following:

```
name: price
Red Dream: 79.99
Blue Velvet: 29.99
```

Obviously we forgot to ignore our header line, and the parse(stream, fs=',', rs=nil, &block) method of class CSV::Reader does not offer the ability to ignore it. Hence, we will use open(path, mode, fs=nil, rs=nil, &block) to get an instance of CVS::Reader:

File 161

```
Line 1   csv = CSV.open('products.csv', 'r')
    -    header = csv.shift # Ignore header line.
    -    csv.each { |row| puts "#{row[1]}: #{row[2]}" }
    -    csv.close
```

This produces the following:

```
Red Dream: 79.99
Blue Velvet: 29.99
```

Normally, you would not ignore the header but use it to dynamically create objects or reports. The following program dynamically creates a list of Product classes from our CSV file:

File 159

```
Line 1   require 'csv'
    -    csv = CSV.open('products.csv', 'r')
    -    Product = Struct.new(*(csv.shift.map { |f| f.to_sym }))
    -    products = csv.inject([]) do |products, row|
    5      products << Product[*row]
    -    end
    -    csv.close
    -
    -    products.each do |p|
    10     puts "#{p.name}: #{p.price}"
    -    end
```

This produces the following:

```
Red Dream: 79.99
Blue Velvet: 29.99
```

That's the Ruby way of life, and nearly all the magic comes from line 3, where we create a new Product class on the fly by using class Struct. Let's dissect this line from the inside out: csv.shift.map { |f| f.to_sym } reads the header line from our CSV file and turns all columns into a symbol by calling to_sym(). The result is an array of symbols that is converted into a parameter list using the asterisk. This parameter list is then used to create a new Struct called Product. Our newly created class has accessors for all the header columns (id, name, price, description) and new instances can be created using the new() or [] operator (as shown in line 5).

Skimming the documentation of the CSV library is not a bad idea, because it contains some convenient methods (such as foreach() and readline()) we didn't cover here.

Properties Files

Properties files

Properties files can be often found in Java environments, and it happens sometimes that you have to add a program to an existing enterprise Java project that has to use the same configuration as the project. For example, the HTTP proxy and database parameters are typically the same for many applications running on the same machine.

Simply put, a property is a value associated with a unique key, and a properties file is a file containing such key/value pairs. Keys and values are separated by = or : characters, and logical lines can comprise more than one physical line.

A typical properties file looks like this:

`File 171`

```
! Comments start with '!'...
# ... or with '#'.

ruby = pragmatic

# A property spanning two lines.
broken_value = This value is \
                    long.

colon_prop: hello

# A property spanning three lines.
fruits:    apple, banana, pear, \
           cantaloupe, watermelon, \
           kiwi, mango

http.proxyHost=example.com
http.proxyPort=8080
```

Although the original specification is much more complicated (e.g., it allows : and = characters in keys and Unicode characters), the following class should understand enough of the Java properties syntax to process most properties files out there:

File 170
```
Line 1   class PropertiesFile
    -       def initialize(file_name)
    -         @properties = load_props(file_name)
    -       end
    5
    -       def [](key) @properties[key]; end
    -       def to_hash() @properties; end
    -
    -       private
   10
    -       def load_props(file_name)
    -         properties = {}
    -         file = File.new(file_name)
    -         while !file.eof? do
   15           line = get_line(file)
    -           next if line =~ /^[#!]/ or line =~ /^\s*$/
    -           if line =~ /^\s*(\S+)\s*[=:]\s*(.*)$/
    -             properties[$1] = $2
    -           end
   20         end
    -         file.close
    -         properties
    -       end
    -
   25       def get_line(file)
    -         current_line = file.readline.chomp
    -         while current_line =~ /^(.*)\\$/
    -           next_line = file.readline.chomp
    -           current_line = $1 + next_line.gsub(/^\s*(.*)$/, '\\1')
   30         end
    -         current_line
    -       end
    -     end
```

Here's a simple program to feed the sample file to our class:

```
require 'propfile'
properties = PropertiesFile.new('regular.properties')
properties.to_hash.each do |k,v|
  puts "#{k}: #{v}"
end
```

```
broken_value: This value is long.
http.proxyPort: 8080
fruits: apple, banana, pear, cantaloupe, watermelon, kiwi, mango
colon_prop: hello
ruby: pragmatic
http.proxyHost: example.com
```

Fixed-Length Records

One of the oldest and simplest file formats in the history of computer science is fixed-length records, where every line of a file is divided into several fields having a fixed length. A fixed-length record file containing a credit card number (19 characters), a first name (20 characters), and a surname (30 characters) looks like this:

File 164

```
Line 1    1234-5678-9012-3456Barney              Gumble
     -    1111-2222-3333-4444Homer               Simpson
```

Even in times of seemingly unlimited resources we still have to think about maximum sizes surprisingly often. For instance, relational databases still force us to define the maximum length of columns (how long can a surname or a street name be? In North America? In Iceland?), and therefore database exports are often files containing fixed-length records. But using fixed-length records can also be a natural choice, because the size of a lot of data, e.g., Social Security or credit card numbers, is limited anyway.

Hence, files containing fixed-length records are still in widespread use today, and processing them with Ruby is easy:

File 165

```ruby
class FixedLengthRecordFile
  def FixedLengthRecordFile.open(filename, field_sizes)
    field_pattern = 'a' + field_sizes.join('a')
    IO.foreach(filename) do |line|
      record = line.chomp.unpack(field_pattern)
      record.map { |f| f.strip! }
      yield record
    end
  end
end
```

File 166

```ruby
FixedLengthRecordFile.open('customers.fix', [19, 20, 30]) do |row|
  puts "#{row[1]}, #{row[2]} (#{row[0]})"
end
```

This produces the following:

```
Barney, Gumble (1234-5678-9012-3456)
Homer, Simpson (1111-2222-3333-4444)
```

The main work in our class is done by the unpack(format) method, which is a string tokenizer on steroids, that can be used whenever you have to dissect a string of bytes. It expects a format string consisting of single-letter commands and returns an array of all values extracted from the string.

In our case we dynamically construct a format string that extracts sequences of ASCII characters from a string. An *a* followed by a number means "extract this amount of ASCII characters." For our customer example it is "a19a20a30"; i.e., extract 19 characters, then 20 characters, and finally 30 characters. It should be obvious that it's not possible to process binary data using our class.

YAML Ain't Markup Language (YAML)

You probably won't have to integrate your software with existing YAML documents in your enterprise. But, in the Ruby world, YAML is popular, maybe even more popular than XML. So let's spend a few pages looking at YAML.

YAML stands for "YAML Ain't Markup Language." That's no lie: YAML actually does not define markup sequences the way XML does. Instead, it specifies a small set of simple rules for formatting structured data without much clutter, using plain text. YAML is available not only for Ruby but also for Python, PHP, and Perl.[17]

The following YAML file (themes.yaml) represents a list of wrapping paper themes. It shows examples of array elements, which start with a - symbol and are separated by newline characters:

File 193

```
- red hearts
- lovely smileys
- rainbows
```

To load and parse the file, we use the YAML parser written by *why the lucky stiff*:

File 194

```
Line 1  require 'yaml'
        themes = YAML::load_file('themes.yaml')
        puts themes.class
        puts themes.join("\n")
```

This prints the following:

```
Array
red hearts
lovely smileys
rainbows
```

Obviously, the parser knows how to turn our list back into a native Ruby array, but does it work the other way around, too?

---

[17]http://www.yaml.org

File 194

```
Line 1    include YAML
      -       puts %w(a spectacular example).to_yaml
```

This produces the following:

```
- a
- spectacular
- example
```

When you include YAML, every object will get a to_yaml() method that returns its YAML representation. That whets our appetite; let's see how YAML treats other data types:

File 194

```
Line 1    [
      -       'PragBouquet',
      -       :aSymbol,
      -       42,
      5       3.14,
      -       true,
      -       { 'chunky' => 'bacon', 'answer' => 42},
      -     ].each do |obj|
      -       puts "#{obj.class}#to_yaml:\n#{obj.to_yaml}\n"
      10    end
```

This produces the following:

```
String#to_yaml:
PragBouquet

Symbol#to_yaml:
:aSymbol

Fixnum#to_yaml:
42

Float#to_yaml:
3.14

TrueClass#to_yaml:
true

Hash#to_yaml:
answer: 42
chunky: bacon
```

All the basic data types (Fixnum, Float, Boolean, and String) seem to be encoded as ordinary Ruby literals. The encoding of Hash objects looks intuitive, too.

By default, every sequence of characters starting with an alphanumeric character is a String object in YAML unless it matches the more fine-grained rules for other data types.

As usual, symbols start with a colon (keep in mind that YAML is not specific to Ruby, so it has no specific syntax for symbols, because they do not exist in all dynamic languages). Integer objects are sequences of digits that may start with an optional sign character (+ or -). They may contain commas for better readability, so -1,234 will be interpreted as an integer. Boolean values are represented by true and false. Float objects are two sequences of digits separated by a period (.). They may start with an optional sign character, and in contrast to Ruby's literals for Float objects, the scientific notation for floating-point numbers is allowed in YAML.

Hash objects are represented as key/value pairs where the key and value are separated by a colon and each pair is separated by a newline character.

Now we know how Ruby's standard types are represented in YAML, so let's look at more complex structures. When running this little program:

File 194

```
Line 1    [
              [%w(a nested list)],
              ['another', %w(more deeply), 'nested', 'list'],
              [ 'a', { 'list' => 'of', 3 => 'different' }, 'objects'],
     5        { 'that' => %w(is getting), 'really' => { 'very' => 'complex'}}
          ].each do |obj|
              puts "#{obj.inspect}.to_yaml:\n#{obj.to_yaml}\n"
          end
```

we get the following result:

```
[["a", "nested", "list"]].to_yaml:
- - a
  - nested
  - list

["another", ["more", "deeply"], "nested", "list"].to_yaml:
- another
- - more
  - deeply
- nested
- list

["a", {"list"=>"of", 3=>"different"}, "objects"].to_yaml:
- a
- list: of
  3: different
- objects

{ "that"=>["is", "getting"], "really"=>{"very"=>"complex"}}.to_yaml:
```

```
really:
  very: complex
that:
- is
- getting
```

No big deal: nested arrays and hashes are encoded by indenting the nested elements with leading spaces. The number of characters used for indentation doesn't matter, but it has to be consistent, so if the first element is indented by four characters, the following elements have to be indented by four characters, also.

Because there are no more standard types left, let's look at other interesting objects:

File 194

```
Line 1   Flower = Struct.new(:name, :price)
   -     [
   -       Time.now,
   -       Flower.new('rose', 1.99),
   5       /even regexes/i,
   -       'a'..'f'
   -     ].each do |obj|
   -       puts "#{obj.class}#to_yaml:\n#{obj.to_yaml}\n"
   -     end
```

This is how our objects are "yamlfied":

```
Time#to_yaml:
2005-11-06 13:13:41.536822 +01:00

Flower#to_yaml:
!ruby/struct:Flower
name: rose
price: 1.99

Regexp#to_yaml:
!ruby/regexp /even regexes/i

Range#to_yaml:
!ruby/range
begin: a
end: f
excl: false
```

Timestamps and dates are encoded in ISO-8601 format or—as shown in the previous example—a slight variation where you can put spaces between the date, time, and time zone.

Struct objects begin with !ruby/struct:*struct name*, followed by the members of the Struct object, listed as colon-separated key/value pairs. Regular expressions are encoded by putting !ruby/regexp in front. Finally, the representation of Range objects starts with the !ruby/range sequence, followed by the three attributes begin, end, and excl, corresponding to the range definition.

Now let's see how YAML encodes objects created from the classes you write:

File 194

```
Line 1   class CustomClass
             attr_accessor :a_hash, :an_array, :a_timestamp
         end

5        custom_class = CustomClass.new
         custom_class.a_hash = { 'how' => 'boring' }
         custom_class.an_array = %w(still awake?)
         custom_class.a_timestamp = Time.now
         puts custom_class.to_yaml
```

This prints the following:

```
!ruby/object:CustomClass
a_hash:
  how: boring
a_timestamp: 2005-11-07 19:36:54.477093 +01:00
an_array:
- still
- awake?
```

That should be fairly self-explanatory.

We've looked at YAML serializing data. It can also deserialize data. If, for example, the file demo.yaml is as follows:

File 192

```
- 42
- ~
- null
- true
- 1.2345
- :aSymbol
- 2005-11-07
- 1972-09-30T03:42:17.0+01:00
- !ruby/object:CustomClass
  a_hash:
    how: boring
  a_timestamp: 2005-11-07 19:36:54.477093 +01:00
  an_array:
  - still
  - awake?
```

and we parse it like this:

File 194

```
Line 1   p YAML::load_file('demo.yaml')
```

then we get the following (manually formatted) output:

```
[
  42, nil, nil, true, 1.2345, :aSymbol,
  #<Date: 4907363/2,0,2299161>, Sat Sep 30 03:42:17 CET 1972,
  #<CustomClass:0x392ffc
    @a_hash={"how"=>"boring"},
    @a_timestamp=Mon Nov 07 19:36:54 CET 2005,
    @an_array=["still", "awake?"]>
]
```

Conclusion

YAML is a useful technology, and its Ruby support is excellent. It still has many more useful features we didn't cover here.[18] For example, you can put several documents into a single file, and you can define references to particular entries in a document and use them wherever you want. The next time you need a data format, you should give YAML a chance....

---

[18]Visit http://yaml4r.sourceforge.net/cookbook to learn every little detail.

## Chapter 4

Low-Ceremony Distributed Applications

Few technologies have changed the IT landscape the way networks have. Today networks are ubiquitous. Some key players claim that the network is the computer. Think about it for a moment: when was the last time you switched on your computer and did not immediately connect to the Internet? When was the last time you started your office PC and did not log in to a server using ssh or telnet?

Yes, it's true: networks have changed the way we think about computers significantly. They've changed the way we think about applications, too. Nowadays, even small applications often depend on distributed architectures where parts of a program are made available using network technologies.

That's obvious on the Internet, where you can freely use services offered by Amazon.com or Google. By sending simple HTTP requests, you get back information about a book, or you can search for news about your favorite football team.

Big companies in the banking or telecommunications business were the first to adapt to the distributed applications paradigm. Because these companies often are spread across different continents, they were motivated to find ways to implement a feature or a function only once and to reuse it wherever possible. Today it's so easy to implement interprocess communication that nearly every company can benefit from using the technology.

You do not have to use heavyweight industry standards such as SOAP or CORBA to make your processes talk to each other. In this chapter we'll show you how to use plain sockets and pure HTTP to separate concerns and to distribute business logic across process boundaries.

4.1 "I'd Rather Use a Socket"

During a conference in 2003 someone asked Robert C. Martin about the future of SOAP. After listening to the answers of his panelists, Uncle Bob replied, "I'd rather use a socket."[1] He is right: more often than not it's sufficient to use some plain text files and a socket instead of huge databases and complex middleware. So, let's start by looking at this simple approach.

Using plain sockets in an efficient and platform-independent manner isn't trivial; handling multithreading issues and the like can become fairly complicated. If you're really interested in the nitty-gritty details of socket programming, look at *Unix Network Programming* [Ste98] and the appendix of *Programming Ruby* [TFH05]. Fortunately, a few off-the-shelf solutions are available in Ruby's standard distribution.

Ruby comes with a class called GServer that helps in the creation of generic TCP servers. Written by John W. Small, GServer deals with stuff such as connection handling and distributing requests to different threads, leaving you to implement the business logic. The unavoidable echo server example that sends back everything it gets looks like this:

`File 58`

```
Line 1   require 'gserver'

         class Parrot < GServer
           def initialize(host = 'localhost', port = '3333')
     5       super(port, host)
           end

           def serve(client)
             text = client.gets
    10       client.puts(text)
           end
         end

         lora = Parrot.new
    15   lora.start
         lora.join
```

---

[1]http://www.artima.com/weblogs/viewpost.jsp?thread=4846

On line 3 we derive our class Parrot from GServer, initializing it on line 5. The serve(client) method gets called whenever a client connects to our server. After reading what the client has to say, it sends it back as an echo. As you might have guessed already, start() starts the server, and the join() method ensures that all running threads finish their work before shutting down the server. Here we have a recording from a live performance:

```
mschmidt:/tmp> telnet localhost 3333
⇒    Trying ::1...
     Connected to localhost.
     Escape character is '^]'.
⇐    Do you wanna have a cookie
⇒    Do you wanna have a cookie
     Connection closed by foreign host.

mschmidt:/tmp>
```

The PragBouquet Status Monitor

Because building a server with GServer is so easy, we will try to solve a problem that has been around for a long time now at PragBouquet. Nearly every application running at PragBouquet writes a log file, often used for troubleshooting.

Unfortunately, not all of them (to be exact, no two of them) use the same format, and the files are scattered across several file systems. Even if you're lucky and eventually find the file that should contain the information you need to resolve a trouble ticket initiated by one of your best (and probably most choleric) customers, chances are good that it has been overwritten already and no backup is available.

To overcome this situation we will create a status monitor, a TCP server whose only purpose is to centrally store messages sent by PragBouquet applications. Each message belongs to a certain application and is tagged with a severity level (warn, error, fatal).

You might be wondering "Hey, why rewrite syslogd?" but our little server differs from syslogd in a lot of ways: it's used exclusively by PragBouquet applications, we can decide where and how to store our log messages, special actions can be triggered for certain log levels, and it's platform independent—it will run on Unix boxes as well as on Windows PCs.

Release candidate 1 of status monitor V0.0.1b writes messages only to STDOUT. It looks like this:

File 74

```ruby
Line 1  require 'logger'
   -    require 'gserver'
   -
   -    class StatusMonitor < GServer
   5      def initialize(host = '127.0.0.1', port = '3333')
   -        super(port, host)
   -        @level_map = {
   -          'w' => 'warn', 'e' => 'error', 'f' => 'fatal'
   -        }
   10       @logger = Logger.new(STDOUT)
   -      end
   -
   -      # Expects CSV data in the following format:
   -      # level,application,message.
   15     def serve(client)
   -        level, app, msg = client.readline.chomp.split(',', 3)
   -        if @level_map.has_key?(level)
   -          @logger.send(@level_map[level], "#{app}: #{msg}")
   -          client.puts('0')
   20       else
   -          client.puts('1')
   -        end
   -      end
   -    end
   25   sm = StatusMonitor.new
   -    sm.start
   -    sm.join
```

Let's test it using good old telnet:

```
mschmidt:/tmp> telnet localhost 3333
⇒   Trying ::1...
    Connected to localhost.
    Escape character is '^]'.
⇐   f,billing,Lost connection to payment gateway.
⇒   0
    Connection closed by foreign host.

mschmidt:/tmp>
```

Our request has been successful (0 was returned). The corresponding server output looks like this:

```
F, [2005-09-03T16:32:03.952707 #1124] FATAL -- : billing: \
   Lost connection to payment gateway.
```

Line 18 shows a nice Ruby trick; it dynamically invokes a method on our logger object using send(symbol, (, args...)) (to read more about the Logger class, see Section 6.2, *Logging*, on page 264).

By the way, if you don't want to test your GServer objects using old-fashioned manual prodding with telnet, you can easily use ordinary unit tests, too. Thanks to the magic of duck typing (see the sidebar, on the next page), you can pass any object to the serve() method that responds to the readline() and puts() methods.StringIO works well for this sort of task:

```
Line 1   require 'test/unit'
    -    require 'stringio'
    -    require 'status_monitor'
    -
    5    class StatusMonitorTest < Test::Unit::TestCase
    -        def setup
    -            @server = StatusMonitor.new
    -        end
    -
   10        def test_empty_string
    -            result = simulate_request("\n")
    -            assert_equal('1', result)
    -        end
    -
   15        def test_invalid_level
    -            result = simulate_request("x,foo,invalid level\n")
    -            assert_equal('1', result)
    -        end
    -
   20        def test_normal_case
    -            result = simulate_request("e,foo,normal case\n")
    -            assert_equal('0', result)
    -        end
    -
   25        def simulate_request(request)
    -            client = StringIO.new(request)
    -            @server.serve(client)
    -            client.string[request.size - 2 .. -2]
    -        end
   30   end
```

This produces the following:

```
Loaded suite sm_test
Started
..E, [2005-10-14T08:00:54.960679 #374] ERROR -- : foo: normal case
.
Finished in 0.012851 seconds.

3 tests, 3 assertions, 0 failures, 0 errors
```

For the unit tests, we've initialized StringIO objects with messages that potential clients could send to the status monitor. The Status Monitor's serve() method doesn't care what class its clients belong to and happily reads requests from a StringIO object and writes results to it.

Duck Typing

Ruby is an object-oriented language. Where there are objects, classes and types are usually not far away. However, in contrast to Java or C++ programs, Ruby programs are not cluttered with type declarations. In Ruby, the type of variables, methods, and method parameters do not have to be explicitly declared. Despite this, all Ruby objects have a certain type.

However, when you're programming in a dynamic language, you soon realize that the most important question about a particular object is normally not "What's its class, and what are *all* the methods it responds to?" but instead "Does the object at hand respond to foo()?"

That's where the duck analogy comes from: if it walks like a duck and talks like a duck, then it will be treated as if it is a duck. No matter if it actually is one or not.

This situation is not uncommon even in apparently statically typed languages. For example, Java programmers expect every object to have a toString() method. In Java, this is because all objects are derived from the omnipresent Object class. The implementation is different, but the principle is the same: you want a particular object to respond to a certain message; its class doesn't matter much to you.

Our implementation of the GServer's serve(client) method doesn't care about client's class: it doesn't declare its type, and it doesn't check whether it actually is some kind of TCP socket. It expects client to respond only to methods called readline() and puts(text).

The main work is done by the simulate_request() method. This calls the serve() method, passing it a StringIO object. To read the result on line 28, we have to ignore the message that is still in the StringIO object, and we have to ignore the line feed the server sends at the end of the message.

Status Monitor Clients

The biggest problem with servers is that they are totally useless without a client. In our case, we have to create one for every programming language PragBouquet uses. Although this may seem like a lot of redundancy, it's always a good idea to provide programmers with the highest degree of flexibility. If there is no status monitor client library for Java, they will not use it (the status monitor, of course. Not Java). If you think the status monitor is a Good Thing and you want your colleagues to use it, then you have to make it as painless as possible to do so.

Currently, there are not many Ruby applications in the PragBouquet environment, but we want to be prepared. Feeding our status monitor from Ruby programs can be accomplished using class TCPSocket:

File 78

```ruby
Line 1    require 'socket'

          class StatusMonitorClient
            WARN = 'w'
    5       ERROR = 'e'
            FATAL = 'f'

            def initialize(host, port)
              @sm = TCPSocket.new(host, port)
    10      end

            def warn(app, msg) log(WARN, app, msg); end
            def error(app, msg) log(ERROR, app, msg); end
            def fatal(app, msg) log(FATAL, app, msg); end
    15      def terminate() @sm.close; end

            private

            def log(level, app, msg)
    20        @sm.puts [level, app, msg].join(',')
              @sm.readline
            end
          end
```

At the heart of class Status MonitorClient is the log(level,app,msg) method. It sends a string to the status monitor and reads back the result. Because TCPSocket objects behave like any other IO instance, it's easy to implement. You can use this class as follows:

File 78

```ruby
Line 1    sm = StatusMonitorClient.new('127.0.0.1', 3333)
          # ...
          sm.fatal('billing', 'Lost connection to payment gateway.')
          # ...
    5     sm.terminate
```

One of the most important clients will be the Java client, because it has been the programming language of choice for a long time at Prag-Bouquet. As we did with the Ruby client, we won't go abstracting too much. At the same time, adding a little layer on top of the TCP stack will certainly pay off in the future:

File 71

```
Line 1    import java.io.*;
   -      import java.net.*;
   -
   -      public class StatusMonitor {
   5          public static final String WARN = "w";
   -          public static final String ERROR = "e";
   -          public static final String FATAL = "f";
   -
   -          public StatusMonitor(final String host, final int port)
   10             throws UnknownHostException, IOException
   -          {
   -              _sm = new Socket(host, port);
   -              _out = new PrintWriter(_sm.getOutputStream(), true);
   -              _in = new BufferedReader(
   15                 new InputStreamReader(_sm.getInputStream())
   -              );
   -          }
   -
   -          public int warn(final String app, final String msg)
   20             throws IOException
   -          {
   -              return log(WARN, app, msg);
   -          }
   -
   25         public int error(final String app, final String msg)
   -             throws IOException
   -          {
   -              return log(ERROR, app, msg);
   -          }
   30
   -          public int fatal(final String app, final String msg)
   -             throws IOException
   -          {
   -              return log(FATAL, app, msg);
   35         }
   -
   -          public void terminate() throws IOException {
   -              _out.close();
   -              _in.close();
   40             _sm.close();
   -          }
   -
   -          private int log(
   -              final String level,
   45             final String app,
   -              final String msg) throws IOException
   -          {
   -              final String DEL = ",";
   -              _out.println(level + DEL + app + DEL + msg);
   50             final String response = _in.readLine();
   -              int return_code = 1;
```

```
-         try {
-             return_code = Integer.parseInt(response);
-         }
55        catch(NumberFormatException ignoreMe) {}
-         return return_code;
-     }
-
-     private Socket _sm;
60    private PrintWriter _out;
-     private BufferedReader _in;
- }
```

Again, most of the work takes place in the log(level,app,msg) method. Because this is a book about Ruby, we will not go into all the nitty-gritty details of the StatusMonitor class. However, we will demonstrate how to use it:

```
Line 1   public class StatusMonitorTest {
-            public static void main(String[] args) {
-                try {
-                    final StatusMonitor sm = new StatusMonitor(
5                        "127.0.0.1",
-                        3333
-                    );
-                    final int result = sm.debug("billing", "ALAAARM!!");
-                    System.out.println(result);
10                   sm.terminate();
-                }
-                catch(Exception e) {
-                    System.err.println(
-                        "An error occurred: " + e.getMessage()
15                   );
-                }
-            }
-        }
```

Oh, and we shouldn't forget the ragged hordes of Perl programmers who inhabited our IT department in the past. All the poor guys who have to maintain their legacy code have the right to use our amazing status monitor, too:

```
Line 1   package StatusMonitor;
-
-        use strict;
-        use IO::Socket;
5
-        use constant WARN  => 'w';
-        use constant ERROR => 'e';
-        use constant FATAL => 'f';
-
```

```
10    sub new {
 -        my $class = shift;
 -        my ($host, $port) = @_;
 -        my $self = {};
 -        my $sm = IO::Socket::INET->new("$host:$port");
15        die "Could not connect to status monitor: $!\n" unless $sm;
 -        $self->{'sm'} = $sm;
 -        bless $self, $class;
 -    }
 -
20    sub warn() {
 -        my ($self, $app, $msg) = @_;
 -        $self->_log(WARN, $app, $msg);
 -    }
 -
25    sub error() {
 -        my ($self, $app, $msg) = @_;
 -        $self->_log(ERROR, $app, $msg);
 -    }
 -
30    sub fatal() {
 -        my ($self, $app, $msg) = @_;
 -        $self->_log(FATAL, $app, $msg);
 -    }
 -
35    sub _log() {
 -        my ($self, $level, $app, $msg) = @_;
 -        my $sm = $self->{'sm'};
 -        $sm->print("$level,$app,$msg\n");
 -        $sm->getline;
40    }
 -
 -    sub DESTROY {
 -        close($_[0]->{'sm'});
 -    }
45
 -    1;
```

For those who are familiar with Perl (the Pathological Eclectic Rubbish Lister, as its inventor Larry Wall sometimes calls it), the previous lines should be no problem. For all the others it will look like line noise until they have studied Perl for several years. Just believe it: this code achieves the same results as our Ruby and Java code. Here's a little test program to prove it:

File 79

```
use strict;
use status_monitor;

my $sm = StatusMonitor->new('127.0.0.1', 3333);
$sm->error('tracking', 'Lost connection to service.');
```

This produces the following:

```
E, [2005-09-17T17:23:43.216794 #1419] ERROR -- : tracking: \
    Lost connection to service.
```

Admittedly, this is a lot of code that has to be maintained from now on, but it has some valuable benefits. Although we had to implement TCP client code for various languages, we can now add features to the status monitor without touching the client libraries. For example, we can send an e-mail to the operations department whenever an application logs a fatal error. Additionally, to change the transport layer, only the different log(level,app,msg) methods have to be changed.

Adding Better Persistence

Let's illustrate that flexibility by replacing our cheap logger by a full-blown MySQL database. At the same time, we'll add an e-mail feature, too. Our little database (called smon) consists of only one table, log_entries. Its structure should be fairly clear:

File 67

```
create table log_entries(
  id int unsigned not null primary key,
  application varchar(64) not null,
  level enum('warn', 'error', 'fatal'),
  message text,
  created timestamp not null
);
```

We'll access the status monitor database using ActiveRecord:

File 75

```
Line 1  require 'rubygems'
   -    require 'active_record'
   -    require 'gserver'
   -
   5    ActiveRecord::Base.establish_connection(
   -      :adapter => 'mysql',
   -      :host => '127.0.0.1',
   -      :database => 'smon'
   -    )
   10
   -    class LogEntry < ActiveRecord::Base; end
   -
   -    class StatusMonitor < GServer
   -      def initialize(host = '127.0.0.1', port = '3333')
   15      super(port, host)
   -        @level_map = {
   -          'w' => 'warn', 'e' => 'error', 'f' => 'fatal'
   -        }
   -      end
```

```
20      # Expects CSV data in the following format:
   -    # level,application,message.
   -    def serve(client)
   -       level, app, msg = client.readline.chomp.split(',', 3)
25         if @level_map.has_key?(level)
   -          entry = LogEntry.new
   -          entry.application = app
   -          entry.level = @level_map[level]
   -          entry.message = msg
30            entry.save!
   -          client.puts('0')
   -       else
   -          client.puts('1')
   -       end
35      end
   -    end
```

First, we removed the Logger class (maybe we will use it again for logging the status monitor's own status, but for now we try to keep the examples short). Next, we added initialization code for ActiveRecord and the LogEntry class (to learn more about ActiveRecord, see Section 2.3, *ActiveRecord Basics*, on page 34). In our serve(client) method we didn't have to change a lot either. All the logging stuff was replaced by initialization code for a new LogEntry object that gets saved for each request.

None of the client libraries had to be touched. By changing only a few lines of Ruby code, we solved one of our biggest problems—important information is now stored centrally. From now on we do not have to search tons of log files to find vital information; a simple SELECT statement will be sufficient. Provided that your database and system administrators earn their salaries by creating regular database backups, this information will be safe forever.

Sending E-mails

At this point we're unstoppable. Let's add some more code to the status monitor that sends an e-mail to the operations department whenever an application logs a fatal error:

File 76

```
Line 1  require 'rubygems'
   -    require 'active_record'
   -    require 'gserver'
   -    require 'tmail'
5       require 'net/smtp'
   -
   -
```

```ruby
      ActiveRecord::Base.establish_connection(
        :adapter => 'mysql',
10      :host => '127.0.0.1',
        :database => 'smon'
      )

      class LogEntry < ActiveRecord::Base; end
15
      class StatusMonitor < GServer
          def initialize(host = '127.0.0.1', port = '3333')
              super(port, host)
              @level_map = {
20                'w' => 'warn', 'e' => 'error', 'f' => 'fatal'
              }
          end


          # Expects CSV data in the following format:
25        # level,application,message.
          def serve(client)
              level, app, msg = client.readline.chomp.split(',', 3)
              if @level_map.has_key?(level)
                  entry = LogEntry.new
30                entry.application = app
                  entry.level = @level_map[level]
                  entry.message = msg
                  entry.save!

35                inform_helpdesk(app, level, msg) if level == 'f'
                  client.puts('0')
              else
                  client.puts('1')
              end
40        end

        private

        def inform_helpdesk(app, level, msg)
45            subject = "A fatal error occurred in #{app}!"
              subject << " Regret your sins!"
              mail = create_mail(
                  'helpdesk@pragbouquet.com',
                  subject,
50                msg
              )
              send_mail('localhost', mail)
          end

55        def create_mail(to, subject, body)
            mail = TMail::Mail.new
            mail.date = Time.now
            mail.mime_version = '1.0'
```

```
   -            mail.set_content_type 'text', 'plain'
  60            mail.from = 'status_monitor@pragbouquet.com'
   -            mail.to = to
   -            mail.subject = subject
   -            mail.body = body
   -            mail
  65          end
   -
   -          def send_mail(host, mail)
   -            msg = mail.encoded
   -            Net::SMTP.start(host, 25) do |smtp|
  70              smtp.send_mail(msg, mail.from_address, mail.destinations)
   -            end
   -          end
   -        end
```

Sending e-mail can be divided into two parts: creating the SMTP (Simple Mail Transfer Protocol) formatted e-mail and sending that e-mail over a network. To create the SMTP representation, we used Minero Aoki's excellent *tmail* library[2] (you can see how to obtain and install it in Section 6.4, *Deploying with setup.rb*, on page 290).

In the create_mail(to,subject,body) method, we'll make a TMail::Mail object that contains all the attributes we'd expect an e-mail to have. Finally, on line 68, we call encoded(). It returns something like this:

```
Date: Sat, 17 Sep 2005 14:48:30 +0200
From: status_monitor@pragbouquet.com
To: helpdesk@pragbouquet.com
Subject: A fatal error occurred in billing! Regret your sins!
Mime-Version: 1.0
Content-Type: text/plain

Lost connection to payment gateway.
```

Ruby's standard class Net::SMTP is quite handy for sending the e-mail we just created. Lines 69 to 71 of method send_mail(host,mail) show how to accomplish this.

We're done! The application is now backed by a database and sends an e-mail to the operations department whenever a fatal application error occurs.

---

[2]http://raa.ruby-lang.org/project/tmail

4.2 Remote Procedure Calls Using HTTP

Our new status monitor has been a huge success—the system failure rate has dropped down to an all-time low of two per day, each lasting for less than ten minutes. Unfortunately, this is true only for the time between 8 a.m. and 5 p.m., Monday to Friday. Every night three to five fatal application errors still occur, and they don't get solved until the following morning.

Obviously, the status monitor e-mails are read only during office hours. It would increase our quality of service significantly if we could inform our operations department's employees of failures wherever they are and whatever time it is. A good way to do this is to use the Short Messages (SMS) supported by cellular networks: to send the message you simply need a cellular number, and to receive it the employee needs only to keep their cell phone with them.

Waking Up the Operator

To send short messages from a computer to a cell phone, you can do the following:

1. Serially connect a computer and a cellular phone or modem that can be controlled via an AT cellular command interface.
2. Connect to a Short Message Service Center (SMSC) at your network provider. You send messages using a protocol called Short Message Peer-to-peer Protocol (SMPP)[3] to the SMSC. The SMSC is responsible for delivering them to the according mobile devices.
3. Use an existing web service on the Internet.
4. Use an e-mail-to-SMS gateway.

PragBouquet chose the SMSC connection. We already have a server that is capable of sending SMS. This particular piece of software offers a simple interface via HTTP: it supports the single function send(recipient, sender, type, data).

You have to distinguish between Short Messages containing textual or binary data. Set type to text or binary accordingly (text is the default). Binary data has to be transmitted in two-digit hexadecimal ASCII representation, so a binary zero is transmitted as 00 and binary 63 is transmitted as 3f.

---

[3]http://en.wikipedia.org/wiki/SMPP

More Privacy!

Even in the early days of the World Wide Web, security was an important issue. In 1994 Netscape Communications invented a protocol called Secure Sockets Layer (SSL)* that enabled web clients and servers to exchange sensitive data without worries.

The first protocol version and its implementation were full of flaws, but since then, SSL has become a de facto standard and has been improved several times. Currently, its most popular implementation is OpenSSL.† The OpenSSL project has created a C library that has been ported to countless platforms and is the basis for Ruby's SSL support, too.

In the simplest cases it makes nearly no difference whether you use HTTP or HTTPS. For example, printing the index page of the OpenSSL web site can be achieved as follows:

File 94

```
Line 1   require 'net/https'

         h = Net::HTTP.new('www.openssl.org', 443)
         h.use_ssl = true
    5    h.get2('/') { |response| print response.body }
```

You have to set the use_ssl attribute of your Net::HTTP object to true, and you have to use get2(path,initheader=nil,&block) instead of get(path,initheader=nil,dest=nil,&block). Oh, and it's important that you explicitly set the SSL port (443) when opening the connection. Otherwise, the HTTP default port (80) will be used, and your request will probably fail.

Because it's based on the OpenSSL reference implementation, Ruby's support of the SSL protocol is as secure and complete as it can be. You can encrypt and decrypt communication transparently (as we did in the previous example). There are methods for signing and verifying both client and server certificates. For example, peer_cert() returns the server's X.509 certificate, and using cert=(certificate) you can set a client's X.509 certificate. The library allows you to maintain a certificate store in your local file system, too.

---

*http://en.wikipedia.org/wiki/Secure_Sockets_Layer
†http://www.openssl.org

The remaining parameters contain the data to be sent and the recipient's and the sender's phone numbers in international format. If the sender parameter is not set, it will be set to the recipient parameter automatically. This way the recipient thinks he has sent himself a message—in our case that is all right.

The service listens on port 4242 under path /send. It returns its result using the HTTP status code, so 200 means everything went fine and 500 means an error occurred. Let's try it using telnet:

```
mschmidt:/tmp> telnet localhost 4242
  ⇒    Trying ::1...
       Connected to localhost.
       Escape character is '^]'.
  ⇐    GET /send?type=text&recipient=+011234123456&data=hello HTTP/1.0
  ⇒
       HTTP/1.1 200 OK
       Connection: close
       Date: Wed, 14 Sep 2005 20:26:47 GMT
       Content-Type: text/plain
       Server: WEBrick/1.3.1 (Ruby/1.8.2/2004-12-25)
       Content-Length: 0

       Connection closed by foreign host.

mschmidt:/tmp>
```

Hmm, there's no error message from the session, but our cell phone didn't yell "YOU HAVE A NEW MESSAGE!" at full volume as it usually does when it receives an SMS. So, what's wrong? Provided that the SMS server is working properly, the problem must be hidden in our input. Obviously, the type and data parameters are correct, but the recipient's phone number contains a subtle syntax error. All international phone numbers start with one of the following prefixes:[4]

- 00<international area code><national area code>

- +<international area code><national area code>

At first sight, everything seems to be all right with the recipient's phone number, but we forgot that we are using an HTTP service that expects all its parameters in URL-encoded format. Hence, the leading + sign is interpreted as a blank that renders the phone number completely

---

[4]Usually, a leading zero of the national area code is omitted, but you should not blindly follow this rule. For Italy, as an example, you have to explicitly transmit the leading zero of the national area code in international phone numbers.

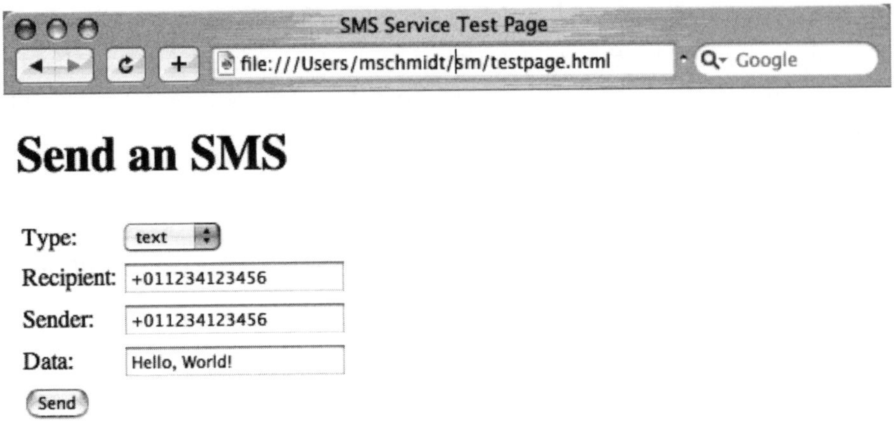

Send an SMS

Type: [text ⬍]
Recipient: [+011234123456]
Sender: [+011234123456]
Data: [Hello, World!]
(Send)

Figure 4.1: TESTING THE SMS SERVER

wrong. Instead of transmitting +011234123456 (an American phone number), ⌴011234123456 (a national phone number with a leading blank) is transmitted.

In the best case, this phone number does not exist, and the SMSC fails to deliver your message. In the worst case, someone could become really angry while you're desperately running your unit test suite over and over again at 2 a.m. on a Saturday night.

When testing complex HTTP services, the telnet command can be a bit tedious. For services expecting GET requests, you're much better off using an ordinary web browser (as shown in Figure 4.1). The browser transparently handles all encoding issues for you (command-line diehards will use wget[5] or curl[6] anyway). An HTML page such as the following is sufficient for testing purposes:

File 80

```
Line 1   <!DOCTYPE html PUBLIC "-//W3C//DTD XHTML 1.0 Strict//EN"
                "http://www.w3.org/TR/xhtml1/DTD/xhtml1-strict.dtd">

         <html>
5          <head>
               <title>SMS Service Test Page</title>
           </head>
           <body>
```

---

[5]http://www.gnu.org/software/wget/wget.html
[6]http://curl.haxx.se

```
  -          <h1>Send an SMS</h1>
 10          <form action="http://localhost:4242/send">
  -            <table>
  -              <tr>
  -                <td>Type:</td>
  -                <td>
 15                  <select name="type">
  -                    <option>text</option>
  -                    <option>binary</option>
  -                  </select>
  -                </td>
 20              </tr>
  -              <tr>
  -                <td>Recipient:</td>
  -                <td><input type="text" name="recipient"/></td>
  -              </tr>
 25              <tr>
  -                <td>Sender:</td>
  -                <td><input type="text" name="sender"/></td>
  -              </tr>
  -              <tr>
 30                <td>Data:</td>
  -                <td><input type="text" name="data"/></td>
  -              </tr>
  -              <tr>
  -                <td colspan="2">
 35                  <input type="submit" value="Send"/>
  -                </td>
  -              </tr>
  -            </table>
  -          </form>
 40        </body>
  -      </html>
```

Another way to circumvent problems like these is to use a mature HTTP
client library, such as the one that comes with the Ruby standard distribution. Let's see how we can perform HTTP requests and encapsulate
the SMS server:

File 69

```
Line 1  require 'net/http'
  -     require 'cgi'
  -
  -     class SmsService
 5       def initialize(host = '127.0.0.1', port = 4242)
  -         @host, @port = host, port
  -       end
  -
  -       def send_text(params)
 10        send_sms(params, 'text')
  -       end
  -
```

```
-          def send_binary(params)
-              send_sms(params, 'binary')
15         end

-          private

-          def send_sms(params, type)
20             result = false
-              Net::HTTP.start(@host, @port) do |http|
-                  query = "type=#{type}"
-                  params.each do |k,v|
-                      query << "&#{k}=#{CGI.escape(v)}"
25                 end
-                  response = http.get("/send?#{query}")
-                  result = response.class == Net::HTTPOK
-              end
-              result
30         end
-      end
```

A small sample program demonstrates the usage of the SmsService class. Finally you (and all your enervated colleagues) can hear it again: "YOU HAVE A NEW MESSAGE!"

File 69

```
Line 1    sms = SmsService.new
-         sms.send_text(
-            :recipient => '+0112341234567',
-            :data => 'Hello, world!'
5         )
```

In send_sms(params,type) of the SmsService class we open a new HTTP connection using the start(host,port) method of class Net::HTTP. It expects a code block that gets passed the current connection. Within the code block the query string for the GET request is prepared (note that we have to use the encode(string) method of the CGI class to URL-encode our query parameters).

Eventually, on line 26 we initiate a GET request that returns an object derived from Net::HTTPResponse. This object encapsulates everything that makes up an HTTP response. Its most important methods are as follows:

- code() returns the HTTP status code.

- message() returns the HTTP status message.

- body() returns the response body.

- The headers hash contains all HTTP headers.

URL Encoding

In the beginning of computer networking everything had to be represented in ASCII characters using only 7 bits. Because of this, nearly all protocols in today's Internet turn non-ASCII data into 7-bit ASCII characters somehow. RFC 1738* painstakingly explains which characters are allowed in URLs:

"Only alphanumerics [0--9a--zA--Z], the special characters [$-_.+!*'(),], and reserved characters used for their reserved purposes may be used unencoded within a URL."

The rules are simple: all ASCII control characters (0x00–0x1f, 0x7f), all non-ASCII characters (0x80–0xff), and all reserved characters ([$&+,/:;=?@]) have to be encoded under all circumstances.

In addition, some characters considered unsafe should be encoded, too: ["?<>#%{}|\^~'] and the square brackets ([,]) themselves (0x5b, 0x5d).

Encoding a single value is easy: you prepend its case-insensitive, two-digit hexadecimal ISO-Latin code by a percent symbol (%).

For example, the blank character is encoded as %20 (for convenience, a blank can also be encoded as a single '+' symbol) and an uppercase 'A' (whose ISO-Latin code is 65) is turned into %41.

*http://www.rfc-editor.org/rfc/rfc1738.txt

There is a separate class for every HTTP status code (yes, this little library defines more than 50 classes), so instead of checking whether code() returns 200, you can alternatively check whether your response object's class is Net::HTTPOK (as we did in line 27).

Integrating the SMS service into StatusMonitor is left as an exercise for the reader. Keep in mind that short messages do have to be short: they shouldn't be more than 160 characters.

Sending Java stack traces is definitely not an option.

If you don't like encoding query parameters manually, you can use HTTP's POST command. In the current example it doesn't make a big difference, though. Here's how send_sms(params,type) would look:

```
File 70        Line 1    def send_sms(params, type)
                  ·        result = false
                  ·        Net::HTTP.start(@host, @port) do |http|
                  ·          query = "type=#{type}"
                  5          params.each { |k,v| query << "&#{k}=#{v}" }
                  ·          response = http.post(
                  ·            '/send',
                  ·            query,
                  ·            'content-type' => 'application/x-www-form-urlencoded'
                  10         )
                  ·          result = response.class == Net::HTTPOK
                  ·        end
                  ·        result
                  ·      end
```

In lines 4 and 5 we build up the query string by concatenating key,
value pairs using the = symbol. The pairs themselves are delimited by
& symbols. That's how input values from an HTML form get transferred
to a server, and therefore, we have set the content type of our POST
request to application/x-www-form-urlencoded. Because the server
now knows how to interpret the data and because we're not sending
it in a URL, we don't have to encode it.

The Other Side of HTTP

We have seen that accessing HTTP services with Ruby is a breeze. This
made us think a bit: shouldn't we make the status monitor available
as an HTTP service, too? It certainly would have some advantages:

- We could get rid of the proprietary CSV parameter list, which
  would make it much easier to add new parameters.

- Adding additional functions would be easier, because we could
  publish them using different URLs—new functions would never
  interfere with existing ones.

- We could access the status monitor with an ordinary web browser.
  This certainly has some advantages when we add statistics or
  query features.

Now that we've convinced ourselves, let's see what the Ruby platform
has to offer for creating HTTP services. Unsurprisingly, it comes with
one of the most advanced and most convenient frameworks currently
available: WEBrick. WEBrick really has it all: you can create generic
HTTP and HTTPS servers. All of them are multithreaded, they support
servlets, and you will find a bunch of useful utility classes and functions, too.

So, let's see how we can turn our status monitor into an HTTP service:

File 77

```ruby
require 'webrick'
include WEBrick
class StatusMonitorServlet < HTTPServlet::AbstractServlet

  # ...

  def do_GET(req, res)
    app = req.query['app']
    msg = req.query['msg']
    level = req.query['level'] || ''
    level.downcase!
    res['content-type'] = 'text/plain'
    if %w(debug info warn error fatal).include?(level)
      entry = LogEntry.new
      entry.application = app
      entry.level = level
      entry.message = msg
      entry.save!
      inform_helpdesk(app, level, msg) if level == 'fatal'
      res.status = 200
      res.body = "Message was logged successfully."
    else
      res.status = 500
      res.body = "An error occurred while logging message!"
    end
  end

  alias do_POST :do_GET

  # ...

end

server = HTTPServer.new(:Port => 4242)
server.mount('/log', StatusMonitorServlet)

%w(INT TERM).each do |signal|
  trap(signal) { server.shutdown }
end

server.start
```

Even if it doesn't seem obvious at first sight, we had to modify our last version only a small amount. The StatusMonitor class has been renamed to StatusMonitorServlet and is derived from WEBrick::HTTPServlet::Abstract-Servlet. initialize(host,port) has been removed, and serve(client) has been replaced by do_GET(request,response). Everything else was left alone.

Whenever the server receives a GET request, do_GET(request,response) is called automatically. The query parameters app, level, and msg are read from the client request. This renders the former CSV solution obsolete, and adding new parameters is trivial now (for better readability we have dropped the level_map hash).

What follows is business as usual. We initialize a new LogEntry object and store it in the database. Instead of sending back 0 or 1 to indicate success or failure, we now set the HTTP status code accordingly in lines 20 and 23. Another way of setting the response status is to raise an exception, so raise HTTPStatus::OK is the same as res.status = 200. In this case it doesn't seem to make a lot of sense, but raising an exception for an error condition such as HTTPStatus::InternalServerError automatically sets the response body to an HTML error page containing a full stack trace. Such a page will be returned for uncaught exceptions, too.

Because there is no reason for the status monitor to care about the request method, we have aliased the method do_GET(request, response) to do_POST(request, response) on line 28. This allows clients to freely choose which request method they want to use.

Naked servlets are nonviable; they depend heavily on a friendly server environment to live in. Hence, we create a servlet environment beginning on line 34. In the next line the StatusMonitorServlet is mounted under the path /log, and lines 37 to 39 install a callback for INT and TERM signals that shuts down the server gracefully when it receives a corresponding signal. After starting the server in the last line, you can point your web browser to http://localhost:4242/log?app= billing&level=info&msg=hello to create a new log message.

Some WEBrick Details

WEBrick's rules for dispatching HTTP requests are simple. When the server receives a command, for example PUT, it calls the corresponding do_XXX method, in this case do_PUT(request,response). WEBrick does not restrict this dispatching mechanism to the official HTTP commands, and you're free to define your own HTTP commands, such as the one in our friendly greeting service below:

File 63

```
Line 1    class FriendlyServlet < HTTPServlet::AbstractServlet
    -         def do_GREET(req, res)
    -             res.status = 200
    -             res.body = "Hello!! Nice to meet you!\n"
    5         end
    -     end
```

HTTP Proxy Servers

Our first HTTP example works fine, because the SMS service is running on a server in the local network.

But in big companies HTTP access to servers on the Internet is often routed through a *proxy server*. Proxies cache frequently requested web sites to decrease network load, and they restrict access to unapproved content.

HTTP clients have to connect to the proxy server instead of the actual server. The proxy server then forwards the client's request and sends back the result.

Using a proxy server with Net::HTTP works as follows:

```
Net::HTTP::Proxy(
    proxy_host,
    proxy_port).start('www.example.com') do |http|
        # http is connected to proxy_host:proxy_port
end
```

If the proxy host is set to nil, no proxy will be used, so it will do no harm if you always use the proxy call.

Sometimes a proxy server expects an authentication via a user name and a password. Such information is passed as follows:

```
Net::HTTP::Proxy(
    proxy_host, proxy_port,
    proxy_user, proxy_pass).start('www.example.com') do |http|
        # http is connected to proxy_host:proxy_port
end
```

```
     server = HTTPServer.new(:Port => 4200)
     server.mount('/', FriendlyServlet)
10   %w(INT TERM).each do |signal|
        trap(signal) { server.shutdown }
     end
     server.start
```

You can use it like any other HTTP command, and you will receive the same request parameters, too (so, if you need a WEBDAV[7] extension, for example, go ahead and build one):

---

[7]http://www.webdav.org

```
mschmidt:/tmp> telnet localhost 4200

 ⇒    Trying ::1...
      Connected to localhost.
      Escape character is '^]'.
 ⇐    GREET / HTTP/1.0
 ⇒
      HTTP/1.1 200 OK
      Connection: close
      Date: Fri, 23 Sep 2005 07:18:19 GMT
      Server: WEBrick/1.3.1 (Ruby/1.8.2/2004-12-25)
      Content-Length: 26

      Hello!! Nice to meet you!
      Connection closed by foreign host.
```

The HEAD and OPTIONS commands have default implementations:

do_HEAD(request,response)

> Returns everything do_GET(request,response) would return except
> the response body. This enables clients to check whether a certain
> document has changed, so it is downloaded only if it is necessary.

do_OPTIONS(request,response)

> Returns a list of all commands available.

All do_XXX methods get passed request and response parameters of
type WEBrick::HTTPRequest and WEBrick::HTTPResponse, respectively. Both of
them provide all the features you'd normally expect. The most important methods and attributes of WEBrick::HTTPRequest are as follows:

- query is a hash object containing all query parameters that have
  been sent by the client. If a parameter is transmitted more than
  once, the corresponding entry in the query hash is an array object
  containing *all* values transmitted.
- header is a hash object containing all HTTP headers sent by the
  client.
- cookies is an array object containing all cookies sent by the client.
  Array elements are WEBrick::Cookie objects.
- Details of the resource requested by the client are available in
  the attributes host, port, request_uri, query_string, script_name, and
  path_info.

WEBrick::HTTPResponse is just as simple:

- Put the overall status of a request into the status attribute.
- Set body to the data you want to send back to the client. Make
  sure it corresponds to the response's content type.

- WEBrick automatically sends back standard HTTP headers such as server and date. The header hash allows you to add your own. For example, the following:
  ```
  response.header['content-type'] = 'text/xml'
  ```
  declares that the server output is an XML document.
- You can send cookies to the client by adding WEBrick::Cookie objects to the cookies array.

There are many more methods and attributes. Most are simply for convenience to provide access to low-level HTTP properties.

It Can Always Be Easier

Although creating your own servlets is easy, WEBrick comes with some default servlet implementations for common tasks such as serving files (we talk about FileHandler in Section 4.2, *WEBricklets*, on page 175) and executing CGI scripts.

Sometimes it seems to be overkill to define a complete servlet class. The WEBrick::HTTPServer class has a highly convenient shortcut:

File 95

```
Line 1    server = HTTPServer.new(:Port => 4100)
          server.mount_proc('/') do |req, res|
              res.status = 200
              res.body = "Hello, #{req.query['name']}!"
     5    end

          %w(INT TERM).each do |signal|
              trap(signal) { server.shutdown }
          end
    10    server.start
```

In line 2 we add a code block using mount_proc(dir,&block) to a server object. These handlers respond to both GET and POST requests and are managed by an instance of class ProcHandler.

Another useful WEBrick handler is CGIHandler. It's invoked automatically by FileHandler when the request URL ends with the extension .cgi. The *Common Gateway Interface* (CGI) defines a simple protocol between web servers and programs that create dynamic content: the web server runs an executable program with the exec() system call, and the CGI protocol specifies a list of environment variables that can be used by the CGI script to get request parameters, and so on. After the program has terminated, the web server sends its output to the web client. Typical companies have tons of old CGI programs (often Perl or bash scripts)

Common Gateway Interface

that "will definitely be replaced as soon as we have some time." Here's
a simple Perl script that creates an XML report of all flowers that are
currently used in our bouquets:

File 42

```perl
Line 1    #!/usr/bin/perl -w

          use strict;
          use DBI;
     5
          sub get_flowers {
            my $result = [];
            my $dbh = DBI->connect('dbi:mysql:webshop', '', '');

    10      my $sql = qq{ SELECT name, price FROM flowers };
            my $sth = $dbh->prepare($sql);
            $sth->execute();
            my ($name, $price);
            $sth->bind_columns( undef, \$name, \$price );
    15
            while($sth->fetch()) {
                    push(@$result, [$name, $price]);
            }

    20      $sth->finish();
            $dbh->disconnect();
            return $result;
          }

    25  print "status: 200\r\n";
        print "content-type: text/xml\r\n\r\n";

        print "<?xml version='1.0' ?>\r\n";
        print "<flowers>\r\n";
    30  my $flowers = get_flowers();
        for (@$flowers) {
          print "  <flower name='$_->[0]' price='$_->[1]' />\r\n";
        }
        print "</flowers>\r\n";
```

To reuse such legacy scripts (do you remember why you switched to
Ruby?), we set up an HTTP server as follows:

File 43

```ruby
Line 1    cgi_dir = File.expand_path('./cgi-bin')
          s = HTTPServer.new(:Port => 2080)
          s.mount('/cgi-bin', HTTPServlet::FileHandler, cgi_dir,
            :FancyIndexing => true
     5    )
```

We installed a FileHandler that manages the content of the cgi-bin directory. Whenever you request a resource ending with .cgi, WEBrick del-
egates the request to CGIHandler, executes the corresponding program,

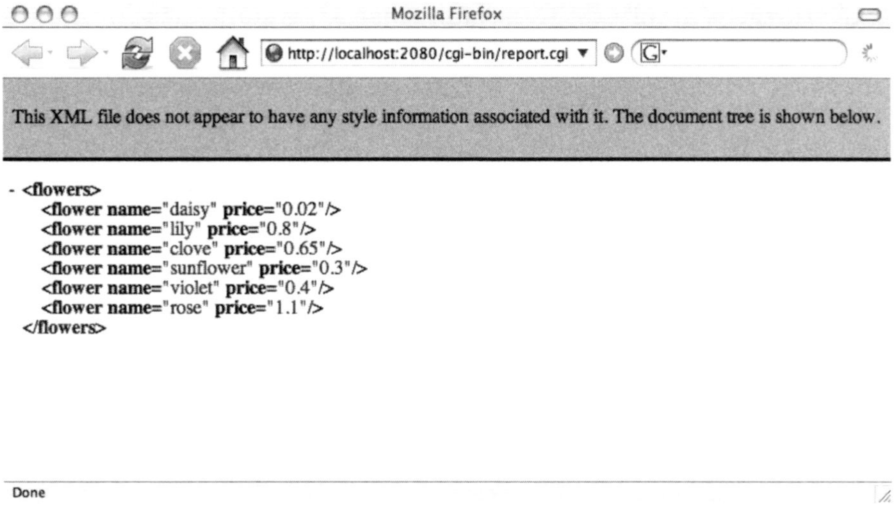

Figure 4.2: WEBRICK'S CGI HANDLER IN ACTION

and returns its output. (You'll learn what the FancyIndexing option is in Section 4.2, *Hiding Little Secrets*, on page 177). The CGI program can set the final HTTP status code by printing the status header (as we did in line 25 of the Perl program).

For the sake of completeness, let's look at the ERBHandler. This is called by the FileHandler when a resource ending with .rhtml is requested. Before the requested file is sent back, it gets processed by the templating engine ERB. To learn the scoop about .rhtml files, have a look at *Agile Web Development with Rails* [TH05].

WEBricklets

You do not have to develop huge applications to benefit from WEBrick. Often little scripts—*WEBricklets*—can significantly improve your life.   *WEBricklets*

For example, when developing Java software for PragBouquet, I often work on a remote host using a Secure Shell. I do this because the host is extremely powerful, and it has the same Java environment as the final production system. My only development tools there are Vim[8] and

---

[8]http://www.vim.org

Ant.[9] I write a lot of unit tests, and I use Ant's junit task to execute them. This task produces nicely formatted HTML pages. In the past I had to copy these pages to my PC using scp in order to view them.

Thanks to WEBrick, these times are long gone. I now run a mini WEBrick-based server on the remote host that allows me to view the pages using the web browser running on my PC:[10]

File 59

```
Line 1    require 'webrick'
          include WEBrick

          dir = Dir::pwd
     5    port = 13000 + (dir.hash % 1000)

          puts "URL: http://#{Socket.gethostname}:#{port}"

          s = HTTPServer.new(
    10        :Port => port,
              :DocumentRoot => dir,
              :ServerType => Daemon
          )

    15    trap('INT') { s.shutdown }
          s.start
```

These 16 lines of Ruby code start an HTTP server on a vaguely random port and provide access to all files in the current directory. The script turns itself into a daemon process. After you run it in the directory the junit task's output goes to, it will serve your test results until you explicitly kill it.

In line 4 we detect the current directory (which is used as the server's document root), and in line 5 a new port is calculated. Then, the file server's URL is printed to the console. Usually, I paste it to my browser's bookmark manager and give it a reasonable name like "JUnit results of project X." It can happen that the program calculates a port that is already in use by another application. In this case, set the port variable temporarily to a constant value, and start the server again.

Beginning in line 9, we create and initialize a new HTTPServer object and pass it two new options. We set DocumentRoot to the current directory, mapping that directory to the path /.

---

[9]http://ant.apache.org
[10]The basis for this example was originally posted by Jim Weirich under http://onestepback.org/index.cgi/Tech/Ruby/WEBrick.rdoc.

Behind the scenes this option installs an HTTPServlet::FileHandler object whose do_GET() method returns every file requested (after determining its MIME type and setting the content-type header correctly).

Option ServerType is set to "Daemon" which—unsurprisingly—turns the server into a daemon (you can learn how to turn your own scripts into a daemon by intensively studying some of H.P. Lovecraft's books at full moon or by referring to Section 6.3, *Creating Daemons and Services*, on page 282).

Hiding Little Secrets

For files such as unit test results, the solution in the preceding section is appropriate, because the files' contents usually contain no secrets (your unit tests results are running constantly at a 100% success rate anyway, aren't they?). As we all know, being paranoid does not mean they aren't after us, so it sometimes makes sense to plug a little security layer to our software.

In the case of our file server, we could add HTTP basic authentication:

File 60

```
Line 1    require 'webrick'
   -      include WEBrick
   -
   -      dir = Dir::pwd
   5      port = 13000 + (dir.hash % 1000)
   -      puts "URL: http://#{Socket.gethostname}:#{port}"
   -
   -      authenticate = Proc.new do |req, res|
   -         HTTPAuth.basic_auth(req, res, "") do |usr, pwd|
  10             usr == 'maik' && pwd == 'secret'
   -         end
   -      end
   -
   -      s = HTTPServer.new(:Port => port, :ServerType => Daemon)
  15      s.mount('/', HTTPServlet::FileHandler, dir,
   -         :FancyIndexing => true,
   -         :HandlerCallback => authenticate
   -      )
   -
  20      trap('INT') { s.shutdown }
   -      s.start
```

Lines 8 to 12 define our authentication logic by creating a Proc object that uses method basic_auth(request,response,realm)[11] of class HTTPAuth.

---

[11]The realm parameter is currently ignored.

This method expects a code block and passes it the user name and password that have been transmitted with the current request. If the authentication fails—basic_auth() returns false—WEBrick automatically returns the HTTP status code 401 and a corresponding HTML error page. If authentication succeeds, WEBrick continues as usual.

Now we have to install the authentication handler. We can't use the call to mount_proc() any longer, because it doesn't allow us to install any hooks. Instead, we have to use a servlet. Fortunately, for our purposes it's not necessary to define a new one—we can use the HTTPServlet::File-Handler class. We add it to the server using mount() and pass several options:

- FancyIndexing defines how directory listings will be handled. If the requested URI refers to a directory and this option is **false** (the default), the HTTP status code 403 (Forbidden) is returned. Otherwise, a directory listing will be displayed.

- HandlerCallback points to a code block that will be called before the do_XXX method belonging to the current request is called.

This solution is far from being perfect. It would increase security only if you put the script into your home directory and grant read permission to no one but yourself.

WEBrick offers more advanced security mechanisms, including support for the same password files the Apache web server[12] uses. These files are usually created with the htpasswd command:

```
mschmidt:/tmp> htpasswd -cdb /tmp/test.pwd scott tiger
Adding password for user scott
mschmidt:/tmp> cat /tmp/test.pwd
scott:Erw4v9nQMuwHQ
mschmidt:/tmp>
```

Here we created a file called test.pwd that contains the encrypted password of the user named *scott*. To use this password database with WEBrick, only the authenticate() method is redefined:

File 61

```
Line 1   authenticator = HTTPAuth::BasicAuth.new(
  -          :UserDB => HTTPAuth::Htpasswd.new('/tmp/test.pwd'),
  -          :Realm => ""
  -      )
  5      authenticate = Proc.new do |req, res|
  -          authenticator.authenticate(req, res)
  -      end
```

---

[12]http://www.apache.org

Instead of hardwiring user names and passwords into your script, they will be read by HTTPAuth::Htpasswd and evaluated by HTTPAuth::BasicAuth.

You can increase the level of security even more if you use htdigest to create passwords. In authenticate(), replace HTTPAuth::Htpasswd with HTTPAuth::Htdigest and HTTPAuth::BasicAuth by HTTPAuth::DigestAuth. Unfortunately, all these mechanisms implement only weak security. For something stronger, use HTTPS right from the beginning:

File 62

```ruby
require 'webrick'
require 'webrick/https'
include WEBrick

dir = Dir::pwd
port = 13000 + (dir.hash % 1000)

puts "URL: http://#{Socket.gethostname}:#{port}"

authenticate = Proc.new do |req, res|
  HTTPAuth.basic_auth(req, res, "") do |usr, pwd|
    usr == 'maik' && pwd == 'secret'
  end
end

s = HTTPServer.new(
  :Port => port,
  :ServerType => Daemon,
  :SSLEnable => true,
  :SSLVerifyClient => ::OpenSSL::SSL::VERIFY_NONE,
  :SSLCertName => [ %w(C US), %w(O PragBouquetSSL.com), %w(CN WWW) ]
)

s.mount(
  '/',
  HTTPServlet::FileHandler,
  dir,
  :FancyIndexing => true,
  :HandlerCallback => authenticate
)

trap('INT') { s.shutdown }
s.start
```

Here we have modified our first version and added support for SSL. We had to require webrick/https, and we had to slightly modify the initialization of our server in lines 19 to 21. For a production system you'd need to get a valid certificate, but we merely wanted to demonstrate the technical details.

Conclusion

HTTP gets abused in countless ways. Because these ways weren't even considered by its inventors, implementations that bend HTTP stray outside of HTTP's design. (There's even a whole RFC called *On the Use of HTTP as a Substrate*[13] dealing with this issue.) Sometimes it's unnecessary to add an HTTP layer to your program, but often it is highly convenient. It may even open your application up to completely unexpected purposes.

In the end it doesn't really matter whether HTTP has been a good choice for a particular application or not. If you have to integrate with an existing HTTP service, you have to use HTTP, too. As you have seen, Ruby supports you in any imaginable way.

Alternatively, if you do want to add an HTTP interface to your own application, WEBrick will prove to be an invaluable companion.

In terms of HTTP support, Ruby is more than ready for prime time.

---

[13]http://www.faqs.org/rfcs/rfc3205.html

## Chapter 5

Distributed Applications with RPC

In the beginning, distributed applications seemed to be some kind of magic to many people, because you had to use rather obscure standards like Sun's Remote Procedure Call (RPC)[1] protocol to make two processes talk to each other.

Today countless protocols, technologies, products, and standards exist for interprocess communication (IPC). Most of them—such as CORBA, XML-RPC, and SOAP—are language neutral, and bindings are available for many programming languages. Still, some protocols do work only with certain programming languages such as Java's *Remote Method Invocation* (RMI) or Distributed Ruby (DRb).

Remote Method Invocation

Theoretically, when building an architecture from scratch, there are many options to choose from (XML-RPC, CORBA, RMI, REST, SOAP, etc.), and chances are good that the company you are working for uses at least two thirds of all protocol standards available worldwide. Ruby supports many of them, and in the following sections we will demonstrate the usage of those that are most frequently used today.

5.1 Another Day, Another Protocol

After studying the market intensively for several years, PragBouquet's marketing department made an astonishing observation: people often add personalized greeting cards to bunches of flowers!

To satisfy this unexpected requirement on a technical level, the following solution has been implemented: in the web shop users can choose

---

[1]http://www.faqs.org/rfcs/rfc1057.html

an image from a list and write a short text, and then the text is printed onto the back of the greeting card in a nice font.

In the past people often got some strange texts on their cards, because their love letters were too long and the old solution did not provide any feedback. Hence, PragBouquet decided to separate the image production process into a server and to add some more logic to it. The web shop client requests the front and back pages of the greeting card from the server and presents them to the user. If everything is fine, the client will ask the server to print the card. Otherwise, it will be deleted.

At the time the current greeting card system was built, the responsible chief software evangelist was convinced that XML-RPC would last forever. Hence, he insisted on plugging an XML-RPC interface to nearly everything during his short employment period. One of the last relics is a C++ server that handles all things related to the creation of greeting cards. This piece of software is a pain in the neck.

It runs only on Windows NT 4, and since the order volume increased significantly at PragBouquet, it cries for Dr. Watson two times a week without an obvious reason. Don't forget that while trying to make it work with a newer, faster laser printer, two people got mad.

Parts of the source code got lost somehow and the company that developed the current solution does not exist any longer. No one has been able to find the programmer who originally created the server (you hope that he has to make a living by creating microcode for toasters today), and consequently it has been decided to reimplement it, at least partially.

The new system still has to support the old XML-RPC interface, because the web shop guys are not able to change their software soon enough. The server has to only care about the image manipulation, because for printing the cards, another system will be built. It only has to transfer the cards to be printed as .pdf files (comprising two pages) into a certain directory where they are picked up by the new printer process (see Figure 5.1, on the facing page).

Luckily, we have found a README file that accurately describes the procedures supported by the server:

- draw_card(order_no,image_id,text) draws a greeting card; i.e., it creates images in GIF format for the front and back pages. It returns the image data and a unique card reference that can be used to

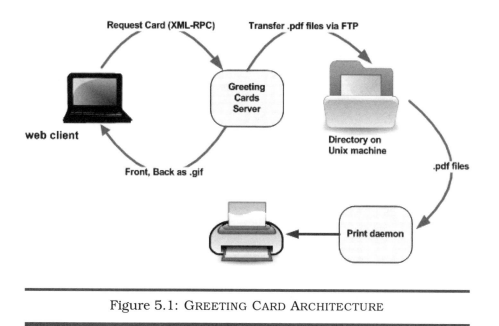

Figure 5.1: GREETING CARD ARCHITECTURE

identify the card later. To identify a greeting card and to put it to the right bouquet, the client has to transmit the according order number as the first parameter. All images used for greeting cards at PragBouquet have an ID that has to be passed as the image_id parameter. text contains the text that should appear on the card.

- print_card(cardref) sends the greeting card identified by cardref to the printer.

- delete_card(cardref) deletes the greeting card identified by cardref.

Before implementing the previous interface, we will briefly describe XML-RPC. If you are already familiar with its bowels, you can safely skip the next section.

XML-RPC in Less Than Eight Minutes

Shortly after XML was born, a lot of people obsessively tried to represent everything using < and > symbols. So it came as no surprise that in 1998/1999 a protocol for Remote Procedure Calls based on XML was defined by Dave Winer. Running out of creativity after a long and exhausting specification process, its inventor called it XML-RPC.[2]

---

[2]http://www.xmlrpc.com

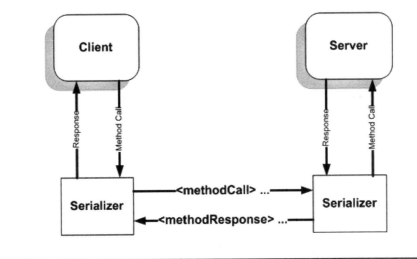

Figure 5.2: XML-RPC Architecture

Simply put, XML-RPC works like any other RPC protocol, but under the hood it is a lot simpler than its binary brothers and sisters. Implementing your own XML-RPC client will not take much more than a boring winter day, but smart people have already done it for you. So, better spend such a day reading trivial stuff while having a good cup of tea.

From an architectural point of view, XML-RPC is a synchronous protocol where every request is followed by a response. Only two types of messages, method calls and method responses, are supported, and both are encoded as XML documents that get transferred on an HTTP layer (see Figure 5.2).

When we call a method to draw a greeting card having the ID 42 and the message text on the back of the card using draw_card(4711, 42, 'Please, forgive me, honeybunch!'), its XML-RPC representation will look like:

File 101

```
Line 1   <methodCall>
    -        <methodName>draw_card</methodName>
    -        <params>
    -            <value><int>4711</int></value>
    5            <value><int>42</int></value>
    -            <value>
    -                <string>Please, forgive me, honeybunch!</string>
    -            </value>
    -        </params>
    10   </methodCall>
```

Type	Values	Tag
Integer	32-bit signed integer	<i4> or <int>
Double	64-bit IEEE 75 floating-point number	<double>
Boolean	false (0) or true (1)	<boolean>
String	Binary string encoded in Base64	<string>
Base64	ASCII string (may contain NULL bytes). Current implementations support Unicode, too	<base64>
DateTime	Absolute specification of date and time without time zone information	<dateTime.iso8601>
nil	Null value (this is an unofficial extension to the standard	<nil>

Figure 5.3: XML-RPC SIMPLE DATA TYPES

The response contains an image file encoded in Base 64 and additionally indicates the type of the file, such as GIF, JPEG, PNG, and so on.

```
Line 1    <methodResponse>
   -        <params>
   -          <value><string>4711_006754</string></value>
   -          <value><string>GIF</string></value>
   5        <value>
   -          <base64>
   -            VGhpcyBpcyBhIHJhdGhlciBsb25nIHRleHQgSSBo
   -            YXZlIHdyaXR0ZW4gdG8gc2ltdWxhdGUgYSBwaWN0
   -            dXJlLiBPZiBjb3Vyc2UsIEkgZGlkIG5vdCB3YW50
   10           IHRvIGZha2UgYSBiYXNlTY0IHN0cmluZyBhbmQg
   -            c28gSSBoYXZlIHVzZWQgUnVieSB0byBidWlsdCBv
   -            bmUgZnJvbS0aGlzIHJlYWxseSBzdHVwaWQgYW5k
   -            IHVzZWxlc3MgdGV4dC4=
   -          </base64>
   15       </value>
   -          <value><nil/></value>
   -        </params>
   -      </methodResponse>
```

XML-RPC supports a fixed set of simple and compound data types (see Figure 5.3, on the preceding page for a list of all simple data types). Because of the nature of XML, all parameter values are tagged, and their values are transmitted as strings. For example, a double value such as -3.14 is encoded as <double>-3.14</double>.

In addition, two compound types are available: arrays and structs. Contrary to array implementations in most programming languages, XML-RPC arrays aggregate a list of elements that must not all be of the same type. Arrays may contain simple data types, structs, and other arrays. For example, [1, 2, 3] is represented like this:

```
<value>
    <array>
        <value><int>1</int></value>
        <value><int>2</int></value>
        <value><int>3</int></value>
    </array>
</value>
```

Structs contain a list of key/value pairs where values might be simple data types, arrays, or structs. The following XML represents the example hash { 'name' => 'maik', 'age' => 32 }:

```
<value>
    <struct>
        <member>
            <name>name</name>
            <value><string>Maik</string></value>
        </member>
        <member>
            <name>age</name>
            <value><int>32</int></value>
        </member>
    </struct>
</value>
```

As a response to a method call, an exception (XML-RPC calls them *faults*) can be raised. Because they can occur only instead of a method response, they are encoded in the same way:

File 96

```
Line 1    <methodResponse>
   -          <fault>
   -              <value>
   -                  <struct>
   5                      <member>
   -                          <name>faultCode</name>
   -                          <value><int>7777</int></value>
   -                      </member>
   -                      <member>
```

```
10          <name>faultString</name>
 -          <value>
 -            <string>Text too short for an apology!</string>
 -          </value>
 -        </member>
15      </struct>
 -    </value>
 -  </fault>
 - </methodResponse>
```

Fault codes have not been standardized, but several XML-RPC implementations use small numbers to indicate errors on the lower transport layers, so you'd better use numbers bigger than 1,000 for your own codes.

All these details should only deepen your understanding of the underlying technology, because for an application developer most of these things happen completely transparently. Usually, you won't even notice that you're calling a procedure on a remote host. An XML-RPC library handles all the low-level stuff, turns method calls into XML documents, transfers these documents via HTTP to a server, gets its XML response, turns the response into a data structure or an exception, and finally returns the result to the caller.

xmlrpc4r

Kudos to Michael Neumann for contributing *xmlrpc4r*—one of the most complete and the most advanced XML-RPC implementations currently available—to the Ruby standard library.

xmlrpc4r

We will use it in the following to develop the new greeting cards server and its according test client. Before diving into the details of xmlrpc4r, let's create a skeleton class for representing two-sided greeting cards:

File 97

```
Line 1  class GreetingCard
 -        attr_reader :card_ref, :front, :back
 -
 -        class << self
 5          def create(order_no, image_id, text)
 -            front = read_image(image_id)
 -            back = create_text_page(text)
 -            card_ref = order_no.to_s + "_" + rand(1000).to_s
 -            store_card(card_ref, front, back)
10            GreetingCard.new(card_ref, front, back)
 -          end
 -
 -          private
 -
```

```
15    def read_image(image_id)
         IO.read("img/#{image_id}.gif")
      end

      def create_text_page(text)
20       return nil unless text
         # Here we have to create the nice-looking
         # text page somehow.
         ""
      end
25
      def store_card(card_ref, front, back)
         # Generate PDF and store cardref.pdf
         # containing front and back images.
      end
30  end

    private

    def initialize(card_ref, front, back)
35     @card_ref, @front, @back  = card_ref, front, back
    end
  end
```

A GreetingCard has only three attributes: a unique reference (cardref), a front page (front), and a back page (back). A factory method called create(image_id,text) creates new GreetingCard objects.

Current versions of xmlrpc4r are based on WEBrick, and the following server should look familiar:

File 99
```
Line 1  require 'webrick'
    -   require 'xmlrpc/server'
    -   require 'net/ftp'
    -   require 'greeting_card'
    5
    -   s = XMLRPC::WEBrickServlet.new

    -   s.add_handler('pragbouquet.draw_card') do |order_no, id, text|
    -     card = GreetingCard.create(order_no, id, text)
   10     {
    -       'cardref' => card.card_ref,
    -       'front' => XMLRPC::Base64.encode(card.front),
    -       'back' => XMLRPC::Base64.encode(card.back)
    -     }
   15   end

    -   s.add_handler('pragbouquet.print_card') do |cardref|
    -     # Transfer cardref.pdf to special directory, where
    -     # it gets picked up and is printed eventually
   20     ftp = Net::FTP.new('ftp.imagehost')
```

```
     -       ftp.login('imageserver', 'secret')
     -       files = ftp.chdir('pub/cards/img')
     -       ftp.putbinaryfile("#{cardref}.pdf")
     -       ftp.close
    25     end
     -
     -     s.add_handler('pragbouquet.delete_card') do |cardref|
     -       File.delete("#{cardref}.pdf")
     -     end
    30
     -     s.set_default_handler do |name, *args|
     -       raise XMLRPC::FaultException.new(
     -         -100,
     -         "Method #{name} missing or wrong number of parameters!"
    35     )
     -     end
     -
     -     server = WEBrick::HTTPServer.new(:Port => 8080)
     -     server.mount('/RPC2', s)
    40   trap('INT') { server.shutdown }
     -
     -     server.start
```

We have created a servlet of class XMLRPC::WEBrickServlet and added handlers for the draw_card(), print_card(), and delete_card() functions. It's not demanded by the specification, but it's good style to give them all a prefix (pragbouquet in our case), and it will pay off later.

draw_card()'s implementation is straightforward using the GreetingCard class. Note that in lines 12 and 13 we had to explicitly convert our images into Base64 format.

The print_card() handler transfers a particular file to the print server via FTP, and delete_card() deletes a particular greeting card.

In line 31 we have installed a so-called default handler that is comparable to Ruby's method_missing() method. It gets called whenever the server receives a request it cannot dispatch for any reason, such as the method name is unknown or the amount of method parameters does not match. In these cases an exception is raised; i.e., a fault response will be returned.

The rest of the server does not differ from initializing and starting any other WEBrick server. By loose convention, XML-RPC services are located under /RPC2, so we mount our servlet there.

All right, the XML-RPC service is listening on port 8080 under the path /RPC2. The following client will test whether it works as expected:

`File 98`

```ruby
require "xmlrpc/client"

server = XMLRPC::Client.new('localhost', '/RPC2', 8080)
begin
  response = server.call(
    'pragbouquet.draw_card',
    4711,
    42,
    'Forgive me!'
  )
rescue XMLRPC::FaultException => e
  puts "An error occurred:"
  puts e.faultCode
  puts e.faultString
end
```

xmlrpc4r's usage is intuitive. To obtain a reference to the server, you have to create an instance of XMLRPC::Client, specifying the host, the path, and the port on which the service is listening. Calling a particular procedure is performed by call(procedure,*args) then. Its result is the decoded server response.

As we all know, there is no Ruby code that could not be made shorter and more expressive:

`File 100`

```ruby
require "xmlrpc/client"

server = XMLRPC::Client.new('localhost', '/RPC2', 8080)
gc = server.proxy2('pragbouquet')
success, cards = gc.draw_card(4711, 42, 'Forgive me!')
if success
  puts cards
else
  puts "An error occurred:"
  puts cards.faultCode
  puts cards.faultString
end
```

In line 4 we have created a proxy for the greeting card service that allows us to use the remote procedures exactly as if they were local ones (here we needed the prefix pragbouquet again). Furthermore, we have suppressed the exception feature; i.e., calling proxy2() makes all remote procedures return a boolean value indicating success or failure. If we had used proxy(), exceptions would be raised. The same applies to call() and call2().

In addition to the WEBrick servlet, you can choose from a variety of different server types that can be configured by several options:

- Server is a stand-alone server that does not depend on WEBrick or anything else.

- CGIServer can be used in a CGI environment; i.e., you can put your XML-RPC implementation into a CGI script that is executed by a web server, whenever it receives an XML-RPC request. To prevent the web server from executing the script over and over again, this server type works with FastCGI,[3] too.

- ModRubyServer allows you to embed your XML-RPC procedures into a web server using mod_ruby.[4]

Conclusion

XML-RPC is fairly popular; e.g., it is supported by many operating systems such as Apple's Mac OS X, and it builds the basis for services like the Blogger API.[5] Its biggest strength compared to competitors such as SOAP or CORBA is its simplicity. When designing a distributed application, XML-RPC is always worth a look especially when you're using Ruby, because xmlrpc4r is extremely powerful and gives you a variety of options for making your remote procedures available to the public quickly.

5.2 We Will Take No REST, Will We?

Remember the LDAP address book we implemented in Section 2.4, *Lightweight Directory Access Protocol (LDAP)*, on page 52? We did it because the web shop guys wanted to give Ruby on Rails a try. Because of some unexpected change requests (what else?), they didn't have enough time to work their way through Ruby and the Rails framework, but the address book is still needed. They know you've already set up an LDAP server and that your Ruby classes are working, too. So they asked you to turn the implementation into an HTTP service that they can access from their Java classes. Although the web shop team said that the details of the interface do not matter much, you know that they'd prefer XML.

You decide that it would be a good idea to map the address book operations (create a new address book, show an address book, add an entry

---

[3]http://www.fastcgi.com
[4]http://www.modruby.net
[5]http://www.blogger.com/developers/api/1_docs

to an existing address book, modify an entry, delete an entry, and delete an address book) to different HTTP methods. To show an address book, for example, we could use the HTTP GET method. To delete an entry or a complete address book, we can use an HTTP DELETE. We'll pass parameters as XML documents.

Let's create the main infrastructure first: a WEBrick server that will be the basis for our service:

File 64

```ruby
Line 1  require 'rexml/document'
   -    require 'addressbook'
   -    require 'ldap'
   -    require 'thread'
   5    require 'cgi'
   -    require 'webrick'
   -    include WEBrick
   -    class AddressBookServlet < HTTPServlet::AbstractServlet
   -      @@instance = nil
  10      @@instance_creation_mutex = Mutex.new
   -
   -      def self.get_instance(config, *options)
   -        @@instance_creation_mutex.synchronize do
   -          @@instance ||= self.new(config, *options)
  15        end
   -      end
   -
   -      def initialize(config, ldap_conn)
   -        super
  20        @ldap_conn = ldap_conn
   -        @ldap_mutex = Mutex.new
   -      end
   -    end
   -    connection = Conn.new
  25    connection.set_option(LDAP_OPT_PROTOCOL_VERSION, 3)
   -    connection.bind('cn=root,dc=pragbouquet,dc=com', 'secret')
   -
   -    server = HTTPServer.new(:Port => 4242)
   -    server.mount('/ab', AddressBookServlet, connection)
  30
   -    %w(INT TERM).each do |signal|
   -      trap(signal) { server.shutdown }
   -    end
   -
  35    server.start
```

This server differs a bit from the servers we have used so far. The servlet is a bit more complicated because we're working with an expensive resource, the connection to the LDAP server. By default, a new servlet instance will be created for every request. This is convenient, because you do not have to care about multithreading issues, but it can waste a lot of resources, too.

The WEBrick inventors were aware of this problem, so they provided the get_instance(config,*options) method. This gives you complete control over the servlet creation process.

We used it to implement a singleton pattern that creates only a single instance of the AddressBookServlet class, but you can come up with any resource management strategy you prefer or need. For example, you could instead implement a servlet pool.

Our solution is much simpler. In line 13 we synchronize the creation of the one and only servlet instance (to prevent a race condition when two requests arrive simultaneously before the instance is created), and in the following line we actually create a new instance if it does not exist already.

For the first time we've defined an initialize() method for our servlet. We had to do this because we want to configure it before we actually mount it. In line 29 we pass it the LDAP connection. In addition, we create a Mutex object in line 21 that we will use for synchronizing access to the LDAP server.

Initializing the server is business as usual. We create a connection to the LDAP server, initialize a servlet, and mount it at /ab (*ab* is an abbreviation for *address book*).

Before adding handlers for the different HTTP methods, we add to_xml() methods to the Recipient and AddressBook classes that return XML representations of their according instances:

File 64

```
Line 1   class Recipient
   -       def to_xml
   -          recipient = REXML::Element.new('recipient')
   -          recipient.add_attribute('forename', forename)
   5          recipient.add_attribute('surname', surname)
   -          address = recipient.add_element('address')
   -          address.add_element('street').add_text(street)
   -          address.add_element('postal-code').add_text(postal_code)
   -          address.add_element('city').add_text(city)
   10         address.add_element('state').add_text(state)
   -          recipient.add_element('description').add_text(description)
   -          recipient
   -       end
   -    end
   15
```

```
     -    class AddressBook
     -      def to_xml
     -        addressbook = REXML::Element.new('address-book')
     -        addressbook.add_attribute('uid', user.uid)
    20        each_recipient { |r| addressbook.add_element(r.to_xml) }
     -        addressbook
     -      end
     -    end
```

We use REXML to turn our objects into XML. This is convenient, because the to_xml() methods return REXML::Element objects, not strings, so we can easily add elements and attributes if needed (of course, we will).

Now we have everything prepared, so let's implement the first HTTP method handler. This returns the complete address book belonging to a particular uid. Our server expects a request of the form http://host:port/ab/(uid), so to get the address book belonging to uid 4711, you send a GET request to http://host:port/ab/4711:

File 64

```
Line 1  class AddressBookServlet
     -    # Return all entries belonging to a particular address book.
     -    def do_GET(req, res)
     -      res['content-type'] = 'text/xml'
     5      uid = get_uid(req)
     -      @ldap_mutex.synchronize do
     -        begin
     -          ab = AddressBook.new(@ldap_conn, User.new(uid))
     -          entries = ab.to_xml
    10          entries.each_element('recipient') do |r|
     -            cn = to_cn(
     -              r.attributes['forename'],
     -              r.attributes['surname']
     -            )
    15            link = r.add_element('link')
     -            link.add_text(
     -              "http://#{req.host}:#{req.port}/ab/#{uid}/#{cn}"
     -            )
     -          end
    20          entries.write(res.body, 0)
     -          res.body << "\n"
     -          res.status = 200
     -        rescue ResultError
     -          res.status = 404
    25        end
     -      end
     -    end
     -
     -    def get_uid(req)
    30      req.path_info =~ /\/(\d+)$/ ? $1 : nil
     -    end
```

```
     def to_cn(forename, surname)
       CGI.escape(forename + " " + surname)
35     end
   end
```

Admittedly, this is a lot of code, but it's not difficult to understand. Let's dissect it, line by line. First, we extract the uid from the URL. This is done in the get_uid() method.

Because we need it two lines later to read the address book, in line 6 we synchronize the access to the LDAP server. Then we convert the address book into an XML element with our new to_xml() method.

The iterator starting on line 10 adds a *<link>* element to each address book entry (that's the reason why to_xml() does not return a string, but a REXML::Element object). This element tells the client how to refer to the entry on the server. To build the URL we append the common name (cn) of the entry to the address book's URL, and therefore we have to URL-encode it in the to_cn() method.

Eventually, we create a nicely formatted version of our XML document in line 20 and send it back to the client. If we could not find the address book requested, we leave the body empty and set the status to *File Not Found* in line 24.

Let's test the method with the command-line tool curl (the -i option instructs curl to print the HTTP headers, too):

```
mschmidt:/tmp> curl -i http://localhost:4242/ab/4711
HTTP/1.1 200 OK
Connection: Keep-Alive
Date: Sun, 13 Nov 2005 09:02:52 GMT
Content-Type: text/xml
Server: WEBrick/1.3.1 (Ruby/1.8.3/2005-09-21)
Content-Length: 739

<address-book uid='4711'>
  <recipient forename='P.H.' surname='Beans'>
    <address>
      <street>Nuclear Powerplant Road 1</street>
      <postal-code>65801</postal-code>
      <city>Springfield</city>
      <state>MO</state>
    </address>
    <description>My boss.</description>
    <link>http://localhost:4242/ab/4711/P.H.+Beans</link>
  </recipient>
  <recipient forename='Marge' surname='Jackson'>
```

```
<address>
  <street>Evergreen Terrace 42</street>
  <postal-code>62701</postal-code>
  <city>Springfield</city>
  <state>IL</state>
</address>
<description>
  Don&apos;t forget our wedding anniversary!
</description>
<link>http://localhost:4242/ab/4711/Marge+Jackson</link>
  </recipient>
</address-book>
```

Representational State Transfer

Everything looks good, but you may ask yourself, what does all this have to do with REST—*Representational State Transfer*?[6] Isn't it an ordinary HTTP service? Yes, it is! The main thing that differs from the services we have built so far is the use of URLs. They do not contain actions such as *send_sms* or *store_address*, but they refer to resources such as address books on the server.

Another difference with REST is that we no longer use just GET and POST requests. To delete an address book entry or a complete address book, we use the DELETE method, for example:

File 64

```
Line 1   class AddressBookServlet
    -      def do_DELETE(req, res)
    -        if req.path_info =~ /\/(\d+)\/(.+)$/
    -          delete_recipient($1, $2)
    5        elsif req.path_info =~ /\/(\d+)$/
    -          delete_address_book($1)
    -        end
    -        res.status = 204 # No Content
    -      end
    10
    -      def delete_recipient(uid, common_name)
    -        @ldap_mutex.synchronize do
    -          ab = AddressBook.new(@ldap_conn, User.new(uid))
    -          cn = CGI.unescape(common_name)
    15          surname = cn.split(/.* (\w+)$/)[1]
    -          forename = cn[0 .. -(surname.size + 1)]
    -          ab.remove(Recipient.new(forename, surname))
    -        end
    -      end
    20
    -      def delete_address_book(uid)
    -        @ldap_mutex.synchronize do
    -          ab = AddressBook.new(@ldap_conn, User.new(uid))
```

---

[6]http://en.wikipedia.org/wiki/Representational_State_Transfer

```
   -             ab.each_recipient { |r| ab.remove(r) }
25               ab.delete
   -           end
   -         end
   -       end
```

At the beginning of the do_DELETE(req,res) method, we check whether
we have to delete a single address book entry or a complete address
book. Depending on the URL format, we delegate work to either the
delete_address_book(uid) or to delete_recipient(uid, common_name). Then
in lines 14 to 16 we extract the forename and surname of the recipient
to be deleted from the common name passed in the URL.

The following session first demonstrates how to delete Marge Jackson
from the address book belonging to user 4711 and then how to delete
the entire address book (curl's -X option lets us specify which HTTP
request to use):

```
mschmidt:/tmp> curl -i http://localhost:4242/ab/4711/Marge+Jackson \
> -X DELETE
HTTP/1.1 204 No Content
Date: Sun, 13 Nov 2005 13:20:42 GMT
Server: WEBrick/1.3.1 (Ruby/1.8.3/2005-09-21)

mschmidt:/tmp> curl -i http://localhost:4242/ab/4711
HTTP/1.1 200 OK
Connection: Keep-Alive
Date: Sun, 13 Nov 2005 13:24:02 GMT
Content-Type: text/xml
Server: WEBrick/1.3.1 (Ruby/1.8.3/2005-09-21)
Content-Length: 373

<address-book uid='4711'>
  <recipient forename='P.H.' surname='Beans'>
    <address>
      <street>Nuclear Powerplant Road 1</street>
      <postal-code>65801</postal-code>
      <city>Springfield</city>
      <state>MO</state>
    </address>
    <description>My boss.</description>
    <link>http://localhost:4242/ab/4711/P.H.+Beans</link>
  </recipient>
</address-book>

mschmidt:/tmp> curl -i http://localhost:4242/ab/4711 -X DELETE
HTTP/1.1 204 No Content
Date: Sun, 13 Nov 2005 13:20:55 GMT
Server: WEBrick/1.3.1 (Ruby/1.8.3/2005-09-21)
```

```
mschmidt:/tmp> curl -i http://localhost:4242/ab/4711
HTTP/1.1 404 Not Found
Connection: Keep-Alive
Date: Sun, 13 Nov 2005 13:24:40 GMT
Content-Type: text/xml
Server: WEBrick/1.3.1 (Ruby/1.8.3/2005-09-21)
Content-Length: 0
```

It looks like our delete methods work. Now let's balance the books by
creating new entries:

File 64

```ruby
class AddressBookServlet
  def do_POST(req, res)
    doc = REXML::Document.new(req.body)
    if doc.root.name == 'recipient'
      create_recipient(doc, req, res)
    else
      create_address_book(doc, req, res)
    end
  end

  def create_address_book(doc, req, res)
    user = parse_user(doc)
    @ldap_mutex.synchronize do
      AddressBook.create(@ldap_conn, user)
    end
    res.status = 201
    res['Location'] = "/ab/#{user.uid}"
  end

  def create_recipient(doc, req, res, update = false)
    uid = get_uid(req)
    recipient = parse_recipient(doc)
    @ldap_mutex.synchronize do
      begin
        ab = AddressBook.new(@ldap_conn, User.new(uid))
        if update
          ab.modify(recipient)
        else
          ab.add(recipient)
        end
        cn = to_cn(recipient.forename, recipient.surname)
        res.status = 201 # Created
        res['Location'] = "/ab/#{uid}/#{cn}"
      rescue ResultError => ex
        @logger.info ex
        res.status = 404
      end
    end
  end
```

```
  -        def parse_user(doc)
  -          attributes = doc.root.attributes
  -          User.new(
  -            attributes['uid'],
 45            attributes['forename'],
  -            attributes['surname']
  -          )
  -        end
  -
 50        def parse_recipient(doc)
  -          attributes = doc.root.attributes
  -          Recipient.new(
  -            attributes['forename'],
  -            attributes['surname'],
 55            attributes['street'],
  -            attributes['postal-code'],
  -            attributes['city'],
  -            attributes['state'],
  -            attributes['description']
 60          )
  -        end
  -      end
```

New objects are created using the POST request. First, we check whether a new address book or a new address book entry should be created. In both cases we read the attributes of the object to be created from an XML document that is passed with the request. Attributes for a new address book will be read by parse_user(doc), and attributes for a new address book entry will be read by parse_recipient(doc).

The create_recipient(doc,req,res,update=false) method is a bit special. It's not only able to create new recipient objects, but it can also modify existing ones. You can change its behavior using the update flag.

Both methods, create_address_book() and create_recipient(), set the Location header in the HTTP response. This contains a link to the object that we just created. This is a REST convention.

The following session creates a new address book and a new address book entry:

```
mschmidt:/tmp> curl -i http://localhost:4242/ab/23 -X POST -d \
> "<address-book uid='23' forename='Homer' surname='Simpson'/>"
HTTP/1.1 201 Created
Connection: Keep-Alive
Date: Sun, 13 Nov 2005 18:46:54 GMT
Server: WEBrick/1.3.1 (Ruby/1.8.3/2005-09-21)
Content-Length: 0
Location: http://localhost:4242/ab/23
```

```
mschmidt:/tmp> curl -i http://localhost:4242/ab/23 -X POST -d \
> "<recipient forename='Barney' surname='Gumble' street='Musterstr. 42' \
> postal-code='11011' city='Berlin' state='n/a' \
> description='My best friend.' />"
HTTP/1.1 201 Created
Connection: Keep-Alive
Date: Sun, 13 Nov 2005 18:48:46 GMT
Server: WEBrick/1.3.1 (Ruby/1.8.3/2005-09-21)
Content-Length: 0
Location: http://localhost:4242/ab/23/Barney+Gumble

mschmidt:/tmp> curl -i http://localhost:4242/ab/23
HTTP/1.1 200 OK
Connection: Keep-Alive
Date: Sun, 13 Nov 2005 18:49:41 GMT
Content-Type: text/xml
Server: WEBrick/1.3.1 (Ruby/1.8.3/2005-09-21)
Content-Length: 366

<address-book uid='23'>
  <recipient forename='Barney' surname='Gumble'>
    <address>
      <street>Musterstr. 42</street>
      <postal-code>11011</postal-code>
      <city>Berlin</city>
      <state>n/a</state>
    </address>
    <description>My best friend.</description>
    <link>http://localhost:4242/ab/23/Barney+Gumble</link>
  </recipient>
</address-book>
```

Now we can create new objects. It would be nice to be able to modify
existing entries, too:

File 64

```
Line 1    class AddressBookServlet
   -        def do_PUT(req, res)
   -          doc = REXML::Document.new(req.body)
   -          create_recipient(doc, req, res, true)
   5        end
   -      end
```

This code is short, because we could reuse the create_recipient() method
that we used to create new entries. Note that to update existing entries,
we use the PUT request. If, for example, Barney becomes Homer's very
best friend, we can change the description attribute as follows:

```
mschmidt:/tmp> curl -i http://localhost:4242/ab/23 -X PUT -d \
> "<recipient forename='Barney' surname='Gumble' \
> street='Musterstr. 42' postal-code='11011' \
> city='Berlin' state='n/a' \
> description='My very best friend.' />"
```

CRUD Action	HTTP Method
Create	POST
Retrieve	GET
Update	PUT
Delete	DELETE

Figure 5.4: MAPPING CRUD TO REST

```
HTTP/1.1 201 Created
Connection: Keep-Alive
Date: Sun, 13 Nov 2005 19:02:07 GMT
Server: WEBrick/1.3.1 (Ruby/1.8.3/2005-09-21)
Content-Length: 0
Location: http://localhost:4242/ab/23/Barney+Gumble

mschmidt:/tmp> curl -i http://localhost:4242/ab/23
HTTP/1.1 200 OK
Connection: Keep-Alive
Date: Sun, 13 Nov 2005 19:03:46 GMT
Content-Type: text/xml
Server: WEBrick/1.3.1 (Ruby/1.8.3/2005-09-21)
Content-Length: 371

<address-book uid='23'>
  <recipient forename='Barney' surname='Gumble'>
    <address>
      <street>Musterstr. 42</street>
      <postal-code>11011</postal-code>
      <city>Berlin</city>
      <state>n/a</state>
    </address>
    <description>My very best friend.</description>
    <link>http://localhost:4242/ab/23/Barney+Gumble</link>
  </recipient>
</address-book>
```

Perfect! We now have methods for all the CRUD actions. Figure 5.4 shows how we mapped them to HTTP request types. At the risk of destroying your faith in technology, we have a confession to make. There is no REST standard. REST is an architectural style that depends on a lot of other standards such as HTTP and XML. It recommends representing entities on a server as XML documents that can be referred to by URLs. But that's about it. There is no such thing as a REST service framework. But, because Ruby has excellent support for HTTP and XML, it also has excellent support for REST services. Maybe you've already implemented a REST service without noticing it.

5.3 SOAP

Today you gave a little presentation of the Stock class we developed in Section 2.3, *What Do We Have in Stock?*, on page 42, to the clerks and the team that develops PragBouquet's financial applications. They were all very impressed, so you've landed the job to work out the details of the final system with Jeff, the leader of the financial applications team.

Jeff told you that Microsoft's .NET environment is their preferred development platform. Processes and components on this platform often communicate via SOAP, so Jeff's life would be easier if the Stock class were available as a SOAP service, too. You don't have much experience with SOAP and absolutely no experience with Ruby and SOAP, but you are sure that there will be an easy way to turn the Stock class into a SOAP service.

Refactoring the Stock Class API

First, we have to refactor the API of the Stock class a bit, because Jeff made some useful suggestions. For example, he wants to remove the Bouquet class, because in his opinion, a flower stock should not have to know anything about bouquets. At least it should be possible to remove flowers without putting them into a bouquet first. He also thinks that the print_report() method should be replaced with a get_report() method that actually returns a stock report instead of printing it.

After 90 minutes of discussion, you both agree upon the following API:

create_flower(name,price,quantity)
> Creates an entry for a new flower called name in the database and sets an initial price and an initial quantity.

add_flowers(name,quantity)
> Adds quantity flowers called name to the stock. It returns the quantity of flowers called name in stock.

remove_flowers(name,quantity)
> Removes quantity flowers called name from the stock. It returns the quantity of flowers called name in stock.

set_price(name,price)
> Sets the price of the flower called name to price.

get_report()
> Returns a hash containing a two-element array for each flower, in

stock. The first array entry is the quantity of the flower and the second is the current price. A typical example looks like this:

```
{
    'rose' => [1000, 2.99],
    'sunflower' => [500, 1.79]
}
```

All price information is stored in U.S. dollars. Every method can raise an exception if it gets invalid arguments or runs into a database error. "That's great!" you think. "I don't have to make any changes to the database schema."[7] Before we deal with any "soapy" things, we will drop the Bouquet class and completely refactor our Stock. If SOAP is worthy of all the hype surrounding it, we won't have to modify our class again later. Our database access layer looks like this:

File 92

```
Line 1   require 'rubygems'
    -    require 'active_record'
    -
    -    ActiveRecord::Base.establish_connection(
    5        :adapter => 'mysql',
    -        :host => '127.0.0.1',
    -        :database => 'webshop'
    -    )
    -    class Flower < ActiveRecord::Base
    10       belongs_to :stock_item
    -    end
    -    class StockItem < ActiveRecord::Base
    -        has_one :flower
    -    end
```

No big surprises here: the Bouquet class and all its dependencies are gone. Let's implement our API specification:

File 92

```
Line 1   class Stock
    -        def create_flower(name, price, quantity)
    -            flower = Flower.find_by_name(name)
    -            raise "#{name} already exists!" if !flower.nil?
    5            si = StockItem.new(:quantity => quantity)
    -            si.save
    -            si.create_flower(:name => name, :price => price)
    -            quantity
    -        end
    10
    -        def add_flowers(name, quantity)
    -            adjust_quantity(name, quantity)
    -        end
```

---

[7]Still thinking the old way, eh? With ActiveRecord these changes would have been a piece of cake anyway. :-)

```
15    def remove_flowers(name, quantity)
        adjust_quantity(name, -quantity)
      end

      def set_price(name, price)
20      flower = Flower.find_by_name(name)
        raise "#{name} is unknown!" if flower.nil?
        flower.price = price
        flower.save
        price
25    end

      def get_report
        StockItem.find(:all).inject({}) do |r,si|
          r[si.flower.name] = [si.quantity, si.flower.price]; r
30        end
      end

      private

35    def adjust_quantity(name, difference)
        flower = Flower.find_by_name(name)
        raise "#{name} is unknown!" if flower.nil?
        si = StockItem.find(flower.stock_item_id)
        si.quantity += difference
40      raise 'Not enough flowers!' if si.quantity < 0
        si.save
        si.quantity
      end
    end
```

As expected, the Ruby implementation reads like the API description itself, and ActiveRecord makes the code pure, short, and simple.

A Look Under the Hood of SOAP

In doing some research on SOAP, you might have come across the draft W3C specification:[8]

"SOAP is a lightweight protocol for exchange of information in a decentralized, distributed environment. It is an XML-based protocol that consists of three parts: an envelope that defines a framework for describing what is in a message and how to process it, a set of encoding rules for expressing instances of application-defined datatypes, and a convention for representing remote procedure calls and responses."

---

[8]http://www.w3.org/TR/2000/NOTE-SOAP-20000508

Simply put, SOAP is XML-RPC after it has been ground by the mills of a standards committee.[9] Like XML-RPC, SOAP specifies a way to implement a remote procedure call architecture where all requests and responses are encoded as XML documents. Compared to XML-RPC, it has a more flexible data type system, deals with encoding and authentication issues, and is meant to be used on different transport layers, not only HTTP.

Let's see how it works in the real world. A method call such as create_flower('rose', 1.99, 1000) gets converted into the following document:

```
<?xml version="1.0" encoding="utf-8"?>
<env:Envelope xmlns:xsd="http://www.w3.org/2001/XMLSchema"
              xmlns:env="http://schemas.xmlsoap.org/soap/envelope/"
              xmlns:xsi="http://www.w3.org/2001/XMLSchema-instance">
  <env:Body>
    <n1:create_flower xmlns:n1="urn:Stock"
                      env:encodingStyle="http://schemas.xmlsoap.org/soap/encoding/">
      <name xsi:type="xsd:string">rose</name>
      <price xsi:type="xsd:double">+1.99</price>
      <quantity xsi:type="xsd:int">1000</quantity>
    </n1:create_flower>
  </env:Body>
</env:Envelope>
```

If we leave out all the namespace stuff, it becomes easier to see how it works:[10]

```
<?xml version="1.0"?>
<Envelope>
  <Body>
    <create_flower>
      <name type="string">rose</name>
      <price type="double">+1.99</price>
      <quantity type="int">1000</quantity>
    </create_flower>
  </Body>
</Envelope>
```

Obviously, every method call gets translated into its own element (in our case, it's *<create_flower>*). All the method's parameters are turned into elements, too, and they become child elements of the method call

---

[9]In the beginning SOAP stood for "Simple Object Access Protocol," but today it only means SOAP. Have a look at the current specification, and you can easily see why the committee decided to drop the "Simple."

[10]We remove the namespaces only for better readability. When you are actually working with SOAP, you have to use them!

element. They all have a type= attribute that specifies the data type of the parameter using XmlSchema.[11]

The return value of our method call looks like this:

```
<?xml version="1.0" encoding="utf-8"?>
<env:Envelope xmlns:xsd="http://www.w3.org/2001/XMLSchema"
      xmlns:env="http://schemas.xmlsoap.org/soap/envelope/"
      xmlns:xsi="http://www.w3.org/2001/XMLSchema-instance">
 <env:Body>
      <n1:create_flowerResponse xmlns:n1="urn:Stock"
       env:encodingStyle="http://schemas.xmlsoap.org/soap/encoding/">
              <return xsi:type="xsd:int">1000</return>
      </n1:create_flowerResponse>
    </env:Body>
 </env:Envelope>
```

Removing all the namespace clutter will help again:

```
<?xml version="1.0"?>
<Envelope>
  <Body>
    <create_flowerResponse>
      <return type="int">1000</return>
    </create_flowerResponse>
  </Body>
</Envelope>
```

To encode a method's return value, a new element is created and its name is built by appending *Response* to the name of the method that was called. The return value itself is encoded as a child called <*return*> of the newly created element. Its data type is specified the same way as the data type of method parameters.

SOAP is much more than this (see *Programming Web Services with SOAP* [STK02], for example), but for our purposes it's sufficient to know how method calls and responses are encoded. (There are more details in Section 5.3, *SOAP Headers*, on page 215.) To call the create_flower() method, we could create an XML document such as the previous example and send it using Ruby's HTTP library. We could then parse the response using REXML. Actually, lots of clients out there work exactly this way. We will follow a more flexible approach and use Ruby's standard SOAP library, called soap4r.

---

[11]http://www.w3.org/XML/Schema

SOAP the Hard Way

To turn the Stock class into a SOAP service, we use Hiroshi Nakamura's soap4r library. It is part of the Ruby standard library, implements SOAP version 1.1,[12] and makes the creation of web services really easy:

File 89

```
Line 1  require 'soap/rpc/standaloneServer'
        require 'stock'

        class StockServer < SOAP::RPC::StandaloneServer
5         def on_init
            @stock = Stock.new
            @log.level = Logger::Severity::DEBUG
            add_method(self, 'create_flower', 'name', 'price', 'quantity')
            add_method(self, 'add_flowers', 'name', 'quantity')
10          add_method(self, 'remove_flowers', 'name', 'quantity')
            add_method(self, 'set_price', 'name', 'price')
            add_method(self, 'get_report')
          end

15        def create_flower(name, price, quantity)
            @stock.create_flower(name, price, quantity)
          end

          def add_flowers(name, quantity)
20          @stock.add_flowers(name, quantity)
          end

          def remove_flowers(name, quantity)
            @stock.remove_flowers(name, quantity)
25        end

          def set_price(name, price)
            @stock.set_price(name, price)
          end
30
          def get_report
            @stock.get_report
          end
        end
35
        server = StockServer.new('stock', 'urn:Stock', '0.0.0.0', 2000)
        trap(:INT) { server.shutdown }
        server.start
```

We didn't actually have to touch the Stock class to make its functionality available in our first SOAP server. In fact, we didn't have to do very much at all.

---

[12]W3C has a recommendation for version 1.2, but it's currently not in widespread use.

First, we derived our StockServer class from a standard SOAP4R class called SOAP::RPC::StandaloneServer. This is one of several ways to create SOAP services with soap4r.

The on_init() method gets called when the server is initialized, so we use it to create our Stock instance, configure the logging system (you'll need a lot of debug output, especially in the beginning), and declare all the remote methods we're going to support. All the remaining methods simply delegate their work to their counterparts in the Stock class.

In line 36 we create a server instance. The constructor gets four parameters:

- The application name.

- URN of the application.

- The name or IP address of the host the service is running on. 0.0.0.0 means that the service is listening on all interfaces.

- The port the service is running on.

In line 37 we make sure the server gets terminated when it receives a SIGINT signal. Finally, on the last line, we start the server.

At this point you could ask a member of Jeff's team to try to use and test the new service, but you're afraid that if it doesn't run properly, it could ruin your newly gained reputation. Better write your own test client:

File 87

```
Line 1    require 'soap/rpc/driver'

          stock = SOAP::RPC::Driver.new('http://localhost:2000', 'urn:Stock')
          [
     5      %w(create_flower name price quantity),
            %w(add_flowers name quantity),
            %w(remove_flowers name quantity),
            %w(set_price name price),
            %w(get_report)
    10    ].each do |signature|
            stock.add_method(*signature)
          end

          begin
    15      stock.create_flower('rose', 1.99, 1000)
            stock.create_flower('orchid', 3.14, 200)
            puts "Created 'rose' and 'orchid'."
            p stock.get_report

    20      stock.remove_flowers('rose', 5)
```

```
   -        puts 'Removed 5 roses.'
   -        p stock.get_report
   -
   -        stock.add_flowers('orchid', 100)
  25        puts 'Added 100 orchids.'
   -        p stock.get_report
   -
   -        stock.set_price('orchid', 3.01)
   -        puts 'Changed orchid price to $3.01.'
  30        p stock.get_report
   -      rescue Exception => ex
   -        puts ex
   -      end
```

This produces the following output (after we have deleted all records from the flowers table):

```
Created 'rose' and 'orchid'.
{"orchid"=>[200, 3.14], "rose"=>[1000, 1.99]}
Removed 5 roses.
{"orchid"=>[200, 3.14], "rose"=>[995, 1.99]}
Added 100 orchids.
{"orchid"=>[300, 3.14], "rose"=>[995, 1.99]}
Changed orchid price to $3.01.
{"orchid"=>[300, 3.01], "rose"=>[995, 1.99]}
```

That wasn't too difficult either. We obtained a proxy for the stock service by creating a SOAP::RPC::Driver instance, passing it the address and the URN of the service we want to access. In lines 4 to 12 we tell the proxy which methods we'd like to use. From then on we could treat the proxy as if it were an instance of the Stock class.

So far, so good, but our current implementation of the server does not meet our high coding standards. Why do we have to repeat the Stock class's API in the SOAP server? Ruby is supposed to be a dynamic language. Isn't it possible to create the server automatically from the Stock class? Fortunately, it is:

File 90

```
Line 1    class StockServer < SOAP::RPC::StandaloneServer
   -        def initialize(*args)
   -          super
   -          @log.level = Logger::Severity::DEBUG
  5          add_servant(Stock.new)
   -        end
   -      end
```

Sweet, isn't it? Instead of adding every single remote method with add_method(), you can make all the methods of a particular class available by passing an instance of the class to add_servant().

Web Services Description Language

Did you notice that we are still violating the DRY principle? In the client we call add_method() for every method of the Stock class to define the interface we want to use. Wouldn't it be nice if we could generate the boring and tedious interface code from a more abstract definition?

Web Services Description Language

In CORBA environments you can use the Interface Definition Language (IDL) to describe interfaces and to generate stubs and skeletons for servers and clients. SOAP uses the *Web Services Description Language* (WSDL) for this purpose. It's an XML dialect made for describing the interface of remote services.

With WSDL you can describe the service itself, its interface, and its bindings. It's not required, but it's good practice to separate the service description from the interface description. Our service description looks as follows:

File 91

```
Line 1   <?xml version="1.0"?>
   -     <definitions name="StockServiceImplementationDescription"
   -         targetNamespace="http://www.pragbouquet.com/wsdl/StockService.wsdl"
   -         xmlns="http://schemas.xmlsoap.org/wsdl/"
   5         xmlns:soap="http://schemas.xmlsoap.org/wsdl/soap/"
   -         xmlns:tns="http://www.pragbouquet.com/wsdl/StockService.wsdl"
   -         xmlns:xsd="http://www.w3.org/2001/XMLSchema">
   -
   -         <import namespace="urn:Stock" location="stock.wsdl"/>
   10
   -         <service name="StockService">
   -             <documentation>
   -                 The stock service allows you to manage PragBouquet's flower
   -                 stock.
   15             </documentation>
   -             <port binding="tns:StockBinding" name="StockPort">
   -                 <soap:address location="http://localhost:2000"/>
   -             </port>
   -         </service>
   20   </definitions>
```

The biggest problem with WSDL files is that they are often cluttered with XML namespaces. If you ignore them the rest is easy to read. In line 9 we import the interface definition of the stock service that we are going to describe next. We then use the *<service>* element to briefly describe it. With the *<documentation>* element, we explain a bit about the purpose of our service, and the *<port>* element tells us where it can be found.

Describing the service's interface is a bit more complex but still not difficult:

```
File 93   Line 1   <?xml version="1.0"?>
              -    <definitions name="StockServiceInterfaceDescription"
              -        targetNamespace="http://www.pragbouquet.com/wsdl/StockService.wsdl"
              -        xmlns="http://schemas.xmlsoap.org/wsdl/"
              5        xmlns:soap="http://schemas.xmlsoap.org/wsdl/soap/"
              -        xmlns:tns="http://www.pragbouquet.com/wsdl/StockService.wsdl"
              -        xmlns:xsd="http://www.w3.org/2001/XMLSchema">
              -
              -        <message name="set_price_in">
             10            <part name="name" type="xsd:string"/>
              -            <part name="price" type="xsd:double"/>
              -        </message>
              -
              -        <message name="set_price_out">
             15            <part name="price" type="xsd:double"/>
              -        </message>
              -
              -        <portType name="StockInterface">
              -            <operation name="set_price">
             20                <input message="tns:set_price_in"/>
              -                <output message="tns:set_price_out"/>
              -            </operation>
              -        </portType>
              -
             25        <binding name="StockBinding" type="tns:StockInterface">
              -            <soap:binding style="rpc"
              -                transport="http://schemas.xmlsoap.org/soap/http"/>
              -            <operation name="set_price">
              -                <soap:operation soapAction="set_price"/>
             30                <input>
              -                    <soap:body
              -                        encodingStyle="http://schemas.xmlsoap.org/soap/encoding/"
              -                        namespace="urn:Stock"
              -                        use="encoded"/>
             35                </input>
              -                <output>
              -                    <soap:body
              -                        encodingStyle="http://schemas.xmlsoap.org/soap/encoding/"
              -                        namespace="urn:Stock"
             40                        use="encoded"/>
              -                </output>
              -            </operation>
              -        </binding>
              -    </definitions>
```

WSDL does not force us to declare the whole interface at once, so we declared only the set_price(name,price) method. Let's dissect it element by element.

We use the <*message*> elements to declare the signatures and return values of all methods we are going to describe. In SOAP everything is a message—a method gets a message containing its parameters, and it sends back its return value as a message. The set_price(name,price) method receives a message called set_price_in that consists of two parts: a string called name and a double called price. A set_price_out message containing a double object named price is returned.

It may look a bit awkward to declare our Ruby methods this way, but SOAP was meant to be interoperable, so the standards committee had to agree upon the data types that are available in most (static) programming languages. Hence, data types in SOAP can be everything you are used to in object-oriented languages such as Java and C++: atomic types such as int and double, arrays, structs, and even full-blown objects. They are described using XmlSchema[13] and reside in the xsd namespace.

We describe the methods (or *operations* as SOAP calls them) offered by the service with the <*portType*> element beginning on line 18. In our case this is simple: we have an operation called set_price() that expects a message of type set_price_in and returns a set_price_out message.

The rest of the WSDL file deals with the so-called service binding. It's possible to declare several implementations of the same interface in a single WSDL file. For example, there could be different SOAP implementations of our Stock servicer: one that uses HTTP as its transport layer and another one that uses HTTPS. Both services would have the same interface, but they would have different bindings. (In fact, they don't even have to be SOAP services at all.) But our Stock service is a plain old SOAP service running on top of HTTP.

Now that we have this abstract, omnipotent XML description of our stock, only a single question remains: what the heck can we do with it? Simple answer: we can use it to generate all the boring code we had to write manually before:

```
mschmidt:/tmp> ls
sd_stock.wsdl    stock.wsdl
mschmidt:/tmp> wsdl2ruby.rb --type client --wsdl sd_stock.wsdl
I, [2005-12-31T12:29:39.745796 #567]  INFO -- app: Creating class \
  definition.
I, [2005-12-31T12:29:39.786257 #567]  INFO -- app: Creates file \
  'StockServiceImplementationDescription.rb'.
```

---

[13]http://www.w3.org/XML/Schema

```
I, [2005-12-31T12:29:39.789094 #567]  INFO -- app: Creating driver.
I, [2005-12-31T12:29:39.790492 #567]  INFO -- app: Creates file \
  'StockServiceImplementationDescriptionDriver.rb'.
I, [2005-12-31T12:29:39.796227 #567]  INFO -- app: Creating client \
  skelton.
I, [2005-12-31T12:29:39.797680 #567]  INFO -- app: Creates file \
  'StockServiceClient.rb'.
I, [2005-12-31T12:29:39.800845 #567]  INFO -- app: End of app.\
  (status: 0)
mschmidt:/tmp> ls
StockServiceClient.rb
StockServiceImplementationDescription.rb
StockServiceImplementationDescriptionDriver.rb
sd_stock.wsdl
stock.wsdl
mschmidt:/tmp>
```

wsdl2ruby.rb turns .wsdl files into Ruby code. Although it is part of soap4r,
it is not part of the Ruby standard distribution and has to be installed
separately.[14]

You can specify the .wsdl file to be compiled with the --wsdl option. Using
the --type option, you can choose whether you want client or server code.
We were interested in client code this time, and wsdl2ruby.rb has generated three files for us. The most interesting one is StockServiceClient.rb:

File 81

```
Line 1   #!/usr/bin/env ruby
   -     require 'StockServiceImplementationDescriptionDriver.rb'
   -
   -     endpoint_url = ARGV.shift
   5     obj = StockInterface.new(endpoint_url)
   -
   -     # run ruby with -d to see SOAP wiredumps.
   -     obj.wiredump_dev = STDERR if $DEBUG
   -
   10    # SYNOPSIS
   -     #   set_price(name, price)
   -     #
   -     # ARGS
   -     #   name               String - {http://www.w3.org/2001/XMLSchema}string
   15    #   price              Double - {http://www.w3.org/2001/XMLSchema}double
   -     #
   -     # RETURNS
   -     #   price              Double - {http://www.w3.org/2001/XMLSchema}double
   -     #
   20    name = price = nil
   -     puts obj.set_price(name, price)
```

---

[14]SOAP4R's home page is http://dev.ctor.org/soap4r.

How convenient: replace name and price in line 20 with actual values, and you are done.

All the other files that have been created are not meant to be touched. The file ending with *Driver* contains the proxy (or driver, as SOAP4R calls it) for the SOAP service. The remaining file contains those classes needed by the driver. Whenever the .wsdl file changes, they have to be generated anew.

For the sake of completeness, let's generate the server side, too:

```
mschmidt:/tmp> ls
sd_stock.wsdl    stock.wsdl
mschmidt:/tmp> wsdl2ruby.rb --type server --wsdl sd_stock.wsdl
I, [2005-12-31T14:33:09.426067 #701]  INFO -- app: Creating class \
  definition.
I, [2005-12-31T14:33:09.428748 #701]  INFO -- app: Creates file \
  'StockServiceImplementationDescription.rb'.
I, [2005-12-31T14:33:09.431321 #701]  INFO -- app: Creating servant \
  skelton.
I, [2005-12-31T14:33:09.432716 #701]  INFO -- app: Creates file \
  'StockServiceImplementationDescriptionServant.rb'.
I, [2005-12-31T14:33:09.436486 #701]  INFO -- app: Creating standalone \
  stub.
I, [2005-12-31T14:33:09.438000 #701]  INFO -- app: Creates file \
  'StockService.rb'.
- Standalone stub can have only 1 port for now. So creating stub for \
  the first port and rests are ignored.
- Standalone server stub ignores port location defined in WSDL. \
  Location is http://localhost:10080/ by default. Generated client \
  from WSDL must be configured to point this endpoint manually.
I, [2005-12-31T14:33:09.474488 #701]  INFO -- app: End of app. \
  (status: 0)
mschmidt:/tmp> ls
StockService.rb
StockServiceImplementationDescription.rb
StockServiceImplementationDescriptionServant.rb
sd_stock.wsdl
stock.wsdl
mschmidt:/tmp>
```

The skeleton for our server can be found in StockServiceImplementation-DescriptionServant.rb:

File 82

```
Line 1    require 'StockServiceImplementationDescription.rb'

          class StockInterface
            # SYNOPSIS
      5     #    set_price(name, price)
            #
            # ARGS
```

```
  -        #    name           String - {http://www.w3.org/2001/XMLSchema}string
  -        #    price          Double - {http://www.w3.org/2001/XMLSchema}double
 10        #
  -        # RETURNS
  -        #    price          Double - {http://www.w3.org/2001/XMLSchema}double
  -        #
  -        def set_price(name, price)
 15          p [name, price]
  -          raise NotImplementedError.new
  -        end
  -     end
```

Generating the server skeleton is normally interesting only if you're developing a SOAP service from scratch. If you already have an implementation (like our Stock class), it's easier to "soapify" it with the method add_servant(). Despite all this, it's always a good idea to design your software without having a certain technology for distributed applications in mind. It may change sooner than you think....

There's an even easier way to automatically create client code from a .wsdl file:

```
Line 1   require 'soap/wsdlDriver'
  -      wsdl = 'sd_stock.wsdl'
  -      stock = SOAP::WSDLDriverFactory.new(wsdl).create_rpc_driver
  -      stock.set_price('orchid', 2.42)
```

The constructor of the SOAP::WSDLDriverFactory accepts the file name of a WSDL file or a URL that points to one. Its create_rpc_driver() method returns a proxy for the service described in the WSDL file.

We cannot simplify the client anymore, so it's time to start the server and to send the .wsdl files to Jeff and his guys. They'll know what to do with 'em....

SOAP Headers

The stock control server is a vital component of PragBouquet's infrastructure. It would certainly cause a lot of problems if someone could manipulate the number of items in stock. To protect against this, you decide to add some kind of authentication to the service.

Authentication for SOAP services can be added at several levels. Typically, you have to decide whether to implement authentication at the transport or at the application layer. Many SOAP services run on top of HTTP, so it's only natural to think about HTTP's authentication mechanisms, such as basic authentication.

Unfortunately, support for HTTP authentication is weak in SOAP4R. At the moment it is not possible to set up a SOAP server that requires basic authentication, regardless of whether you use HTTP or HTTPS.

It is, however, possible to create SOAP clients that are capable of using basic authentication. First, you have to install http-access2.[15] Then you have to set the protocol.http.basic_auth option of your driver:

```
url = 'http://localhost:2000'
stock = SOAP::RPC::Driver.new(url, 'urn:Stock')
stock.options['protocol.http.basic_auth'] << [url, 'username', 'password']
```

Of course, relying on the transport layer's authentication mechanism means you're tied to that transport layer. As an alternative, we could add some kind of authentication to the application layer. For example, we could define a login(userid,password) method for each service. Before doing anything else, users of our application would have to call login() to obtain a session ID. From then on, they'd have to pass this session ID as a parameter to any other method they'd like to use.[16]

Because this approach is ugly, SOAP has a much better solution: using *headers* to transport meta information such as session IDs. In Section 5.3, *A Look Under the Hood of SOAP*, on page 204, we showed what typical SOAP messages look like. What we didn't mention is that as well as having a *<Body>* element, SOAP messages also have a *<Header>* element. Headers transport meta information such as login data or session IDs in parallel to method calls and responses. SOAP4R provides an easy way to manage them. In this section you'll learn how to use them.

Regardless how we transport user IDs and passwords, we have to create a piece of software that actually determines whether a particular user is allowed to invoke a particular method. Usually, such a class manages a set of session IDs that are created whenever a user logs into the application. Our Authenticator class looks like this:

File 83

```
Line 1   require 'digest/md5'

         class Authenticator
           def initialize
      5      @users = {
                 'scott' => 'tiger', 'maik' => 'secret'
               }
```

---

[15]http://raa.ruby-lang.org/project/http-access2
[16]I've seen SOAP interfaces where *every* method expects a user ID and password!

```
  -           @sessions = {}
  -         end
 10
  -         def login(userid, password)
  -           userid and password and @users[userid] == password
  -         end
  -
 15         def authenticate(sessionid)
  -           @sessions[sessionid] # -> userid
  -         end
  -
  -         def create_session(userid)
 20           while true
  -             sessionid = create_sessionid
  -             break unless @sessions[sessionid]
  -           end
  -           @sessions[sessionid] = userid
 25           sessionid
  -         end
  -
  -         def destroy_session(sessionid)
  -           @sessions.delete(sessionid)
 30         end
  -
  -         private
  -
  -         def create_sessionid
 35           Digest::MD5.hexdigest(Time.now.usec.to_s)
  -         end
  -       end
```

In a real application we'd add a persistence layer (probably a database or an LDAP repository) to store the different user accounts, and you wouldn't store passwords unencrypted. For demonstration purposes, the Authenticator is sufficient. It stores all known users and their passwords in the @users hash and all active sessions in the @sessions hash.

The login(userid,password) method checks whether a certain combination of user ID and password is valid. authenticate(userid) determines whether there is a valid session for a given user ID, and the method create_session(userid) creates a new session ID for a user ID.

Our session IDs are not too sophisticated, but at least we use an MD5 digest to increase the security level a bit.

How can we integrate our Authenticator into our stock server? The idea was to transport login data in a SOAP header. In SOAP4R we manage headers with the SOAP::Header::SimpleHandler class:

File 84

```
Line 1   require 'soap/header/simplehandler'

         class AuthHeaderHandler < SOAP::Header::SimpleHandler
           AuthHeaderName = XSD::QName.new(
     5       'http://pragbouquet.com/authHeader',
             'auth'
           )


           def initialize
    10       super(AuthHeaderName)
           end
         end
```

Because we need an implementation of our new header on both the server side and the client side, we created a base class called Auth-HeaderHandler. It is derived from SOAP::Header::SimpleHandler, and it defines an XSD::QName object that represents the qualified name of our new header. It's called auth and resides in the namespace http://pragbouquet.com/authHeader. Now we implement the handler that processes the <auth> header on the server side:

File 86

```
Line 1   require 'authenticator'
         require 'authheader'

         class ServerAuthHeaderHandler < AuthHeaderHandler
     5     @authenticator = Authenticator.new

           def self.create
             new(@authenticator)
           end
    10
           def initialize(authenticator)
             super()
             @authenticator = authenticator
             @userid = @sessionid = nil
    15       @mustunderstand = true
           end


           def on_simple_inbound(auth_header, mustunderstand)
             authenticated = false
    20       userid = auth_header['userid']
             passwd = auth_header['passwd']
             if @authenticator.login(userid, passwd)
               authenticated = true
             elsif sessionid = auth_header['sessionid']
    25         if userid = @authenticator.authenticate(sessionid)
                 @authenticator.destroy_session(sessionid)
                 authenticated = true
               end
             end
```

```
30        unless authenticated
              raise RuntimeError.new('Authentication failed!')
          end
          @userid = userid
          @sessionid = @authenticator.create_session(userid)
35        end

          def on_simple_outbound
              { 'sessionid' => @sessionid }
          end
40      end
```

That's a lot of code, but it's all necessary. SOAP4R expects all header handler classes to be factory classes, so in line 7 we define a class method called create() that returns a fully initialized instance of our ServerAuthHeaderHandler class.

In the following code we define the two most important methods for header handlers:

on_simple_inbound(header,mustunderstand)

Is called for every incoming SOAP message. header contains the value of the header for which the class is responsible. It can be a hash, a string, or nil. If the SOAP header looks like this:

```
<env:Header>
  <n1:auth xmlns:n1="http://pragbouquet.com/authHeader"
           env:mustUnderstand="1">
    <n1:passwd>tiger</n1:passwd>
    <n1:userid>scott</n1:userid>
  </n1:auth>
</env:Header>
```

we get the hash { 'userid' => 'scott', 'passwd' => 'tiger' }.

The logic of our on_simple_inbound() method is easy: if the client sends the parameters userid and passwd, we try to authenticate them with the Authenticator class. If this wasn't successful, we see whether the client has sent a valid sessionid. If yes, we create a new one to prevent session hijacking. Otherwise, we raise an exception.

The mustunderstand parameter specifies whether the application must understand a particular header. Sometimes some headers are optional—an application might or might not use them. In these cases mustunderstand is false. In our class we set @mustunderstand to true in line 15, because our clients must understand the auth header.

on_simple_outbound( )

> Is used to set a header in an outgoing SOAP message. It returns the header values to be sent back as a hash, a string, or nil. The resulting SOAP document fragment looks like this for our sessionid:

```
<env:Header>
  <n1:auth xmlns:n1="http://pragbouquet.com/authHeader"
           env:mustUnderstand="1">
    <n1:sessionid>0068f34003a3912b6843ee549659fb94</n1:sessionid>
  </n1:auth>
</env:Header>
```

Adding the header handler to our existing server is easy:

File 86

```
Line 1    require 'soap/rpc/standaloneServer'
      -   require 'stock'
      -
      -   class StockServer < SOAP::RPC::StandaloneServer
      5     def initialize(*args)
      -       super
      -       @log.level = Logger::Severity::DEBUG
      -       namespace = 'http://pragbouquet.com/stockPort'
      -       add_servant(Stock.new, namespace)
      10      add_request_headerhandler(ServerAuthHeaderHandler)
      -     end
      -   end
```

We added just a single line: in line 10 we add the handler for our new header. Now our server always expects a valid user ID/password combination or a valid session ID for every method call. Hence, our client needs a header handler, too:

File 85

```
Line 1    require 'authheader'
      -
      -   class ClientAuthHeaderHandler < AuthHeaderHandler
      -     def initialize(userid, passwd)
      5       super()
      -       @userid, @passwd = userid, passwd
      -       @sessionid, @mustunderstand = nil, true
      -     end
      -     def on_simple_outbound
      10      if @sessionid
      -         { 'sessionid' => @sessionid }
      -       else
      -         { 'userid' => @userid, 'passwd' => @passwd }
      -       end
      15    end
      -     def on_simple_inbound(auth_header, mustunderstand)
      -       @sessionid = auth_header['sessionid']
      -     end
      -   end
```

In the on_simple_inbound() method we store the session ID that was transmitted in the header. In on_simple_outbound() we send back this session ID or—if it doesn't exist—the user ID and the password. Here's a simple usage example:

```
Line 1   require 'soap/rpc/driver'

         namespace = 'http://pragbouquet.com/stockPort'
         stock = SOAP::RPC::Driver.new('http://localhost:7000', namespace)
    5    stock.add_method('get_report')
         stock.add_method('create_flower', 'name', 'price', 'quantity')
         stock.headerhandler << ClientAuthHeaderHandler.new(
           'scott',
           'tiger'
   10    )
         stock.wiredump_dev = STDOUT
         begin
           stock.create_flower('rose', 1.99, 1000)
           p stock.get_report
   15    rescue Exception => ex
           puts ex
         end
```

We initialized the client as usual. On line 7, we add an instance of the ClientAuthHeaderHandler to the list of header handlers (there can be as many header handlers as you need).

The message that our client sends first looks as follows:

```
<env:Envelope xmlns:xsd="http://www.w3.org/2001/XMLSchema"
        xmlns:env="http://schemas.xmlsoap.org/soap/envelope/"
        xmlns:xsi="http://www.w3.org/2001/XMLSchema-instance">

<env:Header>
    <n1:auth xmlns:n1="http://pragbouquet.com/authHeader"
          env:mustUnderstand="1">
     <n1:passwd>tiger</n1:passwd>
     <n1:userid>scott</n1:userid>
    </n1:auth>
</env:Header>

<env:Body>
   <n2:create_flower xmlns:n2="http://pragbouquet.com/stockPort"
          env:encodingStyle="http://schemas.xmlsoap.org/soap/encoding/">
     <name xsi:type="xsd:string">rose</name>
     <price xsi:type="xsd:double">+1.99</price>
     <quantity xsi:type="xsd:int">1000</quantity>
   </n2:create_flower>
  </env:Body>
</env:Envelope>
```

Everything looks as expected. The body is the same as before, but the SOAP message contains a *<Header>* element with our newly defined *<auth>* element. The server return the following response:

```
<env:Envelope xmlns:xsd="http://www.w3.org/2001/XMLSchema"
            xmlns:env="http://schemas.xmlsoap.org/soap/envelope/"
            xmlns:xsi="http://www.w3.org/2001/XMLSchema-instance">

    <env:Header>
        <n1:auth xmlns:n1="http://pragbouquet.com/authHeader"
                env:mustUnderstand="1">
            <n1:sessionid>523069cbf5351bb1a670183f873b9de1</n1:sessionid>
        </n1:auth>
    </env:Header>

    <env:Body>
        <n2:create_flowerResponse xmlns:n2="http://pragbouquet.com/stockPort
                env:encodingStyle="http://schemas.xmlsoap.org/soap/encoding/">
            <return xsi:type="xsd:int">1000</return>
        </n2:create_flowerResponse>
    </env:Body>
</env:Envelope>
```

It works! The server has sent us a session ID that the client has to transfer back to the server in the next request. Then it will get a new session ID, and so on.

SOAP headers are a useful part of the standard and are well supported by SOAP4R. They are often used for authentication purposes but can be used for all tasks that should be handled outside the normal processing of the application itself.

Conclusion

After the inevitable hype dissipated, SOAP quickly became a standard technology in the industry. If you haven't used it already, the chances are good that you'll have to use or build a SOAP service someday. For most applications, SOAP is complete overkill. Sometimes, though, it makes sense (and there will always be pointy-haired bosses who force you to use a certain technology even when it's absolutely inappropriate).

With Ruby it doesn't matter whether SOAP is appropriate, because SOAP4R completely hides all the nasty details, allowing you to fully concentrate on your application domain.

5.4 CORBA, RMI, and Friends

With the advent of the Internet, textual protocols such as SMTP, HTTP became the norm and so it comes as no surprise that the most popular web services protocols such as SOAP and XML-RPC are textual protocols, too.

Some years ago the situation looked a bit different, and many organizations and companies tried to establish their own "standard" for building distributed architectures. Sun, e.g., has defined the *Remote Method Invocation* (RMI) protocol for Java, and the *Object Management Group* (OMG)[17] has specified CORBA.

Remote Method Invocation

Object Management Group

All these approaches suffered from the same problems: they were way too complex, and they all relied upon binary protocols. Only big companies such as Sun, Borland, and IBM had the power to implement such specifications and even for them it was sometimes too difficult to do it right. Consequentially, the situation today is a mess: there are implementations for only a few programming languages, many systems do not interact as they should because of proprietary vendor extensions, and all in all the former "standards" have been superseded by their young and fresh fellows like XML-RPC anyway.

Despite this, many companies have created CORBA components and RMI services during that short period of time, and chances are good that you still have to use some of these relics. Unfortunately, there is no CORBA or RMI implementation for Ruby (and probably there never will be one), but instead of implementing a CORBA or RMI protocol stack in Ruby, it's much more comfortable to reuse an existing implementation like the one for Java, for example.

Hence, this section mainly deals with integrating Ruby and Java, and we will show you how you can still use the gigabytes of .jar files that you have collected and created during the last years. Although our main example deals with CORBA, it explains all the techniques necessary for accessing your good old RMI services, too.

CORBA, Java, and Ruby

CORBA stands for *Common Object Request Broker Architecture* and is a language-neutral standard for object-oriented interprocess communication. Simply put, it allows you to instantiate remote objects and

---

[17]Read more about the OMG and its work at `http://www.omg.org`.

invoke methods on them transparently over a network. It has been popular in the industry at the end of the nineties, so chances are good that you can find some CORBA services in any company that has survived the dot-com bubble burst.[18]

Object Request Broker

At the core of every CORBA system is the *Object Request Broker* (ORB). All service objects register themselves at the ORB, and clients ask the ORB for particular services. To make network transparency possible, all the marshaling and demarshaling code for all objects is generated from an abstract interface definition. Interfaces of CORBA objects are defined using the *Interface Definition Language* (IDL). Such interfaces are compiled using an IDL compiler that generates *stubs* for the clients and *skeletons* for the server objects. Stubs and skeletons act as proxies and convert method calls into network traffic, and vice versa.

Interface Definition Language

stubs

skeletons

CORBA implementations usually come with a lot of standard services such as a naming service. Hence, clients do not have to know exact network addresses to obtain a reference to a particular service; they have to know only its name and have to ask the ORB to find the service (they do have to know the address of the ORB, of course). It is even possible that different ORBs communicate to find a particular service. Therefore the *Internet Inter ORB Protocol* (IIOP) was invented. See Figure 5.5, on the facing page, for an overview.

Internet Inter ORB Protocol

The SMS Server Again

Before drowning you in theory, we will show you how to access CORBA services with Ruby. Do you remember the HTTP server that allowed us to send short messages in cellular networks (if not, you should read Section 4.2, *Waking Up the Operator*, on page 161, now)? I have to admit that I've tricked you a bit: there is no such thing like an HTTP interface for this server. It's a CORBA service, and I've wrapped it with a thin HTTP layer.

The CORBA interface definition of the SMS service we have used looks like this:

File 48

```
Line 1   #ifndef SMS_IDL__
    -    #define SMS_IDL__
    -
    -    module sms {
    5
```

---

[18]http://en.wikipedia.org/wiki/Dot-com

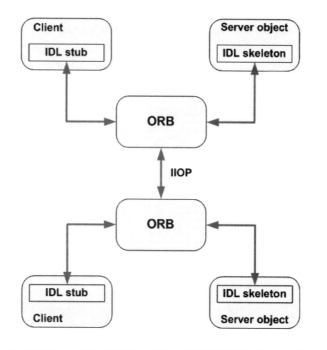

Figure 5.5: CORBA OVERVIEW

```
-       exception IOError {};
-
-       interface SmsService {
-           /* Sends a textual short message and returns the amount
10          * of characters sent.
-           */
-           short send_text(
-               in string recipient,
-               in string sender,
15              in string data) raises (IOError);
-
-           /* Sends a binary short message (the data has to be
-            * encoded as two-digit, case-insensitive hexadecimal
-            * values). Returns the amount of bytes sent.
20          */
-           short send_binary(
-               in string recipient,
-               in string sender,
-               in string data) raises (IOError);
25      };
-   };
-
-   #endif
```

Even if you've never seen an .idl file before, you should have no problems understanding it. We define an interface called SmsService that declares an exception called IOError and exports two methods for sending short messages. All these elements belong to the sms module.

An IDL compiler turns such an interface definition into stub and skeleton code for a particular programming language and generates everything that is needed to transport data types, method calls, and exceptions in a transparent manner.

Unfortunately, there is no native CORBA binding for Ruby (to be concise, there is not even a standardized IDL mapping. Standardized mappings exist for C, C++, Java, COBOL, Smalltalk, Ada, Lisp, Python, and IDLscript), and consequentially there is no IDL compiler for Ruby. That's not a big problem because there are many for Java, and it's easy for us to use one of them.[19]

Our approach is to build the client code with Java and embed it into Ruby. One of the nice features of CORBA is that it doesn't matter whether the server has been implemented in C++ or Java. You can always write or use a Java client, which is usually easier than fiddling around with C++ compiler options and the like.

The idlj command shipping with the Java SDK turns our .idl file into a bunch of .java files (the -fall option generates both client and server code):

```
mschmidt:~/sms> idlj -fall sms.idl
mschmidt:~/sms> ls sms
IOError.java                 SmsServiceHolder.java
IOErrorHelper.java           SmsServiceOperations.java
IOErrorHolder.java           SmsServicePOA.java
SmsService.java              _SmsServiceStub.java
SmsServiceHelper.java
```

We'll create a dummy implementation of the SMS service that makes testing easier and prevents us from sending short messages frequently. Our implementation has to be derived from class SmsServicePOA and looks as follows:

File 47

```
Line 1    import sms.*;

          class SmsServiceImpl extends SmsServicePOA {
              public short send_text(
```

---

[19]At http://java.sun.com/j2se/1.4.2/docs/guide/idl/GShome.html you can find a nice Java/CORBA tutorial.

```
 5            final String recipient,
 ·            final String sender,
 ·            final String data) throws IOError
 ·       {
 ·            // Send SMS somehow...
10            final short text_length = (short)data.length();
 ·            final short bit_amount = (short)(text_length * 7);
 ·            short byte_amount = (short)(bit_amount / 8);
 ·            if (bit_amount % 8 != 0)
 ·                byte_amount++;
15            return byte_amount;
 ·       }


 ·       public short send_binary(
 ·            final String recipient,
20            final String sender,
 ·            final String data) throws IOError
 ·       {
 ·            if (data.length() % 2 != 0)
 ·                throw new IOError("Odd length of binary data!");
25
 ·            // Send SMS somehow...
 ·            return (short)(data.length() / 2);
 ·       }
 ·   }
```

This implementation of the sendTextSms() and sendBinarySms() does not do a lot, but for testing purposes it's sufficient. Both methods calculate the number of bytes that would have been transmitted if we actually had sent a short message. For binary messages it's easy, because we encode the binary data as a string of two-digit, case-insensitive hexadecimal values. Hence, we have to divide the string length by 2 to get the byte count. The calculation for text messages is a bit more complicated, because the character set encodings for short messages usually use only 7 bits per character:

File 45

```
Line 1   import org.omg.CosNaming.*;
 ·       import org.omg.CORBA.*;
 ·       import org.omg.PortableServer.*;
 ·       import sms.*;
 5
 ·       public class SmsServer {
 ·           public static void main(final String args[]) {
 ·               try {
 ·                   final ORB orb = ORB.init(args, null);
10                   final POA rootpoa = POAHelper.narrow(
 ·                       orb.resolve_initial_references("RootPOA")
 ·                   );
 ·                   rootpoa.the_POAManager().activate();
 ·
```

```
15          final org.omg.CORBA.Object ref =
 -              rootpoa.servant_to_reference(new SmsServiceImpl());
 -          final org.omg.CORBA.Object objRef =
 -              orb.resolve_initial_references("NameService");
 -
20          final NamingContextExt ncRef =
 -              NamingContextExtHelper.narrow(objRef);
 -          final NameComponent path[] =
 -              ncRef.to_name("SmsService");
 -          ncRef.rebind(path, SmsServiceHelper.narrow(ref));
25
 -          System.out.println("SMS server is starting ...");
 -          orb.run();
 -        }
 -      catch(Exception e) {
30          System.err.println("An exception occurred: " + e);
 -          e.printStackTrace(System.err);
 -        }
 -      }
 -    }
 -  }
```

If you're a CORBA pro, the previous lines will be totally clear to you.
All the others have to believe me: these lines register the services of the
SmsServer class at the ORB under the name SmsService. So, every client
that wants to use our service has to ask the ORB for a reference to the
service called SmsService.

Before actually starting and registering the SmsServer object, we have to
start the ORB itself. For our purposes Sun's reference implementation
called orbd is everything we need:

```
mschmidt:~/sms> orbd -ORBInitialPort 1050 -ORBInitialHost localhost &
```

The standard port for ORBs is 900, but we did not want to start the
service as the root user, so we chose port 1050.

Let's start the server and register our service object at the ORB:

```
mschmidt:~/sms> javac SmsServer.java sms/*.java
mschmidt:~/sms> java SmsServer -ORBInitialHost localhost \
> -ORBInitialPort 1050 &
SMS server is starting ...
```

The CORBA Client

Now that the whole infrastructure is up and running, we can implement
our client:

File 46

```
Line 1    import sms.*;
 -        import org.omg.CosNaming.*;
 -        import org.omg.CORBA.*;
```

```
 5   public class SmsServiceClient {
         public SmsServiceClient() throws Exception {
             this("localhost", 1050);
         }

10       public SmsServiceClient(
             final String host,
             final int    port) throws Exception
         {
             _smsService = getSmsService(host, port);
15       }

         public short sendTextSms(
             final String recipient,
             final String sender,
20           final String data) throws IOError
         {
             return _smsService.send_text(recipient, sender, data);
         }

25       public short sendBinarySms(
             final String recipient,
             final String sender,
             final String data) throws IOError
         {
30           return _smsService.send_binary(recipient, sender, data);
         }

         private SmsService getSmsService(
             final String host,
35           final int port) throws Exception
         {
             final String[] args = new String[] {
                 "-ORBInitialHost", host,
                 "-ORBInitialPort", "" + port
40           };
             final ORB orb = ORB.init(args, null);

             final org.omg.CORBA.Object objRef =
                 orb.resolve_initial_references("NameService");
45           final NamingContextExt ncRef =
                 NamingContextExtHelper.narrow(objRef);

             final String name = "SmsService";
             return SmsServiceHelper.narrow(ncRef.resolve_str(name));
50       }

         private final SmsService _smsService;
     }
```

To demonstrate the usage of class SmsServiceClient in Java, we have written a small command-line tool that allows us to send textual short messages from the shell:

File 44

```
Line 1   public class SendSms {
             public static void main(final String args[]) {
                 try {
                     final String recipient = args[0];
      5              final String sender = args[1];
                     final String data = args[2];
                     final SmsServiceClient smsServiceClient =
                         new SmsServiceClient();
                     short bytes = smsServiceClient.sendTextSms(
     10                  recipient,
                         sender,
                         data
                     );
                     System.out.println(bytes + " bytes have been sent.");
     15          }
                 catch(Exception e) {
                     System.err.println("An exception occurred: " + e) ;
                     e.printStackTrace(System.err);
                 }
     20      }
         }
```

This little program expects three command-line arguments: the phone number of the recipient, the phone number of the sender, and the text to be sent (do not forget to put the text in quotes if it contains blanks.

Otherwise, the shell will interpret parts of your text as separate arguments.) It is compiled and run as follows:

```
mschmidt:~/sms> javac SmsServiceClient.java SendSms.java sms/*.java
mschmidt:~/sms> java SendSms +0112345 +0198765 Hello
5 bytes have been sent.
```

Bridging the Gap

We have everything available now: a running CORBA service and the appropriate client code. The only task left to do is integrating the client code with Ruby. Thanks to a project called Ruby Java Bridge,[20] this is really a piece of cake, as you'll see in the code following the sidebar.

---

[20]http://raa.ruby-lang.org/project/rjb

Ruby and Java

One of the features that makes Java as popular as it is, is its virtual machine (JVM). Instead of generating code for a particular CPU, Java source code is compiled into byte code for a virtual processor. Hence, to run Java programs on a new hardware platform or a new operating system, you only have to write a new interpreter for the Java byte code.

Many projects have successfully built interpreters for languages targeting the Java Virtual Machine. For example, Jython[*] is a Java implementation of the Python interpreter and Groovy[†] is a new dynamic language—similar to Ruby in many respects—that has been built for the JVM from the beginning.

Simply put, for integrating an arbitrary programming language with the JVM you have two options: you can choose the Jython or Groovy approach and translate the language directly into Java byte code, or you can embed the JVM using the *Java Native Interface* (JNI).[‡] Sun has created a Java Specification Request (JSR)[§] that deals with the integration of the JVM and scripting languages.

It's only natural that Ruby developers also tried to reuse all the fine stuff that is available in the Java world, so there are many projects dealing with this topic:

- JRuby[¶] is an implementation of a Ruby interpreter in Java. It's useful for embedding Ruby in Java and vice versa.

- rjb (Ruby Java Bridge)[‖] uses JNI to access Java objects in Ruby programs. We will use it in this book, because it's relatively lightweight and is a perfect fit for integration purposes.

- yajb (Yet Another Java Bridge)[**] uses a network approach to access Java objects in Ruby programs; i.e., it implements a Ruby client and a Java server that communicate using some kind of XML-RPC.

---

[*]http://www.jython.org
[†]http://groovy.codehaus.org
[‡]http://java.sun.com/docs/books/tutorial/native1.1
[§]http://www.jcp.org/en/jsr/detail?id=223
[¶]http://jruby.sourceforge.net
[‖]http://raa.ruby-lang.org/project/rjb
[**]http://raa.ruby-lang.org/project/yajb

File 49

```
Line 1   require 'rjb'
   -
   -     sms_service_client_class = Rjb::import('SmsServiceClient')
   -     sms_service = sms_service_client_class.new('localhost', 1050)
   5     begin
   -       puts sms_service.sendTextSms('+0112345', '+0198765', 'hello')
   -       puts sms_service.sendBinarySms('+0112345', '+0198765', 'caffe')
   -     rescue IOError => ex
   -       puts "An exception occurred: #{ex}"
   10    end
```

It produces the following:

```
mschmidt:~/sms> ruby sms_client.rb
5
An exception occurred: IDL:sms/IOError:1.0
```

The whole integration happens in two lines of code.

Rjb::import(classname) returns a reference to the SmsServiceClient class, and then we create an instance as usual. Afterward, we can forget that it actually is a Java class.

In the following lines we send a text message and a binary message. To provoke an exception, we send an invalid binary message and catch the exception in line 8.

It's nearly unbelievable, but that's all you have to do to use arbitrary Java classes in your Ruby programs, and the API of the Rjb library is really lightweight:

- load(classpath='.',jvmargs=()) explicitly loads the JVM (Java Virtual Machine). classpath contains a list of directories separated by the host's path separator. This list is prepended to ENV['CLASSPATH']. jvmargs is an array of strings containing all arguments to be passed to the JVM. For example, the following statement:
  ```
  Rjb::load(
    '.:lib/servlet.jar',
    [
      '-Dhttp.proxyHost=example.com',
      '-Dhttp.proxyPort=8080'
    ]
  )
  ```
  loads the JVM, prepends the current directory and the file lib/servlet.jar to the class path, and sets the system properties for an HTTP proxy. If the JVM is not loaded explicitly by calling load(), it will be loaded automatically, before the first call to import(). Hence, you can write hybrid Ruby/Java one-liners:

```
ruby -rrjb -e "Rjb::import(' java.lang.System' ).out.println(' Strange, eh?' )"
```

This prints the following:

```
Strange, eh?
```

- unload() removes the Java Virtual Machine from memory.
- import(classname) turns the Java class called classname into a Ruby class. If we have the following Java class:

File 65

```
package com.pragbouquet;

public class Flower {
    public Flower(final String name, final double price) {
        _name = name;
        _price = price;
    }

    public String getName() { return _name; }

    public double getPrice() { return _price; }
    public void setPrice(final double price) {
        _price = price;
    }

    private double _price;
    private String _name;
}
```

we can use it like this:

File 66

```
flower = Rjb::import(' com.pragbouquet.Flower' )
f = flower.new(' rose' , 2.49)
puts "A #{f.getName()} costs $#{f.getPrice()}. "
```

and the code produces the following:

```
A rose costs $2.49.
```

- bind() allows you to associate a Ruby class with a Java interface. For example, the following program defines a FileFilter in Ruby that gets passed to the listFiles(filter) method of Java's File class:

File 66

```
Line 1  class FileFilter
    -       def accept(file)
    -           !(file.toString =~ /\.java$/).nil?
    -       end
    5   end

    -   filter = FileFilter.new
    -   filter = Rjb::bind(filter, 'java.io.FileFilter' )
    -   java_file = Rjb::import(' java.io.File' )
    10  jf = java_file.new(' .' )
    -   jf.listFiles(filter).each { |f| puts f.toString }
```

This produces the following:

```
./BindDemo.java
./Flower.java
```

- throw() throws a Java exception. When you extend a Java class that has been converted into a Ruby class, it can be necessary to "simulate" a Java exception:

```
def foo(argument)
  if argument.nil?
    Rjb::throw('java.lang.NullPointerException', 'argument is null.')
  end
end
```

All classes returned by Rjb::import(classname) automatically have the following methods:

- new_with_sig(signature,(arg)+) allows you to call typed Java constructors from Ruby. Java is a statically typed language, and therefore you sometimes have to explicitly say which constructor you want to use. Rjb tries to automatically determine the signature you want according to the following rules:

  1. First, Rjb checks whether the number of arguments matches.

  2. All arguments that are instances of the same class match.

  3. Ruby Fixnum arguments match Java byte, char, double, float, int, long, and short parameters.

  4. Ruby String arguments match java.lang.String parameters.

  5. true and false match Java boolean parameters.

  6. Ruby arrays match Java arrays.

  7. Every Ruby object matches the Java Object class.

If there still is an ambiguity, you can call the constructor you want by passing the type information explicitly. Therefore you have to encode the signature using Java's type encoding[21] (see Figure 5.6, on the facing page):

File 66

```
Line 1   flower = Rjb::import('com.pragbouquet.Flower')
    -    f = flower.new_with_sig('Ljava.lang.String;D', 'rose', 2.49)
    -    puts "A #{f.getName()} costs $#{f.getPrice()}."
```

To encode the signature of an array, you have to prepend a [character to the type encoding. The following irb session demonstrates how to call Java's String(byte() bytes,String charsetName) constructor:

---

[21]http://java.sun.com/j2se/1.5.0/docs/api/java/lang/Class.html#getName()

Element Type	Encoding	Element Type	Encoding
boolean	Z	byte	B
char	C	class	L\<classname\>;
interface	L\<interface name\>;	double	D
float	F	int	I
long	J	short	S

Figure 5.6: ENCODING OF JAVA TYPES

```
irb(main):001:0> require 'rjb'
=> true
irb(main):002:0> Str = Rjb::import('java.lang.String')
=> #<Rjb::Java_lang_String:0x337b04>
irb(main):003:0> ruby = Str.new_with_sig(
irb(main):004:1*   '[BLjava.lang.String;',
irb(main):005:1*   [82, 117, 98, 121],
irb(main):006:1*   'iso-8859-1'
irb(main):007:1> )
=> #<#<Class:0x34739c>:0x328b90>
irb(main):008:0> p ruby.toString
"Ruby"
=> nil
```

- _invoke(method_name,signature,(arg)+) invokes a method_name having the signature signature on the current object and passes it the appropriate arguments. For details about the signature mechanism, see the description of new_with_sig(signature,(arg)+).

- _classname() returns the class name as a string:

File 66
```
Line 1   str = Rjb::import('java.lang.String')
    -    instance = str.new('Hello, world!')
    -    puts instance._classname
```

This produces the following:

```
java.lang.String
```

CORBA Is Coming Home...

Finally, we implement an HTTP server using WEBrick that forwards incoming requests to the CORBA service:

File 50
```
Line 1   require 'rjb'
    -    require 'webrick'
    -    include WEBrick
    -
```

```
 5  Rjb::load
 -  sms_service_client_class = Rjb::import('SmsServiceClient')
 -  sms_service = sms_service_client_class.new('localhost', 1050)
 -
 -  sms_server = HTTPServer.new(:Port => 4242)
10  sms_server.mount_proc('/send') do |req, res|
 -      type = req.query['type'] || 'text'
 -      recipient = req.query['recipient']
 -      sender = req.query['sender'] || recipient
 -      data = req.query['data']
15
 -      res['Content-Type'] = 'text/plain'
 -      res.status = 200
 -      res.body = 'Message was sent successfully.'
 -      method = type == 'binary' ? 'sendBinarySms' : 'sendTextSms'
20      begin
 -          sms_service.send(method, recipient, sender, data)
 -      rescue IOError => ex
 -          res.status = 500
 -          res.body = 'Message could not be sent.'
25      end
 -  end
 -
 -  trap("INT") { sms_server.shutdown }
 -  sms_server.start
```

If you have read carefully, the previous program should be perfectly clear to you, and with less than 30 lines of Ruby code we have turned our CORBA service into an HTTP service.

C++ CORBA Services

For CORBA clients, in theory it doesn't matter whether the service they want to use has been written in C++, Java, or COBOL. If you absolutely want to (or have to) use a C++ client, you can use an approach similar to our previous Java example: generate the C++ client stub from the .idl file using the idl2cpp command, and compile the resulting code into a shared object. Then, integrate the shared object using the Ruby native interface, SWIG[22], or Ruby/DL.[23]

We won't cover this topic here, because you can find tons of tutorials about integrating Ruby with C/C++ code on the Internet, and in *Programming Ruby* [TFH05] there is a whole chapter about it, too.

---

[22]http://www.swig.org
[23]http://raa.ruby-lang.org/project/ruby-dl

Distributed Ruby (dRuby)

As soon as a programming language offered dynamic features (such as reflection or code that's interpreted at runtime), it was pretty much guaranteed that someone would invent a system for distributing objects over a network. It's so easy: create methods that marshal and unmarshal objects, put the resulting byte streams into an envelope, and transfer them between processes using TCP (or any other protocol, for that matter).

The Ruby community fell to the temptation, so Masatoshi Seki developed the Distributed Ruby (dRuby or DRb) module.[24] dRuby is similar to Java's RMI in many respects, including its use of a proprietary binary format to encode messages. It's simple to use and usually does not require any modifications to the classes you want to distribute.

To see how it works, we'll implement a distributed sequence object. Back in the sidebar, on page 30, we complained about the weak support for artificial primary keys in modern databases. Now it's time to roll up our sleeves and fix the problem once and for all—at least for our Ruby applications:

File 57

```ruby
Line 1  require 'drb'

        class Sequence
          def initialize(start_value = 0, step = 1)
     5      @value, @step = start_value - step, step
          end

          def next_value
            @value += @step
    10    end
        end

        DRb.start_service('druby://localhost:9000', Sequence.new)
        DRb.thread.join
```

As promised, we did not have to use any special tricks to turn the Sequence class into a network service. To make an object available on a network with dRuby, you have to pass it to DRb.start_service(url,object) (see line 13). This method expects a dRuby URL and the object to be distributed.

It's easy to use our distributed sequence:

---

[24]http://www2a.biglobe.ne.jp/~seki/ruby/druby.en.html

File 55

```
Line 1    require 'drb'
   -
   -      DRb.start_service
   -      puts "Sequence #1:"
   5      sequence = DRbObject.new(nil, 'druby://localhost:9000')
   -      2.times { puts sequence.next_value }
   -
   -      puts "Sequence #2:"
   -      sequence2 = DRbObject.new(nil, 'druby://localhost:9000')
   10     2.times { puts sequence.next_value }
```

This produces the following:

```
Sequence #1:
0
1
Sequence #2:
2
3
```

That was too easy, wasn't it? Usually, creating network services is a difficult thing, so where's the catch in our example? Right: it isn't thread-safe. If two clients try to get the next sequence value simultaneously, it's possible that both of them get the same value. We'll fix this by adding some synchronization code:

File 54

```
Line 1    require 'thread'
   -
   -      class Sequence
   -        def initialize(start_value = 0, step = 1)
   5          @value, @step = start_value - step, step
   -          @mutex = Mutex.new
   -        end
   -
   -        def next_value
   10         @mutex.synchronize do
   -            @value += @step
   -          end
   -          @value
   -        end
   15     end
```

This version can be safely used in a multithreaded environment, so are we done? Will a single sequence be sufficient for all our processes and database tables? Probably not. Let's implement a class that manages a set of named sequences:

File 53

```
Line 1    require 'drb'
   -      require 'sequence'
   -
   -      class SequenceManager
```

```
 5    def initialize
 -      @sequences = {}
 -      @mutex = Mutex.new
 -    end
 -
10    def create(name, start_value, step)
 -      @mutex.synchronize do
 -        if !@sequences.has_key?(name)
 -          @sequences[name] = Sequence.new(start_value, step)
 -        end
15      end
 -      @sequences[name]
 -    end
 -
 -    def get(name)
20      @sequences[name]
 -    end
 -  end
 -
 -  DRb.start_service('druby://localhost:9000', SequenceManager.new)
25  DRb.thread.join
```

Let's see whether it works as expected:

File 56

```
Line 1  require 'drb'
 -      require 'sequence'
 -
 -      DRb.start_service
 5      factory = DRbObject.new(nil, 'druby://localhost:9000')
 -
 -      puts "Sequence #1:"
 -      sequence = factory.create('order_table', 5, 2)
 -      2.times { puts sequence.next_value }
10
 -      puts "Sequence #2:"
 -      sequence2 = factory.get('order_table')
 -      2.times { puts sequence2.next_value }
```

This produces the following:

```
Sequence #1:
5
7
Sequence #2:
5
7
```

Hmm, we have a problem here. It's because dRuby normally passes objects by value. In our case the Sequence objects created by the SequenceManager are copied before being transmitted, so changes to the local instances aren't seen on the server. In line 8, we create a sequence called order_table and get two values from it in the following line. These changes are made only to the local object. When we get the order_table sequence again in line 12, it's another copy of the original on the server.

What we actually need is a remote reference to a Sequence object on the server. Fortunately, dRuby makes it possible: just mix DRbUndumped into classes you want to transfer by reference:

File 54

```
Line 1    class Sequence
              include DRbUndumped
          end
```

Class DRbUndumped creates a proxy that communicates with the real object. Instead of marshaling the whole object and passing it by value, only the proxy will be transferred. This explains why you have to execute DRb.start_service in your clients, too: every client has to be prepared to act as a server for incoming proxy calls.

After restarting the modified server, our client works as expected:

```
Sequence #1:
5
7
Sequence #2:
9
11
```

For the final solution, you'd probably add a thin persistence layer that stores the current sequence values in a database or file system, but from a networking point of view we are done.

The implementation of dRuby is a perfect example of Ruby's strengths, demonstrating how easy it is to create a complete distributed object system with some nice bells and whistles in less than 3,000 lines of code. If necessary, you can run it over a secure SSL connection and across firewalls.[25] In addition, it is surprisingly fast, because it uses Ruby's internal marshaling mechanism that's written in C.

dRuby finds uses all over the place. Folks often use it for prototyping new architectures. You'll also find it in Ruby on Rails,[26] where it's used to implement the remote breakpoint facility.

Despite all this, dRuby shares the same disadvantages as all other language-specific systems.

---

[25]See http://www.rubygarden.org/ruby?DrbTutorial for more details.
[26]http://api.rubyonrails.com/classes/Breakpoint.html

Distributed Ruby and Security

dRuby passes (references to) real Ruby objects. In terms of security this is a big problem. For example, running the following code:

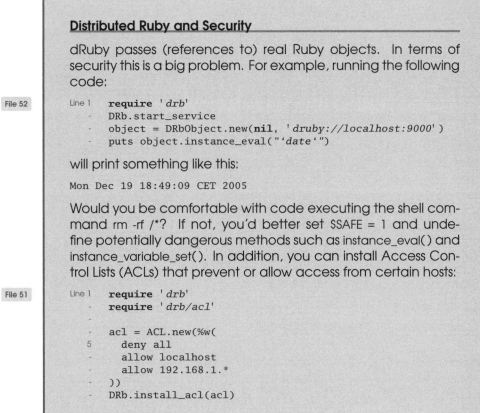

File 52

```
Line 1   require 'drb'
    -    DRb.start_service
    -    object = DRbObject.new(nil, 'druby://localhost:9000')
    -    puts object.instance_eval("'date'")
```

will print something like this:

```
Mon Dec 19 18:49:09 CET 2005
```

Would you be comfortable with code executing the shell command rm -rf /*? If not, you'd better set $SAFE = 1 and undefine potentially dangerous methods such as instance_eval() and instance_variable_set(). In addition, you can install Access Control Lists (ACLs) that prevent or allow access from certain hosts:

File 51

```
Line 1   require 'drb'
    -    require 'drb/acl'
    -
    -    acl = ACL.new(%w(
    5      deny all
    -      allow localhost
    -      allow 192.168.1.*
    -    ))
    -    DRb.install_acl(acl)
```

In particular, to access a dRuby service you have to use a Ruby client. Although we think that Ruby is currently the best programming language available, we're sure that it'll be improved or replaced by a better one someday. To prepare your distributed objects for the unpredictable future, you might want to consider using a standard technology such as HTTP.

Chapter 6

Tools and Techniques

A programming language alone will not make you more productive in an enterprise environment. Ruby will certainly increase your development speed, because it supports a lot of advanced concepts (pure object-oriented programming, iterators, and meta-programming, to name a few), but that's less than half the battle.

Especially in enterprise environments, you face a lot of challenges that are not directly related to your programming language of choice but that are typical for every piece of enterprise software. For example, enterprise software often comes in the shape of servers and daemon processes without any user interface. They have to be deployed somehow into the production system. To indicate that they are still alive and working, they usually write into external log files. In addition, enterprise software often has to fulfill the needs of clients coming from different countries, speaking different languages, and paying in strange currencies.

Hence, in this chapter you will learn how to overcome internationalization problems, how to create sophisticated logging strategies, how to create your own daemon processes, and how to automatically deploy your software.

6.1 Internationalization and Localization

The world is getting smaller. For enterprise applications, internationalization (i18n) and localization (l10n)[1] have become important topics.

---

[1] i18n is an abbreviation for internationalization. The word starts with an *i*, ends with an *n*, and in between are 18 letters. Guess what l10n means....

You now have to be prepared to have people use your application in foreign countries—you'll have to deal with different character sets, date formats, address formats, number formats, etc.

There is no official definition of the terms *internationalization* and *localization*. We'll define them as follows:

- Your software is *internationalized* if it runs correctly in all locales it has to run in. If, for example, you have developed and tested a program in the United States and it runs correctly in your target markets Germany and Japan without modifying it, it is internationalized.

- Your software is *localized* if it is internationalized and reflects the peculiarities of the locale it is running in—it outputs messages in the correct language; prints numbers, dates, and currencies in the right format; and so on.

Perhaps you have worked with Java or C# before, and now you are impatiently waiting for easy answers to all your i18n questions. You've skimmed the documentation of the Ruby standard library and did not instantly find the counterparts of Locale, DateFormat, InputStream, and so on. In this chapter we will reveal an ugly truth: i18n is not supported very well in Ruby. Enterprise platforms such as J2EE and .NET come with a huge number of classes that deal with this topic and even have standardized formats for resource bundles, and so on. Ruby does not.

This is not as bad as it may seem in the beginning, but you will have to perform a lot of tasks manually that you took for granted in other programming languages. But you can always find a solution.

Character Sets and Encodings

Character sets and encodings are different. The Unicode code character set, for example, contains nearly all known characters. It can be encoded in more than one way: UTF-8, UTF-16, and UTF-32.[2] Because of its Japanese roots, Ruby in principle supports different encodings such as EUC, SJIS, and UTF-8. Unfortunately, many of its classes do not.

---

[2]For more information about character sets and their encodings, see the following:

- http://www.w3.org/International/resource-index.html
- http://www.joelonsoftware.com/articles/Unicode.html

What's $KCODE?

You can specify Ruby's internal character set by assigning EUC, SJIS, UTF8, or NONE (which means use the default character set) to the global variable $KCODE. Alternatively, pass e, s, or u to the -K option of the Ruby interpreter.

$KCODE determines which characters are allowed in identifiers (variable names, method names, etc.) and literals. To see what implications it has, run the following UTF-8 program without telling Ruby that it is encoded in UTF-8:

File 113

```
Line 1   class Circle < Struct.new(:x, :y, :r)
    -       def area
    -         π = Math::PI
    -         π * r * r
    5       end
    -     end
    -
    -     c = Circle.new(0, 0, 1)
    -     puts c.area
```

You will get the following result (in a UTF-8 terminal):

```
mschmidt:/tmp> ruby circle.rb
circle.rb:3: Invalid char '\317' in expression
circle.rb:3: Invalid char '\200' in expression
circle.rb:3: parse error, unexpected '='
    π = Math::PI
       ^
circle.rb:4: Invalid char '\317' in expression
circle.rb:4: Invalid char '\200' in expression
circle.rb:4: parse error, unexpected '*', expecting '='
π * r * r
^
```

Obviously, 'π' has not been recognized as a valid word character. Tell Ruby that it is an UTF-8 program and everything is fine:

```
mschmidt:/tmp> ruby -Ku circle.rb
3.14159265358979
```

Note, though, that the $KCODE does not affect the behavior of the String class, so the length() method, for example, still returns the number of bytes, not characters:

```
mschmidt:/tmp> ruby -Ku -e 'puts "Motörhead".length'
10
```

One of the biggest problems with i18n is that developers do not know—and often do not care—what encoding their textual data has. If you get text from an external source such as a database, an LDAP repository, a socket, or a plain file, you always have to ask, "What encoding does this data use?"

In fact, the situation is even worse: you also have to ask yourself which encoding your text editor uses to store your source code files. The Ruby lexer treats everything between single or double quotes as a String—it copies all the *bytes* between quotes into a String object. Hence, it makes a big difference whether these bytes represent characters of a single-byte encoding such as ASCII or a multibyte encoding such as UTF-8.

To see the difference, store the following statement as UTF-8 text[3] and run it:

File 119

```
puts 'Über-Programmer'.length
```

It will print 16, although our string has only 15 characters. That's because the German umlaut Ü needs two bytes in UTF-8. Store the file using the ISO-8859-1 encoding, and it will print 15.

We have to realize that Ruby's String class is nothing more than a byte array with a convenient API. It doesn't know anything about the character concept. That becomes even more obvious when we try methods such as upcase(). When we store the following source code as an UTF-8 file and run it like this:

File 128

```
puts 'Müller'.upcase
```

it produces the following:

```
MüLLER
```

When we store the same source code in ISO-8859-1, it prints the following:[4]

```
M?LLER
```

Both versions produce an incorrect result: the correct uppercase version of Müller is MÜLLER. Fortunately, the German alphabet has only four additional characters: ä, ö, ü, and ß. Their uppercase versions are Ä, Ö, Ü, and SS, so we can write a correct upcase() method ourselves:

---

[3]If your text editor does not support UTF-8, go get a new one. No excuses!

[4]I'm working with an UTF-8 terminal that prints ? for every character it doesn't recognize. In this case ? stands for 0xfc, which is a lowercase ü in ISO-8859-1 and is invalid in UTF-8.

It really is that complicated...

If you've never had to deal with characters outside the ASCII set then you might be surprised how complicated things get when you want to perform apparently simple operations such as converting a string to uppercase or sorting words.

Although the German alphabet has only four additional letters, they cause a lot of trouble and debate. We have three umlauts ä, ö, ü, and we have the letter ß ("sharp s"). The uppercase equivalents of the umlauts are 'Ä', 'Ö', and 'Ü', but 'ß' becomes 'SS' when it's turned into uppercase, i.e. the size of an uppercase string can be bigger than the size of the original string!

A few years ago, the rules were even more complicated. When turning a string to uppercase, it was acceptable to convert ß to SZ, if SS had otherwise led to a misunderstanding (for example in the uppercase versions of Busse (plural form of the German word for bus) and Buße (German for expiation).

Another big problem is sort order (collation). Usually, you ignore the umlaut—if you have two words that only differ in the dots (such as the German verbs "fallen" and "fällen"), the not-dotted version comes first. But there's also an industry standard (DIN 5007) that turns all German umlauts into their "non-dotted" equivalents (ae for ä, oe for ö, and ue for ü) and sorts them lexically. In this case "faellen" would come before "fallen".

le 115

```ruby
Line 1  def german_upcase(text)
   -      uc = text.upcase
   -      uc.tr('äöü', 'ÄÖÜ')
   -      uc.gsub('ß', 'SS')
   5    end
   -
   -    str = 'Märchenstraße'
   -    puts str
   -    puts german_upcase(str)
```

The previous program outputs the following:[5]

```
Märchenstraße
MÄRCHENSTRASSE
```

---

[5]Märchen is the German word for fairy tale and Straße is German for street.

All right, we have corrected one method, but what about downcase(), index(), reverse(), and so on? All of them fail with multibyte characters:

File 126

```
Line 1   str = 'Märchen'
     -   puts 'Ouch!' if str.length != 7
     -   puts 'Ouch again!' if str.reverse != 'nehcräM'
```

This prints the following:

```
Ouch!
Ouch again!
```

Hmmm, things are getting complicated. Ruby supports different character sets, but you have to do a lot yourself. To determine the correct length of an UTF-8 string, for example, you could use the unpack() method with the format specifier U*, which stands for *unsigned integer values representing UTF-8 characters*:

```
puts 'Motörhead'.unpack('U*').length # -> 9
```

To manipulate each character (not byte!) of a UTF-8 string, you can use a regular expression that knows about UTF-8:

File 125

```
str = 'Motörhead'
p str.scan(/./)
p str.scan(/./u)
```

This produces the following:

```
["M", "o", "t", "\303", "\266", "r", "h", "e", "a", "d"]
["M", "o", "t", "\303\266", "r", "h", "e", "a", "d"]
```

When you add the u-modifier to a regular expression, you get each UTF-8 character as a string (these strings can contain more than one byte!). Without the u-modifier, you get every byte separately. This works for EUC (modifier: e) and SJIS (modifier: s), too.

Now let's turn our newly gained knowledge into a class that represents UTF-8 strings in Ruby:[6].

File 129

```
Line 1   class UString < String
     -       def length; self.unpack('U*').length end
     -
     -       def reverse; self.scan(/./u).reverse.join end
     5
     -       def inspect; "u#{super}" end
     -   end
     -
```

---

[6]This example was originally published by *why the lucky stiff*: http://redhanded. hobix.com/inspect/closingInOnUnicodeWithJcode.html

```
     module Kernel
10     def u(str)
         UString.new str.gsub(/U\+([0-9a-fA-F]{4})/u) {
           ["#$1".hex].pack('U*')
         }
       end
15   end
```

Our UString class demonstrates some of Ruby's biggest strengths. First, we can override the methods of one of the most important standard classes (String) by subclassing it. Then, we override the length() and reverse() methods with our UTF-8 implementations. In addition, we changed the inspect() method so we can distinguish String and UString objects.

Finally, we added a new method called u(str) to Kernel. It allows us to create UTF-8 strings that can contain hexadecimal character literals beginning with U+. Here's a small usage example:

```
Line 1   str = u'Märchen'
         puts str.length == 7
         puts str.reverse == 'nehcräM'

5        str = u'MU+00fcnchen'
         puts str
         puts str.length
```

It prints the following:

```
true
true
München
7
```

UString could be the basis for a full-blown UTF-8 string class, but you'd have to add a lot of code. Rather than writing your own implementation like this, you're better off using an existing one. We'll introduce some options in the following sections. None of them is perfect—they all have their strengths and weaknesses—so if you need stronger encoding support, choose carefully.

jcode

jcode is a standard library that modifies Ruby's String class. Depending on the value of the global variable $KCODE (see the sidebar, on page 245) jcode updates the methods chop!(), chop(), delete!(), delete(), squeeze!(), squeeze(), succ!(), succ(), tr!(), tr(), tr_s!(), and tr_s(). Additionally, it adds

> ### Don't Panic!
>
> We have to admit it: Ruby is still in its infancy when it comes to internationalization, and it will take some time until the situation gets better.*
>
> But don't panic! Keep in mind that all this is relevant only if you have to manipulate, compare, or sort strings. If all you do is read them from an external source and write them to another (such as displaying database data in a web browser) without touching a single byte, you are safe. And for special domains such as the Ruby on Rails framework, i18n solutions will probably be available soon.
>
> Even if you absolutely have to manipulate Unicode strings, there is a good chance that you might find what you need in an open source library such as ICU4R. It might not be convenient, but at least it will work.
>
> ---
> *http://redhanded.hobix.com/inspect/futurismUnicodeInRuby.html shows what Matz wants to do.

methods such as jlength(), jcount(), and each_char(), but it does not provide correct implementations for upcase(), downcase(), and so on:

File 118

```
Line 1   $KCODE = 'UTF8'
     -   require 'jcode'
     -   str = 'Köln' # Cologne, a big city in Germany.
     -   puts "Ruby length: #{str.length}."
     5   puts "jcode length: #{str.jlength}."
     -   str.each_char { |c| print c.inspect, ' ' }
     -   puts
```

This prints the following:

```
Ruby length: 5.
jcode length: 4.
"K" "ö" "l" "n"
```

jcode's biggest advantage is that it is part of every Ruby installation. In other respects it is severely limited and will be sufficient only for the simplest transformations.

Unicode

For the sake of completeness we mention Yoshida Masato's unicode project.[7] It complements jcode somewhat, because it offers methods that allow you to compare UTF-8 strings and change them to uppercase or lowercase:

```
Line 1    require 'rubygems'
    -     require 'unicode'
    -
    -     puts Unicode::downcase('HOFBRÄUHAUS')
    5     puts Unicode::upcase('straße')
```

This prints the following:

```
hofbräuhaus
STRAßE
```

Unfortunately, our trivial example does not work correctly, because the ß letter has not been converted properly. In addition, the library seems not to be maintained any longer, so I recommend not using it.

ICU4R

ICU4R[8] is (as I write this) a new project created by Nikolai Lugovoi that looks very promising. It is a C extension for IBM's International Component for Unicode (ICU).[9] It provides two classes: UString and URegexp. UString is a feature-rich implementation of strings encoded in UTF-16:

```
Line 1    require 'ustring'
    -
    -     str = u'Märchenstraße'
    -     puts "Length is #{str.length} characters."
    5     puts str.downcase
    -     puts str.upcase
    -     p str.to_s('ISO-8859-1').scan(/./)
```

This produces the following:

```
Length is 13 characters.
märchenstraße
MÄRCHENSTRASSE
["M", "\344", "r", "c", "h", "e", "n", "s", "t", "r", "a", "\337", "e"]
```

In line 3 we create a new UString object with the u(string) method (you can turn a String object into a UString object by calling its to_u() or u()

---

[7]http://raa.ruby-lang.org/project/unicode
[8]http://rubyforge.org/projects/icu4r
[9]http://ibm.com/software/globalization/icu

method). We then print its length and change its case, and finally we turn back our UString object into a String by invoking to_s(encoding), which accepts an encoding for the result now.

After you have created a UString, you can do a lot of useful things with it. For example, you can iterate over its characters and words:

File 130

```
Line 1    str = u'Märchenstraße'
    -     str.each_char('de_DE') { |c| puts c.inspect_names }
    -     "Hello, world!".u.each_word('en_US') { |w| puts "'#{w}'" }
```

Here's the output of the previous program:

```
<U00004D>LATIN CAPITAL LETTER M
<U0000E4>LATIN SMALL LETTER A WITH DIAERESIS
<U000072>LATIN SMALL LETTER R
<U000063>LATIN SMALL LETTER C
<U000068>LATIN SMALL LETTER H
<U000065>LATIN SMALL LETTER E
<U00006E>LATIN SMALL LETTER N
<U000073>LATIN SMALL LETTER S
<U000074>LATIN SMALL LETTER T
<U000072>LATIN SMALL LETTER R
<U000061>LATIN SMALL LETTER A
<U0000DF>LATIN SMALL LETTER SHARP S
<U000065>LATIN SMALL LETTER E

'Hello'
','
' '
'world'
'!'
```

In the first line we iterate over each character using each_char(locale) and print its code and its official name. A lot of ICU methods accept a locale that consists of a two-character language code and a two-character country code separated by an underscore (de_DE, en_GB, en_US, etc.). If you set this locale to an empty string, it uses your machine's default locale. When iterating over characters, the locale is important because of so-called combining marks that are sometimes used to store letters and their accents separately.[10]

The each_word(locale) method lets you iterate over the words in a string. Because the concept of a word greatly differs from language to language, you can pass a locale, too.

---

[10]See http://www.unicode.org/notes/tn2 for the gory details.

Another great feature of the UString class is its fmt(locale,*args) method, which is sprintf() on steroids:

```
Line 1    gb = u"In{0, date, MMMM} it will cost {1, number, currency}."
   -      puts gb.fmt('en_GB', Time.now, 12345.34)
   -      us = u"In{0, date, MMMM} it will cost {1, number, currency}."
   -      puts us.fmt('en_US', Time.now, 12345.34)
   5      de = u"Im{0, date, MMMM} kostet es {1, number, currency}."
   -      puts de.fmt('de_DE', Time.now, 12345.34)
```

This produces the following:

```
In January it will cost £12,345.34.
In January it will cost $12,345.34.
Im Januar kostet es 12.345,34 €.
```

fmt() handles everything nicely: month names are translated, decimal points are chosen correctly, and thousands are separated by the right character. It picks the right currency symbol, and it knows where to put it (did you know where euro symbols go?). Awesome, isn't it? And it gets even better:

```
Line 1    s = u'{0, choice, 0#no chance|1#a chance|1<many chances}.'
   -      0.upto(2) { |i| puts "We have " + s.fmt('de_DE', i) }
```

This produces the following:

```
We have no chance.
We have a chance.
We have many chances.
```

The choice pattern consists of a number of range specifiers separated by |-characters. Every range specifier is compared to the actual argument, and depending on its value, the right one is chosen.[11]

Objects of class URegexp handle Unicode regular expressions and can be created with the ure(str) method:

```
Line 1    puts 'Last character: ' + ure('(.)(.)(.)').match('süß'.u)[3]
   -
   -      strange_csv = 'thisäisästrange'
   -      puts ure('ä').split(strange_csv.to_u, nil)
```

This produces the following:

```
Last character: ß
this
is
strange
```

---

[11]You should look at the ICU4R documentation. There are many more nice features.

ICU4R's biggest disadvantage is that your strings need twice as much memory as before. In addition, a lot of important methods such as tr(), chop(), delete(), etc., are still missing.[12] Despite this, ICU4R is the most advanced Unicode library currently available for Ruby and might well become an important milestone for the internationalization of Ruby programs.

International I/O

We know how strings in Ruby work in general. Now we'd like to see how the I/O classes support different character set encodings.

For our first experiment, take your favorite text editor, set its encoding to UTF-8, and create a file called utf8.txt containing only the German surname Müller. Six characters, no newline.

Then store the same file using the ISO-8859-1 character set, or use the iconv utility to convert it:[13]

```
mschmidt:/tmp/data> iconv -f UTF-8 -t iso-8859-1 utf8.txt > \
> iso-8859-1.txt
mschmidt:/tmp/data> ls -l
total 16
-rw-r--r--   1 mschmidt  mschmidt   6 Jan  3 19:26 iso-8859-1.txt
-rw-r--r--   1 mschmidt  mschmidt   7 Jan  3 19:25 utf8.txt
```

Notice that the ISO-8859-1 file is shorter than its UTF-8 counterpart. A hex viewer such as xxd shows us why:

```
mschmidt:/tmp/data> xxd iso-8859-1.txt
0000000: 4dfc 6c6c 6572                          M.ller
mschmidt:/tmp/data> xxd utf8.txt
0000000: 4dc3 bc6c 6c65 72                        M..ller
mschmidt:/tmp/data>
```

In ISO-8859-1 the German umlaut, ü, is encoded with a single byte (0xfc), but in UTF-8 it needs two (0xc3, 0xbc). All the other characters of the string Müller are encoded the same way in both ISO-8859-1 and UTF-8.

Let's see what happens when we feed our files to Ruby's standard IO classes:

---

[12]It is a fairly young project, so that might already have changed by the time you are reading this.

[13]The ISO-8859-1 character set represents all Western European languages.

e 116

```
Line 1  def examine_file(file_name)
    -     content = IO.read(file_name)
    -     puts "Its content is '#{content}'."
    -     puts "Content length is #{content.length} bytes."
    5     a = []; content.each_byte { |b| a << b }; p a
    -   end
    -
    -   puts 'Here we have the ISO-8859-1 file...'
    -   examine_file('data/iso-8859-1.txt')
    10  puts
    -   puts '... and here we have the UTF-8 file:'
    -   examine_file('data/utf8.txt')
```

This produces the following:

```
Here we have the ISO-8859-1 file...
Its content is 'M?ller'.
Content length is 6 bytes.
[77, 252, 108, 108, 101, 114]

... and here we have the UTF-8 file:
Its content is 'Müller'.
Content length is 7 bytes.
[77, 195, 188, 108, 108, 101, 114]
```

That doesn't look very promising. Reading data in our standard character set works, but the IO class and the String class obviously don't know anything about character set encodings. *All* standard Ruby IO methods are strictly byte oriented—you cannot tell them which character set encoding they should use.

This is different in Java, for example, where all strings are encoded with a Unicode encoding internally and all IO classes support different character set encodings. They distinguish between byte streams and character streams.

To read an input stream that uses a particular encoding, you can use a java.io.InputStreamReader and initialize it with an InputStream and a character set encoding:

```
InputStreamReader in = new InputStreamReader(System.in, 'UTF-8');
```

The reader called in in the previous example reads bytes from the console and interprets them as characters encoded in UTF-8.

If we need such a feature in Ruby, we have to do the conversion manually. Thanks to Iconv, this is a piece of cake:

File 117

```
Line 1   require 'iconv'

         class IO
           def IO.i18n_read(name, from_cs = 'utf-8', to_cs = 'iso-8859-1')
     5         converter = Iconv.new(to_cs, from_cs)
               converter.iconv(read(name))
             end
         end

    10   content = IO.i18n_read('data/utf8.txt')
         puts "#{content} (#{content.length} bytes)"
```

In an UTF-8 terminal the previous program prints the following:

```
M?ller (6 bytes)
```

We added a method called i18n_read() to the IO class that allows us to specify an input and an output character set. Now we can specify which character set encoding the creator of the file used and which encoding we'd like to work with.

Iconv is sufficient as long as you don't have to manipulate data. If you want to display it only on a web site, for example, set the character set encoding of the HTML pages and the HTTP header content-type appropriately, or convert the data using Iconv.

Date and Time Formats

Back in the good old days of C programming, you had nothing but the printf() family of functions to format textual data. Sometimes you needed esoteric stuff such as strftime(), but even then you didn't want to know that there were different calendars such as the Gregorian and the Julian, and you didn't want to know that there were people who did not use "am" and "pm" in timestamps.

This kind of thinking no longer cuts it. The creators of platforms such as J2EE and .NET tried to solve typical i18n problems once and for all. Despite this, many programs that run on these platforms are often not capable of dealing with i18n issues. So what's the problem? Are the libraries buggy? Are the developers too stupid? They aren't, but often the APIs of the standard classes are much too complicated. Today you have beasts such as Java's Calendar and DateFormat classes that enable you to calculate your grandma's next 20 birthdays and print them in Klingon standard time, but seemingly simple tasks such as printing the current date need several method calls.

Perhaps surprisingly, in Ruby you have the best-of-breed classes when it comes to time and dates: the Time, Date, and DateTime classes provide everything you're likely to need for date and time management. They even come with excellent documentation.[14] In addition, you can still hack away with sprintf(), strftime(), and friends.[15].

You won't run into serious problems as long as you output dates only in a numerical format such as 2006-01-09 or 30/09/1972. As soon as you want to output the name of a month or the name of a day, you have to manage the names for every language yourself if you use the standard classes. Ruby's Date and Time classes provide only the English names:

File 114

```
Line 1    require 'date'

          birthday = Date.new(1972, 9, 30)
          puts birthday.strftime('It was a %A in %B.')
```

This prints the following:

```
It was a Saturday in September.
```

If you want to print the German translation, do something like the following:

File 114

```
Line 1    MONTHS = {
            :de => %w(
              placeholder Januar Februar März April Mai Juni
              Juli August September Oktober November Dezember
    5       )
          }

          DAYS = {
            :de => %w(
    10        Sonntag Montag Dienstag Mittwoch Donnerstag Freitag Samstag
            )
          }

          month_name = MONTHS[:de][birthday.month]
    15    day_name = DAYS[:de][birthday.wday]
          puts "Es war ein %s im Monat %s." % [day_name, month_name]
```

Then you'll get this result:

```
Es war ein Samstag im Monat September.
```

---

[14]See http://www.ruby-doc.org/stdlib/libdoc/date/rdoc and http://www.ruby-doc.org/stdlib/libdoc/time/rdoc

[15]Isn't it interesting that Sun added sprintf()-like behavior recently to the Java platform? (http://java.sun.com/j2se/1.5.0/docs/api/java/text/MessageFormat.html)

That means you have to manage the translation of month and day names for every language you'd like to support. In the following section you'll learn how to solve this kind of problem (alternatively, you can look at Section 6.1, *ICU4R*, on page 251).

Managing Message Text

One of the most important issues when localizing software is the management of message text. Every program whose source code reaches a critical mass outputs hundreds or even thousands of different messages. No matter whether the program has a text interface, a batch interface, or a GUI, it usually has to ask for input and print results or error messages.

Translating every single message into another language is already a lot of work, so it would be nice if you didn't also have to worry about the technical details of managing the different translations in your programs. Fortunately, the GNU foundation has created the gettext command.[16] Even better: Masao Mutoh has created a Ruby version called Ruby-GetText.[17]

In principle, using the gettext family of commands is simple. To localize all messages of your program, you have to perform the following steps:

1. Pass all hard-coded strings in your program to one of the gettext methods (_(str), gettext(), etc.).

portable object template

2. Run rgettext to create a .pot (*portable object template*) file that contains a list of all messages to be translated.

portable object

3. For every language you'd like to support create a copy of the .pot file, and give it the extension .po (*portable object*).

4. Edit the .po files, and translate every message.

machine objects

5. Turn all portable objects into *machine objects* with the rmsgfmt command. The machine objects have the extension .mo.

When you run the following program:

File 124
```
Line 1   require 'gettext'
  -      include GetText
  -
  -      bindtextdomain('sample')
```

---

[16]http://www.gnu.org/software/gettext
[17]http://gettext.rubyforge.org

```
5   puts _('Our first example!')
-   str = gettext('Translate me!')
-   puts str
```

it prints the following:

```
Our first example!
Translate me!
```

We tell rgettext where to look for a particular translation of our message texts with the bindtextdomain(domain,path=nil,locale=nil,charset=nil) method. This points it to a file that can be found in the following subdirectory: path/locale/LC_MESSAGES/domain.mo. The parameters are as follows:

domain

Is a symbolic name for the translation package.

path

Points to the directory that contains the .mo files. If it's nil and the environment variable GETTEXT_PATH is not set, gettext searches in /usr/share/locale and /usr/local/share/locale.

locale

Specifies the locale (de_DE, en_US, and so on) to be used in the current file. If it is nil, the following environment variables will be checked consecutively: LC_ALL, LC_TYPE, LC_MESSAGES, and LANG. If they are all empty, the system's default language will be used. You should not normally set this value explicitly, because doing so defeats the purpose of gettext.

charset

Sets the output character set of the translated messages. If it is nil and the environment variable OUTPUT_CHARSET is not set, it defaults to the system's character set. You shouldn't set this variable explicitly.

Let's localize our little example step by step, creating a German translation. First, we extract all the messages with rgettext:

```
mschmidt:/tmp> rgettext sample.rb -o sample.pot
```

The newly created file sample.pot looks as follows:

```
msgid ""
msgstr ""
"Project-Id-Version: PACKAGE VERSION\n"
"POT-Creation-Date: 2006-01-12 19:28+0100\n"
"PO-Revision-Date: 2006-01-12 19:28+0100\n"
```

```
"Last-Translator: FULL NAME <EMAIL@ADDRESS>\n"
"Language-Team: LANGUAGE <LL@li.org>\n"
"MIME-Version: 1.0\n"
"Content-Type: text/plain; charset=UTF-8\n"
"Content-Transfer-Encoding: 8bit\n"
"Plural-Forms: nplurals=INTEGER; plural=EXPRESSION;\n"

#: sample.rb:5
msgid "Our first example!"
msgstr ""

#: sample.rb:6
msgid "Translate me!"
msgstr ""
```

It starts with a list of meta-information, followed by all messages that have to be translated. Messages aren't identified by an artificial identifier but by the message text itself.

For every language we'd like to support, we have to create a portable object (.po) file:

```
mschmidt:/tmp> mkdir de
mschmidt:/tmp> cp sample.pot de/sample.po
```

Then we have to translate every message in the .po file. In our case the result looks like this:

File 121
```
msgid ""
msgstr ""
"Project-Id-Version: Sample 0.0.1\n"
"POT-Creation-Date: 2006-01-12 19:28+0100\n"
"PO-Revision-Date: 2006-01-12 19:28+0100\n"
"Last-Translator: Maik Schmidt\n"
"Language-Team: DE <de@li.org>\n"
"MIME-Version: 1.0\n"
"Content-Type: text/plain; charset=UTF-8\n"
"Content-Transfer-Encoding: 8bit\n"
"Plural-Forms: nplurals=INTEGER; plural=EXPRESSION;\n"

#: sample.rb:5
msgid "Our first example!"
msgstr "Unser erstes Beispiel!"

#: sample.rb:6
msgid "Translate me!"
msgstr "Übersetze mich!"
```

Now we turn the translation into a machine object, creating a .mo file that contains a more compact representation. Usually, you will put them into a directory called locale that itself contains a subdirectory for every language supported (actually, we put it under a directory called LC_MESSAGES, which is a convention for affirmative and negative system responses):

```
mschmidt:/tmp> mkdir -p locale/de/LC_MESSAGES
mschmidt:/tmp> rmsgfmt de/sample.po \
> -o ./locale/de/LC_MESSAGES/sample.mo
```

Finally, we test whether everything works as expected:

```
mschmidt:/tmp> export GETTEXT_PATH=./locale
mschmidt:/tmp> LANG=de_DE ruby sample.rb
Unser erstes Beispiel!
Übersetze mich!
```

We set the GETTEXT_PATH environment variable to tell gettext where to search for .mo files (if your program does not work as expected, start it in debug mode with ruby -d). For the runtime of our sample script, we set the LANG variable to a German locale.

For the simplest cases this is all you need, but sometimes messages are a bit more dynamic (for example, when the value of a variable dictates whether you'd choose a plural or singular form of a message):

File 122

```
Line 1   require 'gettext'
     -   include GetText
     -   bindtextdomain("plural")
     -   0.upto(3) do |i|
     5     printf(
     -       n_("%d file was removed.\n", "%d files were removed.\n", i),
     -       i
     -     )
     -   end
```

This prints the following:

```
0 files were removed.
1 file was removed.
2 files were removed.
3 files were removed.
```

You can specify different text for singular and plural forms of a message with the n_(singular,plural,quantity) method. You can define a "plural rule" in the portable object that determines—depending on the value of quantity—which message should be used.

In our current example gettext didn't just help us with translating a message text; it helped choose the right one. Although we did not specify which message text to choose, the output is correct, because by default gettext chooses the first message text only if the parameter value is 1 (usually a good guess for a singular form).

A nice-looking German translation is a bit more difficult, because we need three different texts. Let's create the portable object first:

```
mschmidt:/tmp> rgettext plural.rb -o plural.pot
mschmidt:/tmp> cp plural.pot de/plural.po
```

After editing plural.po, it looks like this:

File 120

```
msgid ""
msgstr ""
"Project-Id-Version: Sample 0.0.1\n"
"POT-Creation-Date: 2006-01-14 10:07+0100\n"
"PO-Revision-Date: 2006-01-14 10:07+0100\n"
"Last-Translator: Maik Schmidt\n"
"Language-Team: DE <de@li.org>\n"
"MIME-Version: 1.0\n"
"Content-Type: text/plain; charset=UTF-8\n"
"Content-Transfer-Encoding: 8bit\n"
"Plural-Forms: nplurals=3; plural=(n < 2 ? n : 2)\n"

#: plural.rb:5
msgid "%d file was removed.\n"
msgid_plural "%d files were removed.\n"
msgstr[0] "Keine Dateien wurden gelöscht.\n"
msgstr[1] "Eine Datei wurde gelöscht.\n"
msgstr[2] "%d Dateien wurden gelöscht.\n"
```

For the first time we had to change one of the portable object headers: Plural-Forms. This header specifies how to determine a plural form. It consists of two parts: nplurals defines how many plural forms a message may have, and plural is set to a piece of Ruby code that returns the index of the message text to be used for a particular parameter value. In our case we have different plural forms for 0, for 1, and for values that are greater than 1. Finally, we have to define the translated message texts in array syntax.

It's time for a final test run:

```
mschmidt:/tmp> rmsgfmt de/plural.po \
> -o ./locale/de/LC_MESSAGES/plural.mo
mschmidt:/tmp> export GETTEXT_PATH=./locale
mschmidt:/tmp> LANG=de_DE ruby plural.rb
Keine Dateien wurden gelöscht.
Eine Datei wurde gelöscht.
2 Dateien wurden gelöscht.
3 Dateien wurden gelöscht.
```

Perfect! gettext is a mature and powerful tool.[18] Its Ruby implementation is comprehensive, and often it will be everything you need to localize your software.

Conclusion

It will take some time until Ruby fully supports all the techniques that are necessary to create fully internationalized applications. Fortunately, it will probably take even longer until all software developers really understand what these techniques are. ;-)

In the meantime you should keep in mind that many important tips and tricks related to internationalization and localization are completely independent of a particular programming language:

- Always test your applications with non-ASCII content from the beginning. The sooner you notice that your program fails miserably when Özgür Müller wants to get some stuff delivered to Düsseldorf, the better the chances that you can quickly fix it.

- Structure data—especially address data—as finely grained as possible, because it's easier to create different output formats when you need them.

- Do not hardwire message texts, icons, and other resources. Use tools like gettext instead.

- Do not hardwire output formats for dates, numbers, currencies, etc.

- If you can specify an encoding (e.g., in HTTP headers or HTML pages), do it. At least it will make you think about it.

- Encapsulate string manipulations carefully so you can replace them easily as soon as Ruby gets better i18n support.

- Delegate i18n issues to external sources if they have better support. If, for example, your database provides a to_upper(text) function that correctly converts a string into uppercase, use it.

---

[18]Read its manual (`http://www.gnu.org/software/gettext/manual/gettext.html`) if you want to get the best out of it. Although it covers the C version, you'll learn a lot of useful tricks for the Ruby version, too.

6.2 Logging

Typical enterprise production systems are often implemented as distributed architectures where lots of server processes that do not have any user interfaces communicate with each other. As a result, enterprise systems are full of log files. You probably already deal with some of these, such as the ones created by the Apache web server or the Unix syslog daemon.

Log files are used for different purposes:

- As a poor man's debugger
- For creating statistics
- For troubleshooting
- For monitoring purposes

If you choose your logging strategy carefully, a whole tool suite can be built around the log files of your program. For the Apache web server, for example, programs can take the logs and create access statistics, click streams, and so on. Because it logs messages in a standard format, this whole process is decoupled from the web server.

In this section we'll introduce the two logging tools that are available for Ruby, Logger and Log4r.

Logging with Logger

The standard distribution of Ruby provides logging support in the form of the Logger class. It's pretty straightforward to use:

File 147

```
require 'logger'
logger = Logger.new(STDOUT)
logger.debug("Look, Ma: I've created my first logger...")
logger.info('... and started a program.')
logger.warn("It's getting boring.")
```

Our first example prints something like this to the console:

File 146

```
D, [2005-03-05T08:11:17.305000 #3012] DEBUG - :
    Look, Ma: I've created my first logger...
I, [2005-03-05T08:11:17.305000 #3012]  INFO - :
    ... and started a program.
W, [2005-03-05T08:11:17.305000 #3012]  WARN - :
    It's getting boring.
```

As expected, we got three output lines. Big deal—we could've achieved the same results using simple puts() statements. But Logger has a lot more to offer than this.

Log Levels

Every message that is logged with Logger has an associated log level:

```
DEBUG < INFO < WARN < ERROR < FATAL < UNKNOWN
```

The log levels are ordered by priority, so a warning message is more important than a debug message. For every log level there is a corresponding method that logs a message with a certain priority. This is especially useful for filtering and suppressing messages. For example, debug messages are good for debugging purposes only, and in a production system they may be annoying or could even slow down your process. Hence, it is possible to set a threshold for a Logger so only messages with a priority bigger or equal to the current threshold value get logged:

File 150

```
Line 1  require 'logger'
     -  logger = Logger.new(STDOUT)
     -  logger.level = Logger::WARN
     -  logger.debug('You will not see me ...')
     5  logger.info('... or me.')
     -  logger.warn("I've warned you!")
     -  logger.error('Ouch!')
```

In line 3 we have set the threshold to WARN, so only the last two messages get logged:

```
W, [2005-09-26T08:59:02.567292 #408]  WARN -- : I've warned you!
E, [2005-09-26T08:59:02.570480 #408] ERROR -- : Ouch!
```

The set of available log levels is fixed, so if you need something other than the six levels provided by Logger, you'll have to use Log4r (see Section 6.2, *Logging with Log4r*, on page 267) instead.

Logging to Files

Printing messages to the console doesn't cut it in a production environment. At the very least we'd like to store the output of our program in a file. Therefore, Logger's new() method accepts a file name or an object derived from IO. This is how the file name variant works:

File 148

```
logger = Logger.new('logger_with_file.log')
logger.info('Logging to a file now.')
```

This example creates a file called logger_with_file.log in the current directory. Your program will log to it until your file system becomes full. To prevent such accidents (and angry calls from your system administrator), Logger supports so-called *rotating loggers* that automatically create generations of log files:

File 149

```
logger = Logger.new('rotating_logger.log', 2, 512)
10.times { logger.info('Wasting space and time...') }
```

This will create a rotating Logger, which renames the current log file whenever its size exceeds 512 bytes after logging a message.[19] The file name will be generated by appending a number, so after running the program, we have two files in the current directory: rotating_logger.log and rotating_logger.log.0.

In addition, it's possible to create new generations of log files depending on periods of time. Logger.new('sys.log', 'daily') will create a Logger that changes the log file daily. Other options are weekly and monthly.

Logging to ordinary files is what you will need 99% of the time, but sometimes it's useful to log to an arbitrary IO object, such as a StringIO in the following example.

File 148

```
require 'stringio'
buffer = StringIO.new
io_logger = Logger.new(buffer)
io_logger.debug('Logging with IO.')
puts buffer.string
```

This produces the following:

```
D, [2005-09-26T09:52:34.393910 #510] DEBUG -- : Logging with IO.
```

By writing your own class derived from IO, it's possible to create sophisticated loggers with Logger, but if you really need such a beast, you might be better off using Log4r.

The Log Line Format

Logger's biggest weakness is its lack of configuration options, especially regarding the format of the log lines. They always look like this:

```
log level, [timestamp #pid] log level -- progname: message
```

The elements are separated by different characters: the abbreviated log level is separated by a comma from the timestamp, timestamp and process ID are put in square brackets, and so on. Wouldn't it be much

---

[19]We set the limit low here to show rotation in action. In production, you're likely to set the size limit to something in the megabyte range.

How and What Should I Log?

Choosing a log file format does not seem like a big decision, but you should consider it carefully. The biggest challenge is to make it suitable for both human readers and automatic processes. If you have to spend minutes (or even hours) watching a log file using less or tail to find an obscure bug, you will be grateful if you don't have to read the same useless debug messages over and over again. You will be even more grateful if you can quickly come up with a little shell script that will do the job for you.

Make sure you always write all vital information into the log file. Nothing is worse than having your application behave unexpectedly but seeing no evidence of a problem in the log file. In an ideal world, the log file should contain everything you need to diagnose the problem. It is a good idea to log every input value your program receives so you can at least create a unit test (and you have lots of them, don't you?) to reproduce the error on your development box.

Especially in enterprise environments, standardizing log file layout and timestamp format pays off quickly.

---

easier to automatically process a log file if its format were a bit more consistent? Unfortunately, you cannot change the format easily.[20]

There is one piece of customization: the timestamp's format can be changed by setting the instance variable datetime_format to a format string supported by strftime(). For example, you could write the following assignment:

```
logger.datetime_format = '%Y-%m-%d %H:%M:%S'
```

Logging with Log4r

For many purposes Logger is sufficient, but sometimes you need more sophisticated features. One of the biggest disadvantages of Logger is the lack of customizable log formats (in the current version) and the inflexibility of log destinations. In a multithreaded environment, for example,

---

[20]At least not in the version that ships with Ruby 1.8.2. The next generation may provide such an option.

it is usually helpful to log the ID of the current thread. In a distributed environment, logging to a local file may not meet your needs. With the basic Logger class, though, you don't have many options.

In the Java, C++, Perl, and Python worlds, the log4* family (log4j, log4cpp, Log4perl, and log4p) sets the standard for logging. Thanks to Leon Torres, we have a Log4r, too. It can be used like this:

File 140

```
Line 1    require 'rubygems'
   -      require 'log4r'
   -      include Log4r

   5      joker = Logger.new('joker')
   -      joker.outputters = Outputter.stdout
   -      joker.info('I am back!')
   -      joker.warn('This is my last warning, Batman!')
```

This produces the following:

```
INFO joker: I am back!
WARN joker: This is my last warning, Batman!
```

For convenience we installed Log4r as a Gem (read more about Gems in Section 6.4, *RubyGems*, on page 302), so we have to require 'rubygems'. To save some keystrokes, we used include to bring the Log4r module into our program's namespace.

We first create a Logger instance on line 5, giving it the name joker. By default, the Logger objects in Log4r do nothing with the messages you give them. To see the messages appear on the console, in a file, and so on, you have to explicitly assign one or more *outputters* to the Logger instance. On line 6 we make sure that Joker's messages can be seen on the console, and in the following lines an information message and a warning are sent to our first Logger. Admittedly, the output is a bit spartan, but we will beautify it later.

Because superheroes are usually a bit short of time, they are interested only in the really important statements and serious threats coming from their archenemies. Log4r allows our heroes to increase the log level by setting joker.level = WARN, so Joker's annoying info and debug messages will be suppressed and so only the really scary stuff will appear on the ticker in the Batcave. Our little program already demonstrates two of the most important classes in the Log4r class hierarchy, Logger and Outputter (the latter is equivalent to log4j's Appender class.) Together with the Formatter class (called Layout in log4j), they form the basis for Log4r. We'll dissect them in the following sections.

Loggers

The Logger class is the interface to the whole logging system. You can create as many Logger objects as you like. Each must have a unique name, because Log4r organizes them in a hierarchy. Usually, you will create a separate Logger for every class with the same name as the class. This is only a convention: you can name your loggers in any way you like.

Logger objects have methods for every log level; debug(), info(), warn(), error(), and fatal(). All take the message to be logged. Every Logger holds a threshold value. When one of these methods is called, the logger checks whether the message's level is bigger or equal to the current threshold. If yes, the message is sent to *all* outputters belonging to the Logger. Otherwise, the message is ignored. Log4r's default levels are as follows:

```
DEBUG < INFO < WARN < ERROR < FATAL
```

Log4r's Level class allows you to completely redefine the log levels. You can add new levels and change the order of existing levels. You could, for example, implement Sun's log-level hierarchy for Java:[21]

```
File 136    Line 1   require 'rubygems'
              -      require 'log4r'
              -      require 'log4r/configurator'
              -      include Log4r
              5
              -      Configurator.custom_levels(
              -          :FINEST, :FINER, :FINE, :CONFIG,
              -          :INFO, :WARNING, :SEVERE
              -      )
             10
              -      logger = Logger.new('java-style')
              -      logger.outputters = Outputter.stdout
              -      logger.finest('Who needs this?')
              -      logger.config('Or this?')
             15      logger.info('yo')
```

This produces the following:

```
FINEST java-style: Who needs this?
CONFIG java-style: Or this?
```

Do not worry if you don't exactly know what a Configurator is—we'll explain it shortly. To define your own hierarchy of log levels, you have

---

[21]http://java.sun.com/j2se/1.5.0/docs/api/java/util/logging/Level.html

to call custom_levels(*levels) and pass it a list of all the levels you want your Logger objects to have. This list has to be in ascending order of the log-level priority. You can use strings or symbols for the level names. Level names have to start with an uppercase letter, but the names of their corresponding log methods will be completely lowercase. You should define your custom levels before you do anything else.

All Logger objects are children of the RootLogger singleton. This can be obtained by calling Logger.root or Logger.global. To navigate through the hierarchy of your Logger objects, you can use path-like structure:

File 141

```
Line 1    Logger.new('abe')
    -     Logger.new('abe::homer')
    -     Logger.new('abe::homer::bart')
    -     Logger['abe'].outputters = Outputter.stdout
    5
    -     Logger['abe'].debug('Once upon a time...')
    -     Logger['abe::homer'].debug("D'oh!")
    -     Logger['abe::homer::bart'].debug('Eat my shorts!')
```

This produces the following:

```
DEBUG abe: Once upon a time...
DEBUG homer: D'oh!
DEBUG bart: Eat my shorts!
```

Here we created a hierarchy of three different Loggers called *abe*, *homer*, and *bart*. By default the logger path delimiter is the *::* sequence (it can be changed by setting LoggerPathDelimiter). In our case we made *homer* a child of *abe*, and *bart* a child of *homer*. Although we have added an Outputter only to *abe*, the debug messages of *homer* and *bart* are logged, too. This happens because all children inherit their parent's outputters by default (you can change this behavior by setting the additive attribute of the parent to false).

Child Loggers also inherit the log-level threshold of their parents. This means that it's possible to change this value for a whole subtree of the Logger hierarchy:

File 141

```
Line 1    Logger['abe::homer'].level = INFO
    -     Logger['abe'].debug('*snore*')
    -     Logger['abe::homer'].debug("Marge!")
    -     Logger['abe::homer::bart'].debug('Ay, caramba!')
```

This produces the following:

```
DEBUG abe: *snore*
```

We have set the log-level threshold to INFO for all Loggers that are descendants of *homer* and therefore only the debug messages of the *abe* Logger are still visible.

Formatters

Until now our log messages have been pretty boring, because only the log level, the logger name, and the log message itself have been printed. So, where's all the fancy stuff that we're been promising? Where are the timestamps, process IDs, and so on? Don't panic! Log4r has it all. Let's start with a simple example:

File 138

```
Line 1   fancy = Logger.new('fancy')
    -    p = PatternFormatter.new(:pattern => "[%5l] %d: %m")
    -    fancy.add(StdoutOutputter.new('stdout', :formatter => p))
    -    fancy.info(%w(cat mouse dog))
    5    fancy.error('I am so nicely formatted!')
```

This produces the following:

```
[ INFO] 2005-09-25 16:33:41: catmousedog
[ERROR] 2005-09-25 16:33:41: I am so nicely formatted!
```

Did you notice that we have passed an array to the info() call? Log4r handles such things nicely, because it calls to_s() on every object that is passed to a log method.

All the formatting stuff Log4r has to offer is performed by the Format and PatternFormat classes. Usually, a pattern format is all you need, because it works the way printf() fans like. On line 2, we create a new Pattern-Format object that prints the log level (in square brackets and with a fixed width of five characters), the current timestamp, and the actual log message. Format strings may contain arbitrary characters and special sequences prefixed by a percent sign. All attributes available are listed in Figure 6.1, on the following page.

Because it's one of the most important pieces of information in log files, Log4r handles the formatting of timestamps separately. If your web shop is new and you do not expect too many requests, the following date format may be sufficient:

File 138

```
Line 1   p = PatternFormatter.new(
    -        :pattern => '[%5l] %d: %m',
    -        :date_pattern => '%Y',
    -    )
    5    fancy.add(StdoutOutputter.new('stdout', :formatter => p))
    -    fancy.info('Oh, our second customer.')
```

Format Specifier	Meaning
c	A Logger's name
C	A Logger's full name up to the RootLogger
d	Current timestamp (in ISO-8601 format by default). Otherwise the format returned by date_pattern() or by date_method() will be used.
t	Name of the file (and line number) that's the origin of the log message. Has the same format as Kernel.caller[0].
m	Whatever is returned when to_s() is called on the log message.
M	Whatever is returned when format_object() in class BasicFormatter is called on the log message. For example, exceptions will be nicely formatted automatically.
l	The log level.
%	The percent sign itself.

Figure 6.1: LOG4R FORMAT SPECIFIERS

This produces the following:

```
[ INFO] 2005: Oh, our second customer.
```

Or maybe you have so many requests that even microseconds matter. No problem, just pass the usec() method of the Time class as date_method to the PatternFormat constructor (date_method expects one of class Time's methods):

File 138

```
Line 1   p = PatternFormatter.new(
    -         :pattern => '[%5l] %d: %m',
    -         :date_method => :usec
    -     )
    5     fancy.add(StdoutOutputter.new('stdout', :formatter => p))
    -     fancy.info('Money, money, money.')
```

This produces the following:

```
[ INFO] 724998: Money, money, money.
```

Still unsatisfied? OK, then let's write a completely new Formatter. The following example formats exceptions in an aggressive manner:

File 135

```
Line 1   class ExceptionFormatter <  Log4r::Formatter
    -       def format(e)
    -           log = "[%5s] %s: %s\n" %
    -               [LNAMES[e.level], Time.now, e.data.to_s]
    5         if e.data.class == Exception
    -               msg = e.data.message
    -               size = msg.size
    -               line = '!' * (size + 6) + "\n"
    -               log << line
   10             log << '! ' + msg.center(size + 2) + " !\n"
    -               log << line
    -           end
    -           log
    -       end
   15    end
    -
    -     custom = Logger.new('my_first_format')
    -     outputter = StdoutOutputter.new(
    -         'stdout',
   20        :formatter => ExceptionFormatter
    -     )
    -     custom.add(outputter)
    -     custom.info(%w(cat mouse dog))
    -     custom.fatal(Exception.new('ALAAARRRRMMM!'))
   25    custom.error('I am so nicely formatted!')
```

This produces the following:

```
[ INFO] Sun Sep 25 18:17:12 CEST 2005: catmousedog
[FATAL] Sun Sep 25 18:17:12 CEST 2005: ALAAARRRRMMM!
```

```
!!!!!!!!!!!!!!!!!!!!
!  ALAAARRRRMMM!   !
!!!!!!!!!!!!!!!!!!!!
[ERROR] Sun Sep 25 18:17:12 CEST 2005: I am so nicely formatted!
```

Writing your own formatter is simple: derive a class from Formatter, and override the format(event) method that gets passed the current log event as an instance of LogEvent. The LogEvent class encapsulates the attributes belonging to a single log message: the log level, the logger name, the message itself, and so on (the LNAMES hash we have used in line 4 maps the numerical log levels to their textual representations). At the end of format(), return a string in your selected format.

Outputters

Log messages are pretty useless if they don't appear somewhere. Log4r supports the concept of outputters that receive log messages and "visualizes" them somehow. You can print them to the console, write them to a file, send them via e-mail, or send them to a syslog daemon (see Figure 6.2, on page 276, for a complete list).

Each Logger can have many outputters. You can add them to the outputters array at any time. In addition to the log level threshold of the Logger, each Outputter has a threshold, too. It can be set with the only_at(*levels) method (for example, outputter.only_at(ERROR, FATAL)).

Log4r comes with a lot of configurable outputters. Usually these will do everything you need. However, you can also create your own outputters if you need something special.

The following class implements a buffered outputter that consumes a certain number of log events and then logs them all at once whenever a configurable threshold value has been reached or a fatal event has been logged:

File 137

```
Line 1    class BufferedOutputter < IOOutputter
     -      def initialize(name, io, options = {})
     -        super(name, io, options)
     -        @out = io
     5        @last_events = []
     -        @max_events = options[:max_events] || 50
     -      end
     -
     -      def canonical_log(event)
     10        @last_events << event
     -        if @last_events.size >= @max_events ||
     -            LNAMES[event.level] == 'FATAL'
```

```
       -              @last_events.each { |e| super(e) }
       -              @last_events = []
      15          end
       -        end
       -      end
       -
       -    logger = Logger.new('buffered-outputter')
      20    outputter = BufferedOutputter.new(
       -        'buffered',
       -        $stdout,
       -        :max_events => 2
       -    )
      25    logger.outputters = outputter
       -    logger.debug('I cannot be seen immediately!')
       -    logger.info('Now both are there!')
```

This produces the following:

```
DEBUG buffered-outputter: I cannot be seen immediately!
 INFO buffered-outputter: Now both are there!
```

Because BufferedOutputter needs a number of IO facilities, we chose to subclass IOOutputter, rather than Outputter. The initialize(name, out, options) method expects the outputter's name, the IO object to write to, and an optional options hash.

Beginning on line 9 we override the canonical_log(logevent) method. This is responsible for handling a log event that has made its way to our outputter.

By the time a log event arrives here, it has passed all log-level checks and is actually meant to be logged. We add every event to our current list of events. Whenever this list exceeds the maximum size or a fatal event is logged, we delegate the logging of every buffered event to Log4r's default implementation by calling super().

In our main program we create new Logger and BufferedOutputter objects. We associate the outputter with $stdout, so all outputs will appear on the console. To make sure we will see anything, we set max_events to 2.

Configuration

Until now we have configured all our Loggers manually in the code. For demonstration purposes this is perfect, but in a production system you want to have configuration files that can be safely edited without touching a single line of your program. Log4r gives you the freedom to choose XML or YAML as the format of your configuration files.

Outputter	Purpose
IOOutputter	Logs to an arbitrary IO object.
StdoutOutputter	Logs to STDOUT.
StderrOutputter	Logs to STDERR.
FileOutputter	Logs to a single file.
RollingFileOutputter	Logs to a file and automatically maintains a generation of log files depending on their size, that is, files will be closed and renamed at a certain size.
DateFileOutputter	Logs to a file and automatically maintains a generation of log files depending on their timestamp: files will be closed and renamed daily, monthly, etc.
SyslogOutputter	Logs to the syslog daemon.
EmailOutputter	Sends log messages via e-mail.
RemoteOutputter	Sends log messages to a remote LogServer instance.

Figure 6.2: LOG4R OUTPUTTERS

Configurator is a central component that controls most of the configuration options (we have already used it in Section 6.2, *Loggers*, on page 269, to configure our own log levels). Its most important methods are load_xml_file(file_name) and load_xml_string(xml_string). These are used to configure Log4r using its XML dialect. A typical example looks like:

File 142

```
Line 1    <log4r_config>
    -        <pre_config>
    -          <custom_levels>
    -            FINEST, FINER, FINE, CONFIG,
    5            INFO, WARNING, SEVERE
    -          </custom_levels>
    -          <global level="FINE"/>
    -        </pre_config>
    -    </log4r_config>
```

Log4r's XML configuration has to be defined under a *<log4r_config>* element. This doesn't have to be the root element in the actual XML file. This allows you to embed the Log4r configuration into your application's global configuration file: you do not have to spread your configuration across several files.

Optionally, the XML file may contain a *<pre_config>* section, where custom log levels, configuration parameters, and a global log level can be defined.

If we store the previous XML configuration file in a file called log4r.xml, we can use it like this:

```
Line 1   Configurator.load_xml_file('log4r.xml')
    -    main = Logger.new('main')
    -    main.outputters = Outputter.stdout
    -    main.finest("That's how my coffee should be!")
    5    main.fine("That's ok, too.")
```

This produces the following:

```
FINE main: That's ok, too.
```

Because we have set the global log level to FINE, only the second message gets logged.

Using parameters defined in the *<pre_config>* section, we can communicate between the Configurator class and the configuration file:

```
<log4r_config>
    <pre_config>
      <parameter name="pattern" value="%l [%d] %m"/>
    </pre_config>

    <outputter name="logfile" level="WARN">
      <type>FileOutputter</type>
      <filename>#{basepath}/main.log</filename>
    </outputter>

    <logger name="main" level="DEBUG" trace="true">
      <outputters>stdout, logfile</outputters>
    </logger>
</log4r_config>
```

We initialize the basepath variable used in the previous configuration file in our Ruby program:

```
Line 1   Configurator['basepath'] = '/tmp'
    -    Configurator.load_xml_file('log4r2.xml')
    -    main = Logger['main']
    -    main.debug('On console only.')
    5    main.warn('On console and in file.')
```

This is where the fun begins! We have configured a Logger with two outputters for the first time. One prints to STDOUT and the other one into a file (/tmp/main.log). On the console we have the following:

```
DEBUG main(pre_config_parameters.rb:11): On console only.
WARN main(pre_config_parameters.rb:12): On console and in file.
```

and /tmp/main.log contains the following:

```
WARN main(pre_config_parameters.rb:12): On console and in file.
```

There are configuration sections for every Log4r object: loggers, formatters, and outputters. As a rule of thumb, all attributes we have used as we have configured our objects manually are also available in the configuration files. Let's examine a complete example:

File 132

```
Line 1   <log4r_config>
    ·        <pre_config>
    ·            <global level="WARN"/>
    ·            <parameter name="pattern" value="%l [%d] %m"/>
    5        </pre_config>
    ·
    ·        <outputter name="console">
    ·          <type>StdoutOutputter</type>
    ·          <formatter type="PatternFormatter" pattern="#{pattern}">
   10            <date_pattern>%Y-%m-%d %H:%M:%S</date_pattern>
    ·          </formatter>
    ·        </outputter>
    ·
    ·        <outputter name="logfile" level="ERROR">
   15          <type>RollingFileOutputter</type>
    ·          <filename>#{basepath}/main.log</filename>
    ·          <maxsize>1048576</maxsize>
    ·          <count>5</count>
    ·          <trunc>false</trunc>
   20          <formatter type="PatternFormatter" pattern="#{pattern}">
    ·            <date_method>usec</date_method>
    ·          </formatter>
    ·        </outputter>
    ·
   25        <logger name="app">
    ·          <outputter>console</outputter>
    ·        </logger>
    ·
    ·        <logger name="db" outputters="logfile"/>
   30   </log4r_config>
```

Here we define two outputters called console and logfile. The first one writes its output to the console using a StdoutOutputter; the other uses a RollingFileOutputter that keeps up to five log files, each with a maximum size of 1MB. Both outputters use a PatternFormatter with the same format. Only the date format differs: for the console we use the date_pattern modifier, and for the log file we use date_method.

Then we define two loggers called app and db. app logs only to the console, and db logs into a log file. Running the following snippet:

```
Line 1    require 'log4r/outputter/rollingfileoutputter'
  -       include Log4r
  -       Configurator['basepath'] = '/tmp'
  -       Configurator.load_xml_file('complete.xml')
  5
  -       app = Logger['app']
  -       app.debug('Look at me!')
  -       app.warn('Look at Roy!')
  -
  10      db = Logger['db']
  -       db.error('DB logs go always into a file.')
  -       db.warn('But not this one.')
```

leaves these messages on our console:

```
WARN [471281] Look at Roy!
```

Because we have set the global log level to WARN in the *<pre_config>* section, only the second message sent to the app object gets logged. Our log file contains something like this:

```
ERROR [163338] DB logs go always into a file.
```

Only the first message is written, because the log level of the logfile outputter is ERROR.

You have to require all Log4r classes you've used in your configuration to prevent problems during the configuration process. For example, we had to explicitly require 'log4r/outputter/rollingfileoutputter'. Annoyingly, for the rolling file outputter, Log4r creates an empty /tmp/main.log file and starts logging in a file called /tmp/main000001.log. Note that we have set trunc to false. If we hadn't, our new log file would be truncated whenever we restart our program. That's usually not what you want.

For those who prefer YAML over XML's verbosity, Log4r has the Yaml-Configurator. Let's translate our previous example into YAML (see Section 3.5, *YAML Ain't Markup Language (YAML)*, on page 141, if you are not familiar with YAML):

```
log4r_config:
  pre_config:
    global:
      level: WARN
    my_pattern:
      - &pat "%l [%d] %m"
```

XML Parameters in Log4r

It's possible to use Ruby variables in Log4r configuration files, and vice versa. To pass a value from Ruby to the configuration, you can use the Configurator class like a hash:

```
Configurator['basepath'] = '/tmp'
```

In the configuration file, you can use it like this then:

```
<log4r_config>
    <pre_config>
        <parameters>
            <basepath>#{basepath}</basepath>
        </parameters>
        <parameter name="pattern" value="[%l] %d: %m"/>
    </pre_config>
</log4r_config>
```

On the other side, you can access parameters defined in the <pre_config> section of the XML configuration file in your Ruby program. For example, you can access the pattern parameter defined previously like this:

```
puts Configurator['pattern']
```

Most Log4r configuration parameters can be expressed in two ways, namely, as a value= attribute or as a child element. For example, the following definition:

```
<outputter name="main" filename="./log/main.log"/>
```

is equivalent to this:

```
<outputter>
  <name>main</name>
  <filename>./log/main.log</filename>
</outputter>
```

```
loggers:
  - name      : app
    outputters:
      - stdout

  - name      : db
    outputters:
      - logfile

outputters:
  - type      : StdoutOutputter
    name      : stdout
    formatter:
      date_pattern: '%Y-%m-%d %H:%M:%S'
      pattern    : *pat
      type       : PatternFormatter

  - type        : RollingFileOutputter
    level        : ERROR
    name         : logfile
    maxsize      : '1048576'
    count        : '5'
    date_pattern: '%Y%m%d'
    trunc        : 'false'
    filename     : "#{basepath}/main.log"
    formatter    :
      date_method : 'usec'
      pattern     : *pat
      type        : PatternFormatter
```

By replacing only the first two lines of the previous XML example, we achieve the same results with our YAML configuration:

```
Line 1   require 'log4r/yamlconfigurator'
   -     YamlConfigurator['basepath'] = '/tmp'
   -     YamlConfigurator.load_yaml_file('complete.yaml')
```

Performance Considerations

Logging is an invaluable tool in enterprise environments. But, like most things in life, logging has a dark side. Excessive logging will slow down your processes significantly, because logging usually causes a lot of I/O, and I/O is expensive. To prevent this, it's a good idea to execute some logging statements only when they are absolutely necessary. To help you do this, Log4r makes it easy for you to check the current log level:

```
Line 1   logger = Logger.new('perf')
   -     logger.outputters = Outputter.stdout
```

```
      long_list = %w(lots of elements)
    5  if logger.debug?
         long_list.each_with_index do |o, i|
           logger.debug("Element #{i}: #{o}")
         end
      end
```

Logging the contents of long_list—especially when it's really long—is an expensive operation, because you have to iterate over all elements and to_s() is called each time. Therefore, it makes sense to execute the appropriate method calls only when the debug log level is actually active. It should not be too surprising that all log methods are capable of processing code blocks, too.

Conclusion

Logger's API is as simple as it could be. Although it is often tempting, you should not use plain puts() statements to print messages even from simple scripts. Use Logger instead, because it's as easy to use as puts() and comes with a lot of benefits.

For bigger software systems that comprise several modules, you will run into Logger's limits soon. In these cases, you're better off using Log4r right from the beginning. It is highly configurable and has everything (and even more) you'd expect from a full-blown logging tool.

6.3 Creating Daemons and Services

On Unix operating systems, daemons are long-living processes that run in the background and do not have a controlling terminal. Often they are started when a computer is booted and then run forever. Their names usually end with d, as in syslogd or httpd. Because daemons are dangerous creatures, you have to tame them with a control script.

The Apache web server, for example, comes with the famous apachectl script that allows you to start, stop, or restart the server. Daemons exist in the Microsoft Windows world, too, but the superstitious folks in Redmond call them *services* instead.

In the following sections we show you how to create them on both platforms with Ruby.

Unix Daemons

According to *Unix Network Programming* [Ste98], you have to perform a lot of complicated tasks to safely create a daemon under Unix. You have to detach from the console, change the current working directory to a specific location (usually to the root directory /), set the file creation mask to 0, and close all unneeded file descriptors. Even for Unix wizards, it's not easy to remember these steps (how they are ordered is significant, too).

To make it even harder, your work isn't done after the daemon is running, because you still need a control script such as apachectl. It's therefore very nice that Thomas Uehlinger has created the Daemons package[22] that transparently handles all this for us. It turns an arbitrary Ruby script into a daemon process and automatically generates the appropriate control script for starting, restarting, and stopping it.

Do you remember the greeting card server from Section 5.1, *Another Day, Another Protocol*, on page 181? We didn't implement the complete architecture that could be seen in Figure 5.1, on page 183. One process is still missing: the one that actually prints the cards. In this section we will develop a daemon process that will do the job. Our print process is a little script that reads a particular directory every ten seconds, sends all .pdf files in the directory to a process called print_card, and deletes them afterward:

```
Line 1  require 'logger'

        path = ARGV[0] || '/tmp'
        interval = ARGV[1] || 10
     5  interval = interval.to_i

        logfile = File.dirname(__FILE__) + '/watcher.log'
        logger = Logger.new(logfile)
        logger.info('Started the watcher...')
    10
        loop do
          files = Dir["#{path}/*.pdf"]
          files.each do |filename|
            logger.info("Processing #{filename}.")
    15      %x(print_card #{filename})
            File.delete(filename)
          end
          sleep(interval)
        end
```

---

[22]http://daemons.rubyforge.org

Our little observer accepts two command-line parameters, the directory to be observed (/tmp by default) and the timer interval measured in seconds (10 by default). Then we create a logger to see what our process is doing. In line 7 we determine the full path name of the log file. This is very important, because we are going to turn our script into a daemon process, and these processes normally change their working directory to / when they start. The path variable has to contain an absolute path if we're to put the log file in the correct place.

The rest is fairly easy. We read the directory's content every interval seconds, execute a system command called print_card, and delete the file. Now let's turn our script into a full-blown Unix daemon process. Put these three lines into a file called watcher_control.rb.

File 112

```
Line 1    require 'rubygems'
    -     require 'daemons'
    -     Daemons.run('watcher.rb')
```

We can use this script to start, stop, or restart our process like this:

```
$ ruby watcher_control.rb start
$ ruby watcher_control.rb restart
$ ruby watcher_control.rb stop
```

To perform all this magic, Daemon writes the process ID into a file called watcher.rb.pid and reads it whenever it's needed.

You can pass command-line options after a double hyphen:

```
$ ruby watcher_control.rb start -- /tmp/cards/img 5
```

This command line starts our daemon process and looks for new .pdf files in the /tmp/cards/img directory every five seconds. It logs its activities into a file called watcher.log that lives in the same directory as the watcher script itself.

The Daemons class allows you to daemonize your programs in several ways. For example, it's possible to turn your script into a daemon by calling Daemons.daemonize at any time, but by doing so you lose the ability to use the _control script to administer your daemon.

For debugging purposes, there is a run option that starts the script in the foreground.

Windows Services

None of the nice things we learned in the preceding section will work on the Microsoft Windows platform, because Unix daemons depend on the fork() system call, which isn't available on Windows. Daniel Berger opened the Windows platform to Ruby programmers with his win32utils project.[23] Part of this project is win32-service. This allows us to create daemons (services) for Win32, too. It is not as convenient as the Daemons package, because it does not have automatic support for control scripts, but it certainly is helpful.

Do you remember our status monitor (see Section 4.1, *The PragBouquet Status Monitor*, on page 149) and the SOAP stock server (see Section 5.3, *SOAP*, on page 202)? To make sure the stock server is working properly, let's create a small script that periodically checks to see if the server is still alive. If it detects any problem, it sends a message to the status monitor. Our checks will not be too sophisticated—we'll test only whether the service is physically available, but for a first solution this approach is sufficient.

Because we install the observer script as a Windows service, we have to (partly) implement the interface of a Windows service:

File 110

```
Line 1   $:.unshift File.dirname(__FILE__)
     -   require 'status_monitor_client'
     -   require 'logger'
     -   require 'soap/rpc/driver'
     5   require 'win32/service'
     -   include Win32
     -
     -   class StockServerObserver < Daemon
     -     def initialize(opts = {})
    10       super()
     -       @opts = opts
     -     end
     -
     -     def service_init
    15       @interval = @opts[:interval] || 60
     -       @logger = Logger.new(@opts[:logfile] || 'c:/observer.log')
     -       @stock = SOAP::RPC::Driver.new(
     -         @opts[:soap_url] || 'http://localhost:2000',
     -         @opts[:soap_urn] || 'urn:Stock'
    20       )
     -       @stock.add_method('get_report')
     -       @sm = StatusMonitorClient.new(
     -         @opts[:sm_host] || '127.0.0.1',
     -         @opts[:sm_port] || 3333
    25       )
     -       @logger.info('Observer has been initialized.')
     -     end
```

---

[23]http://rubyforge.org/projects/win32utils

```
  -      def test_stock_service
 30        @stock.get_report.class == Hash
  -      end
  -
  -      def service_main
  -        @logger.info('Observer has been started.')
 35        sleep 1 while state != RUNNING
  -        while state == RUNNING
  -          if !test_stock_service
  -            msg = 'Stock service is not running.'
  -            @logger.warn(msg)
 40            @sm.warn('stock', msg)
  -          else
  -            @logger.info('Stock service is running.')
  -          end
  -          sleep(@interval)
 45        end
  -        @logger.info('Observer has been stopped.')
  -      end
  -    end
```

All the stuff related to our original task—observing the stock server—is fairly trivial. In the test_stock_service() method we perform a simple test to see whether the stock server is still alive. We call the get_report() method and verify that it returns a hash object. If the remote procedure call works properly, we can be fairly confident that the physical connection to our stock server is working. If it does not, we send a warning message to the status monitor.

We derived our StockServerObserver from the Win32::Daemon class, and we overrode the service_init() and service_main() methods. service_init() gets called when a service is initialized—we use it to create clients for the status monitor and the stock server. In addition, we initialize a Logger for logging the observer's status.

The service_main() method contains the main logic of the daemon. This is typically an "infinite" loop that waits for external events or performs a task periodically. In our case we call test_stock_service() every @interval seconds as long as the daemon's state is RUNNING. If test_stock_service() returns false or an exception is raised, we send a message to the status monitor.

Two facts are very important when developing Windows services:

- Windows services (like Unix daemons) change their working directory when they start, so you must specify all the files you need in

absolute form. To find Ruby libraries outside the standard directories, add the script's directory to Ruby's load path in the first
line.

- You should not rely upon being in a certain state. A lot of things
  regarding Windows services work asynchronously, because services are controlled from the outside with a control script or the
  services panel. Hence, in line 35 we wait until the service is actually running, because sometimes it needs a few seconds.

You cannot simply start our current script and expect that it turns
itself into a service. Every service has to have a name and it has to be
installed properly before starting it:

```
Line 1   require 'win32/service'
  -      include Win32
  -
  -      def install_service(name, display_name, executable)
  5        service = Service.new
  -        service.create_service do |s|
  -          s.service_name = name
  -          s.display_name = display_name
  -          s.binary_path_name = 'ruby ' + File.expand_path(executable)
  10         s.dependencies = []
  -        end
  -        service.close
  -        puts "#{name} has been installed."
  -      end
```

Call install_service() to install any Ruby program you like as a service.
Pass it a unique service name, the name that should be displayed in
the service list, and the path to a Ruby script that should be installed
as a service. The working of the function is fairly obvious, but line 9 is
interesting. Here we specify the program that is going to be installed
using (as is the case with all files referenced by a service) its absolute
file name.

Provided that our stock observer is in a file called stock_observer.rb, we
can now install it like this:

```
irb(main):002:0> service_name = 'StockObserver'
=> "StockObserver"
irb(main):003:0> install_service(
irb(main):004:1*    service_name,
irb(main):005:1*    'PragBouquet Observer',
irb(main):006:1*    'stock_observer.rb'
irb(main):007:1>    )
StockObserver has been installed.
=> nil
```

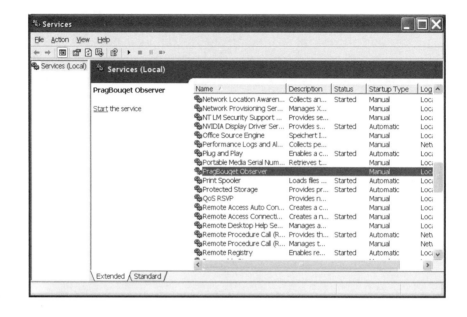

Figure 6.3: PRAGBOUQUET OBSERVER IN THE SERVICE CONTROL PANEL

Our internal service name is *StockObserver*, but in the service list it appears as *PragBouquet Observer*. Even though it's in the service list, it isn't running yet. You could start it using the Windows Services control panel (see Figure 6.3), but isn't it more fun to do it programmatically?

File 109

```
Line 1    def start_service(name)
   -         Service.start(name)
   -         started = false
   -         while !started
   5           s = Service.status(name)
   -           started = (s.current_state == 'running')
   -           break if started
   -           puts 'Trying to start service...'
   -           sleep 1
   10          end
   -         puts "#{name} was started."
   -       end
```

To safely start a service, call the start(name) method of the Service class, and wait until its status turns to *running*:

```
irb(main):004:0> start_service(service_name)
Trying to start service...
StockObserver was started.
 => nil
```

From now on the stock observer will send SOAP requests to the stock
server every minute until the end of time...or until we stop it:

e 109

```
Line 1    def stop_service(name)
    -         Service.stop(name)
    -         stopped = false
    -         while !stopped
    5             s = Service.status(name)
    -             stopped = (s.current_state == 'stopped')
    -             break if stopped
    -             puts 'Trying to stop service.'
    -             sleep 1
    10        end
    -         puts "#{name} was stopped."
    -     end
```

Stopping a service works exactly like starting it: call the stop() method
of the Service class, and wait until the service has the *stopped* state:

```
irb(main):005:0> stop_service(service_name)
StockObserver was stopped.
=> nil
```

Finally, we should be prepared to uninstall a service:

e 109

```
Line 1    def uninstall_service(name)
    -         begin
    -             Service.stop(name)
    -         rescue
    5         end
    -         Service.delete(name)
    -         puts "#{name} was uninstalled."
    -     end
```

That's all you need to turn your Ruby programs into Windows services.
The Daemon class provides many more useful and important methods, and the win32utils project is full of interesting stuff. If you want to
develop Ruby applications on the Windows platform, you must have a
look at it.

6.4 Build and Deployment Process

Compared to deployment processes needed when shipping software on
a CD or DVD to end users, deployment processes in enterprise environments are relatively simple. Often, they can be reduced to copying a
bunch of files from a development or integration platform to a production host. If anything goes wrong, bugs can be fixed in a single place
instead of providing all users with an update.

Additionally, installers for enterprise software do not need colorful wizards with bells and whistles or several hundred kilobytes of End User License Agreements (EULA). Nevertheless, all software—your own and the third-party products and the libraries they depend on—has to be deployed somehow. There are several alternatives for Ruby programs.

Many programming languages encourage developers to produce completely self-contained programs that bring everything they need with them. For example, it's not unusual for companies using Java to have several XML parsers (in dozens of versions) lying around on their production systems, because every application ships with its own xerces-xyz.jar.

Sometimes they are even bundled with their own version of the Java virtual machine. For C++ applications, people often link the required libraries into huge executable images or risk *DLL hell* by shipping the required shared libraries with each of their applications.

Ruby's (and Perl's, Python's, etc.) approach is different. It's oriented toward a more central installation philosophy, where all libraries are installed only once in the same directory. On Unix systems this is by default something like /usr/lib/ruby or /usr/local/lib/ruby and on Microsoft Windows boxes it's c:\Program Files\ruby\lib or c:\ruby\lib. (If you're looking for the source code of a certain library, these places are good starting points.)

You aren't constrained to have a single, central Ruby installation. You can install it wherever you want (and you can have multiple, independent installations on the same machine). On some platforms it's even possible to turn Ruby programs into self-contained executables that do not even depend on an existing Ruby installation.

Deploying with setup.rb

Back in the dark and ancient days of Ruby's childhood, nearly every developer who made available a library or script in the Ruby Application Archive (RAA) [24] wrote yet another proprietary installation program that usually copied some files to the central Ruby lib directory.

These programs were often quick 'n' dirty solutions that failed on many platforms: their authors did not know the nitty-gritty details of every environment their software was going to be installed in.

---

[24]http://raa.ruby-lang.org

Considering that generations of programmers contributed to tools like GNU's autoconf, it's not surprising that an individual Ruby coder would struggle with these issues.

Minero Aoki was fed up with the situation. He built a sophisticated solution, called setup.rb, that over time became extremely powerful. Before the appearance of the RubyGems project, it was the de facto standard for packaging Ruby software. As a result, there are still hundreds of projects out there that depend on it. It's still vital for every serious Ruby programmer to know how it works.

We'll demonstrate the use of setup.rb by installing the tmail library we used in Section 4.1, *"I'd Rather Use a Socket"*, on page 148 (for those who don't read books front to back: tmail is a library that supports the creation of e-mail messages in SMTP format). Before installing tmail, we have to get it somehow. Figure 6.4, on the following page shows how to download and unpack the current tmail distribution (by the way, the terminal application I've used on Mac OS X is iTerm.)[25] To download the file, of course, you can use wget, your favorite web browser, or whatever you prefer instead of the curl command I used.[26]

Part of the tarball is a file called setup.rb. This contains everything needed to install the tmail library on an arbitrary platform. The only prerequisites are Ruby and a C compiler. (The C compiler is necessary because tmail includes code written in C. If the software to be installed does not contain C extensions, a compiler is not needed.)

setup.rb is similar to GNU's autoconf; it divides the installation of software in a Unix environment into three steps.

With autoconf, you do something like the following:

1. ./configure
2. make
3. make install

Step 1 detects the specifics of the current environment: which C compiler is installed, the size of a native int, and so on. The second step builds the software from source. The final step copies everything to its final destination (so this step usually has to be performed by a user having root privileges).

---

[25]http://iterm.sourceforge.net
[26]Whatever you use, keep in mind that you'd usually have to specify a proxy server in an enterprise environment. For curl you'd have to add the option -x proxy_host:proxy_port.

```
● ○ ○                           Default                              ▭
                    ⎧ 1: Default │ 2: Default │ 3: Default ⎫
mschmidt:/tmp $ curl http://i.loveruby.net/archive/tmail/tmail-0.10.8.tar.gz \
> -o tmail-0.10.8.tar.gz
  % Total    % Received % Xferd  Average Speed   Time    Time     Time  Current
                                 Dload  Upload   Total   Spent    Left  Speed
100  122k  100  122k    0     0   18150      0  0:00:06  0:00:06 --:--:-- 24966
mschmidt:/tmp $ tar xfz- tmail-0.10.8.tar.gz
mschmidt:/tmp $ cd tmail-0.10.8
mschmidt:/tmp/tmail-0.10.8 $ ls
0ChangeLog              NEWS                    ext
BUGS                    README.en               install.log
COPYING                 README.ja               lib
ChangeLog               TODO                    sample
DEPENDS                 config.save             setup.rb
Incompatibilities       doc                     test
Incompatibilities.ja    doc.en
Makefile                doc.ja
mschmidt:/tmp/tmail-0.10.8 $ █
```

Figure 6.4: GETTING TMAIL FROM THE INTERNET

setup.rb works in an equivalent fashion—even the meaning of the three steps is the same as in the UNIX installation procedure described previously:[27]

1. ruby setup.rb config
2. ruby setup.rb setup
3. ruby setup.rb install

Let's examine the installation of the tmail library step by step. Figure 6.5, on page 294, shows the output of running ruby setup.rb config. The script automatically explored the environment and created two Makefiles that will be used in the next step to compile all C extensions needed by tmail. Platform-independent Makefiles are created by extconf.rb, which uses the mkmf library to do its dirty work. This step's

---

[27]In older versions an additional file called install.rb was part of the setup.rb project. It's not supported any longer, but you will still find it in many older packages.

output differs from package to package. For example, the majority of Ruby packages don't depend on C extensions; for these, no Makefiles are created.

Usually, the configuration step just detects where the Ruby installation is located on the current system. Its results are stored in a file called config.save that can be edited manually if necessary. On my box it looks as follows (all values starting with a $ sign can be configured during the installation process; you can also view the current configuration by running ruby setup.rb show):

le 151

```
bin-dir=$prefix/bin
site-ruby=$prefix/lib/ruby/site_ruby/1.8
prefix=/usr
ruby-path=/usr/bin/ruby
make-prog=make
rb-dir=$site-ruby
without-ext=no
ruby-prog=/usr/bin/ruby
site-ruby-common=$prefix/lib/ruby/site_ruby
std-ruby=$prefix/lib/ruby/1.8
data-dir=$prefix/share
so-dir=$prefix/lib/ruby/site_ruby/1.8/powerpc-darwin8.0
```

tmail depends on two C extensions (one for encoding and decoding of Base64 strings and one for scanning e-mails). In Figure 6.6, on page 295, you can see how running ruby setup.rb setup compiles these.

In our textbook example everything went fine, and the GNU compiler on my Mac happily produced the object files needed. However, if you have even a small amount of experience with Unix, you'll know that a lot can go wrong during this step.

Tools such as autoconf and setup.rb made it much easier to build and install software even on exotic hardware and operating systems, but there are still potential incompatibilities, and you have to be prepared for compiler warnings, errors, and so on.

This is especially true for the Microsoft Windows platform, where often no C compiler or make command is available. For popular tools and libraries you can sometimes get precompiled binaries, but often you are doomed to have to try to build it yourself. This can be a frustrating (and sleep-depriving) experience....

Finally, tmail has to be copied to the standard Ruby library directory. You can see how this can be achieved in Figure 6.7, on page 296. Nor-

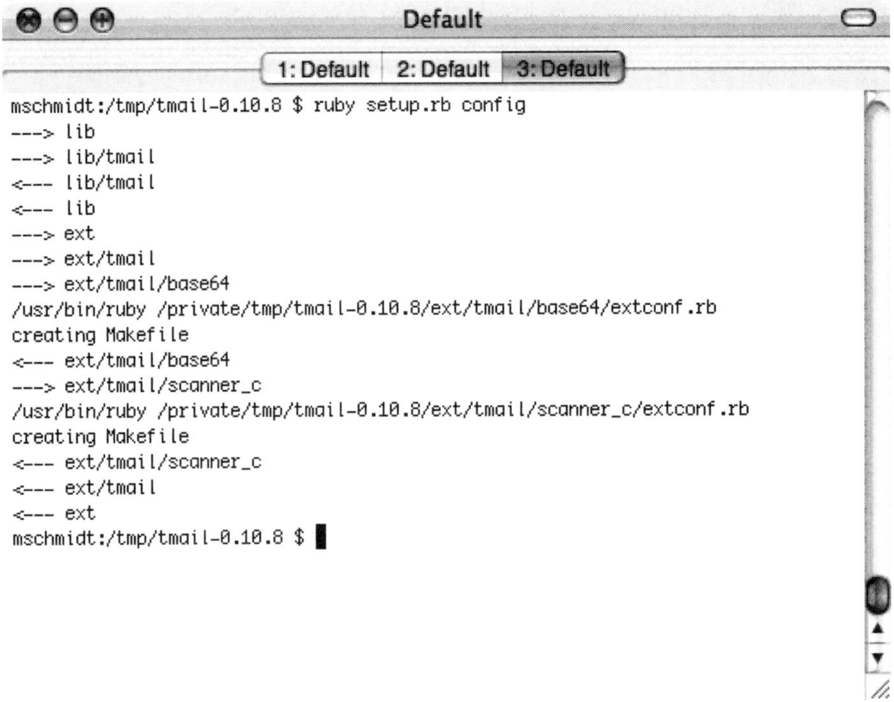

Figure 6.5: CONFIGURING TMAIL

mally Ruby libraries are installed in a systemwide directory, so the final step has to be performed by a user having root privileges.

As good citizens we did not log in as root, but we used the sudo command[28] instead.

Underprivileged?

Sometimes you do not have the root password and have no write permission for some directories. Sometimes you explicitly do not want to install your software in the standard paths for other reasons. setup.rb therefore supports some global options and some task-specific options that allow you to override nearly every setting that would normally be determined automatically. Using these, you can control where stuff goes.

---

[28]http://en.wikipedia.org/wiki/Sudo

```
  ●  ●  ●                    Default (80,28)                    ⬭

                   [ 1: Default | 2: Default | 3: Default ]
mschmidt:/tmp/tmail-0.10.8 $ ruby setup.rb setup
---> lib
---> lib/tmail
<--- lib/tmail
<--- lib
---> ext
---> ext/tmail
---> ext/tmail/base64
make
gcc -fno-common  -arch ppc -g -Os -pipe -fno-common  -arch ppc -pipe -pipe -fno-
common  -I. -I/usr/lib/ruby/1.8/powerpc-darwin8.0 -I/usr/lib/ruby/1.8/powerpc-da
rwin8.0 -I/private/tmp/tmail-0.10.8/ext/tmail/base64   -c base64.c
cc -dynamic -bundle -undefined suppress -flat_namespace  -L"/usr/lib" -o base64.
bundle base64.o  -lpthread -ldl -lobjc
<--- ext/tmail/base64
---> ext/tmail/scanner_c
make
gcc -fno-common  -arch ppc -g -Os -pipe -fno-common  -arch ppc -pipe -pipe -fno-
common  -I. -I/usr/lib/ruby/1.8/powerpc-darwin8.0 -I/usr/lib/ruby/1.8/powerpc-da
rwin8.0 -I/private/tmp/tmail-0.10.8/ext/tmail/scanner_c   -c scanner_c.c
cc -dynamic -bundle -undefined suppress -flat_namespace  -L"/usr/lib" -o scanner
_c.bundle scanner_c.o  -lpthread -ldl -lobjc
<--- ext/tmail/scanner_c
<--- ext/tmail
<--- ext
mschmidt:/tmp/tmail-0.10.8 $ █
```

Figure 6.6: Setting Up tmail

Considering good old Unix traditions, the most important global option is -q or --quiet. This completely mutes the output of setup.rb.

The --prefix option is often useful for the config and install tasks, because it allows you to specify the base directory of the installation. If you want to install a package in the lib/ruby directory right under your home directory, for example, run the following:

```
$ ruby setup.rb config --prefix=~/lib/ruby
```

Afterward, don't forget to set the environment variable RUBYLIB accordingly or to add the path specified in --prefix to your load path (by adding it to $:). Otherwise, the Ruby interpreter will not be able to find your freshly installed stuff.

```
mschmidt:/tmp/tmail-0.10.8 $ sudo ruby setup.rb install
---> lib
mkdir -p /usr/lib/ruby/site_ruby/1.8/
install tmail.rb /usr/lib/ruby/site_ruby/1.8/
---> lib/tmail
mkdir -p /usr/lib/ruby/site_ruby/1.8/tmail
install address.rb /usr/lib/ruby/site_ruby/1.8/tmail
install base64.rb /usr/lib/ruby/site_ruby/1.8/tmail
install compat.rb /usr/lib/ruby/site_ruby/1.8/tmail
install config.rb /usr/lib/ruby/site_ruby/1.8/tmail
install encode.rb /usr/lib/ruby/site_ruby/1.8/tmail
install header.rb /usr/lib/ruby/site_ruby/1.8/tmail
install info.rb /usr/lib/ruby/site_ruby/1.8/tmail
install loader.rb /usr/lib/ruby/site_ruby/1.8/tmail
install mail.rb /usr/lib/ruby/site_ruby/1.8/tmail
install mailbox.rb /usr/lib/ruby/site_ruby/1.8/tmail
install mbox.rb /usr/lib/ruby/site_ruby/1.8/tmail
install net.rb /usr/lib/ruby/site_ruby/1.8/tmail
install obsolete.rb /usr/lib/ruby/site_ruby/1.8/tmail
install parser.rb /usr/lib/ruby/site_ruby/1.8/tmail
install port.rb /usr/lib/ruby/site_ruby/1.8/tmail
install scanner.rb /usr/lib/ruby/site_ruby/1.8/tmail
install scanner_r.rb /usr/lib/ruby/site_ruby/1.8/tmail
install stringio.rb /usr/lib/ruby/site_ruby/1.8/tmail
install textutils.rb /usr/lib/ruby/site_ruby/1.8/tmail
install tmail.rb /usr/lib/ruby/site_ruby/1.8/tmail
install utils.rb /usr/lib/ruby/site_ruby/1.8/tmail
<--- lib/tmail
<--- lib
---> ext
---> ext/tmail
---> ext/tmail/base64
mkdir -p /usr/lib/ruby/site_ruby/1.8/powerpc-darwin8.0/tmail
install base64.bundle /usr/lib/ruby/site_ruby/1.8/powerpc-darwin8.0/tmail
<--- ext/tmail/base64
---> ext/tmail/scanner_c
mkdir -p /usr/lib/ruby/site_ruby/1.8/powerpc-darwin8.0/tmail
install scanner_c.bundle /usr/lib/ruby/site_ruby/1.8/powerpc-darwin8.0/tmail
<--- ext/tmail/scanner_c
<--- ext/tmail
<--- ext
mschmidt:/tmp/tmail-0.10.8 $ ▮
```

Figure 6.7: Installing tmail

It's Not Perfect

By default the Firefox browser* running on my Mac stores files I downloaded from the Internet in the directory ~/Documents/My Downloads. I never experienced any problems with this setting until I tried to install tmail from this particular location in the file system.

After downloading and unpacking the tarball, I ran ruby setup.rb config, which unexpectedly resulted in the following error message:

```
/usr/bin/ruby: No such file or directory -- ~/Documents/My \
    (LoadError)
'system /usr/bin/ruby ~/Documents/My Downloads/tmail-0.10.8/ \
    ext/tmail/base64/extconf.rb ' failed
Try 'ruby setup.rb --help' for detailed usage.
```

Obviously, setup.rb dynamically creates a command-line string that gets executed with the system() method. Unfortunately, this command-line string does not work for directory names containing blanks. The lesson I've learned is this: do not try to run setup.rb (or extconf.rb) from a directory whose name contains spaces!

---

*http://www.mozilla.org/products/firefox

A complete list of all options can be found on setup.rb's web site,[29] but beware: the documentation does not completely match the current state of affairs. For example, the all task is documented but not supported any longer.

Shipping the Status Monitor

Although it took several pages to demonstrate the usage of setup.rb, in reality it's simple. Just run the following commands:

```
$ curl http://i.loveruby.net/archive/tmail/tmail-0.10.8.tar.gz \
> -o tmail-0.10.8.tar.gz
$ tar xfz- tmail-0.10.8.tar.gz
$ cd tmail-0.10.8
$ ruby setup.rb config
$ ruby setup.rb setup
$ sudo ruby setup.rb install
```

---

[29]http://i.loveruby.net/en/man/setup/usage.html

setup.rb   Destination

lib	/usr/local/lib/site_ruby/1.8
bin	/usr/bin
data	/usr/share
ext	/usr/local/lib/site_ruby/1.8/i386-linux

Figure 6.8: Typical Directory Mapping for setup.rb

So where does all the magic come from?

Even Ruby programmers do not believe in magic (although many of them firmly believe that Matz is from outer space. Some concepts are just too advanced...). You may ask yourself what you have to do to package your own stuff and make it available on nearly all platforms currently supported.

The answer is quite simple: probably nothing if you did what good programmers (and that's all of you, isn't it?) do anyway: you have to put your software into a certain directory structure, and you have to add a copy of setup.rb to your project. That's it!

setup.rb expects you to use the following directory layout:

```
project-root/
   setup.rb
   lib/
   bin/
   ext/
   data/
```

The different directories are mapped to certain destinations. A typical setup for Linux running on an Intel processor can be seen in Figure 6.8. These values will differ from platform to platform, but you should get the idea.

It's OK to put more than one module into a package. Simply add subdirectories to your project's root directory. The classic compiler example looks like this (note: the packages directory is mandatory):

```
my-compiler/
    setup.rb
    packages/        --> mandatory directory name!
        scanner/
            bin/
            lib/
            ext/
            data/
        parser/
            bin/
            lib/
            ext/
            data/
        codegen/
            bin/
            lib/
            ext/
            data/
```

So, let's get a bit more concrete and create a package for the status monitor we developed in Section 4.1, *"I'd Rather Use a Socket"*, on page 148. Our directory layout is simple:

```
sm/
    setup.rb
    create_smon.sql
    bin/
        control_sm.sh
    lib/
        pre-install.rb
        sm/
            status_monitor.rb
            status_monitor_client.rb
            sms.rb
```

setup.rb was copied verbatim from Minero Aoki's web site. The script create_smon.sql contains everything to create the MySQL database needed by the status monitor:

File 152

```
create database smon;

use smon;

create table log_entries(
    id int unsigned not null primary key,
    application varchar(64) not null,
    level enum('debug', 'info', 'warn', 'error', 'fatal'),
    message text,
    created timestamp not null
);
```

In the bin directory we placed a shell script called control_sm.sh that controls the status monitor—it lets the users of the monitor start and stop it.

The lib/sm directory contains all the files we created for the status monitor: the status monitor itself (status_monitor.rb), the library that encapsulates the access to the SMS server (sms.rb), and the Ruby library for accessing the status monitor (status_monitor_client.rb).

There's only one file left to be explained: pre-install.rb in the lib directory. setup.rb has a nice feature that makes it possible to execute a Ruby script before and after every installation phase. Such scripts are named (*pre*|*post*)-(*config*|*setup*|*install*).rb. In our case the script gets executed before the status monitor is installed. Unsurprisingly, the script installs the status monitor database:

File 153

```
Line 1    # pre-install.rb creates the status monitor database
    -     # before installing the status monitor itself.
    -
    -     system('mysql < ../create_smon.sql')
```

One of the biggest problems with installation processes is testing them, because you normally don't have access to the final production environment. In addition, installation processes often perform tasks that cannot be reverted easily, such as dropping or modifying databases or files.

Fortunately, setup.rb's inventor was well aware of these restrictions and added useful options that make testing much easier. Probably the most important one is --no-harm, which simulates the installation process without actually touching anything. It will not create or copy any directories or files. In Figure 6.9, on the facing page, you can see a sample run.

Oops! Didn't we say that nothing would be touched? In the lower third of the screenshot MySQL complains about the existence of our smon database. It does already exist, because we installed it for running our local tests. The problem is that setup.rb's philosophy regarding the pre- and post-script mechanism is a bit more local.

setup.rb was not primarily designed for processes installing complete databases, but for creating temporary files that are needed for further steps generating C code by executing commands like lex and yacc.

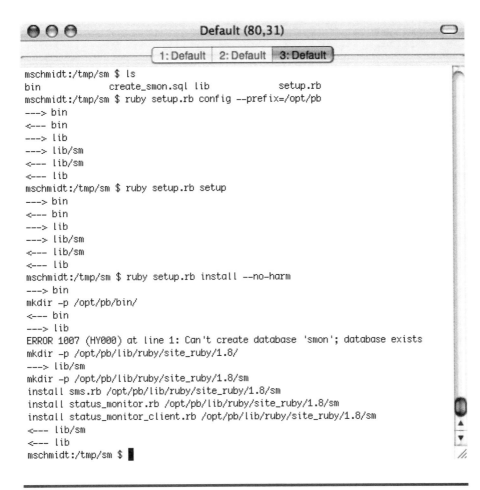

Figure 6.9: SIMULATING STATUS MONITOR INSTALLATION

Fortunately, there is the "Hook Script" API[30] that allows us to read nearly all options that have been passed to setup.rb. For example, calling get_config('prefix') in a pre- or post- script determines the current value of the --prefix option (/opt/pb in our case). Unfortunately, this is true only for configuration options and not for options that have been passed to the different installation steps such as --no-harm.

Open source to the rescue: after examining the source code of setup.rb, I quickly discovered that the hash object @options contains everything we need to make the status monitor installation complete:

---

[30]http://i.loveruby.net/en/man/setup/hookapi.html

File 154

```
Line 1    # pre-install.rb creates the status monitor database
     -    # before installing the status monitor itself.
     -
     -    if @options['no-harm']
     5        puts 'Normally, we would install the database now!'
     -    else
     -        system('mysql < ../create_smon.sql')
     -    end
```

From now on only a polite message will be printed to the console when we run ruby setup.rb install --no-harm.

Of course, relying on the internals of an implementation like this is generally a bad idea, but in this case we will get away with it, because the probability is low that setup.rb is going to change. This is especially true for our local copy.

RubyGems

As Ruby grew in popularity and more and more great libraries were released, it became obvious that a full-blown standardized packaging and installation system was needed. setup.rb does a fairly good job for typical installation tasks, but it lacks a lot of important features. For example, it is not possible to install different versions of a particular package in parallel. Uninstalling packages isn't possible either.

Gems

To create a more advanced solution, David A. Black, Paul Brannan, Chad Fowler, Richard Kilmer, and Jim Weirich sat together during a Ruby conference some years ago and designed (and implemented!) a first version of a new packaging system. They called the packages *Gems* and the package system *RubyGems*.[31]

Since these modest beginnings, RubyGems has been rewritten completely and greatly enhanced. It has become the de facto standard for distributing Ruby libraries and applications. At the time of this writing RubyGems was not part of the official Ruby distribution, but chances are good that things have changed by the time you're reading this. You can see whether RubyGems is installed already by running gem list. This command prints a list of all Gems that are installed on your system. The output should look like this:

```
mschmidt:/tmp> gem list

        *** LOCAL GEMS ***
```

---

[31]http://rubygems.rubyforge.org

```
actionmailer (1.1.3, 1.0.1)
    Service layer for easy email delivery and testing.

actionpack (1.11.0, 1.9.1)
    Web-flow and rendering framework putting the VC in MVC.

actionwebservice (0.9.3, 0.8.1)
    Web service support for Action Pack.

activerecord (1.13.0, 1.11.1)
    Implements the ActiveRecord pattern for ORM.
...

xml-simple (1.0.7)
    A very simple API for XML processing.
```

If instead you get an error message like "gem: No such file or directory," you probably don't have RubyGems installed. You'll need to download and install it. It might be the last Ruby program you have to install manually....

RubyGems comes with an excellent documentation system (try gem -- help, and play around with the options of the list command a bit), there's a great user guide on the project's home page,[32] and Chad Fowler has written a chapter about it in [TFH05]. Because of all this, I'm not going to write yet another full tutorial, but I'd like at least to explain briefly how to use RubyGems.

A Gem is a self-contained package that contains everything belonging to a particular Ruby library or application. It doesn't matter whether it's a program written in pure Ruby or it's a C extension, whether it contains extensive documentation, or whether it comes with a big test suite. Everything belonging to the package can be found in the .gem file. In the next section we will need the rake command that is available as a Gem, so let's install it now:

```
mschmidt:/tmp> sudo gem install rake
Password:
Attempting local installation of 'rake'
Local gem file not found: rake*.gem
Attempting remote installation of 'rake'
Updating Gem source index for: http://gems.rubyforge.org
Successfully installed rake-0.6.2
Installing RDoc documentation for rake-0.6.2...
```

---

[32]http://docs.rubygems.org

Because Gems are usually installed in a central directory (usually in a local tree such as /usr/local/lib/ruby/gems), you have to run gem as the root user. As good citizens we use the sudo command instead of su.

RubyGems tries to find a local installation of the rake Gem first. If it doesn't find one, it tries to get it from the central Gems server.[33] Then it downloads the package, unpacks it, and installs it. The installation process usually is more than a simple cp or install command. Often, C extensions and documentation files are built before copying the result to the central Gems directory.

The update option installs the most current version of an existing package:

```
mschmidt:/tmp> sudo gem update activerecord
Password:
Upgrading installed gems...
Attempting remote upgrade of activerecord
Attempting remote installation of 'activerecord'
Install required dependency activesupport? [Yn]   Y
Successfully installed activerecord-1.13.2
Successfully installed activesupport-1.2.5
Installing RDoc documentation for activerecord-1.13.2...
Installing RDoc documentation for activesupport-1.2.5...
Gems: [activerecord] updated
```

gem automatically downloaded the current ActiveRecord version, along with its dependency ActiveSupport (another important feature of Gems: they can depend on each other, and the gem command knows about it). Then, it installed the two libraries and their documentation, which is freshly generated from RDoc comments in the source code.

To find out which versions of ActiveRecord are installed, we use the list option again:

```
mschmidt:/tmp> gem list activerecord

*** LOCAL GEMS ***

activerecord (1.13.2, 1.13.0, 1.11.1)
Implements the ActiveRecord pattern for ORM.
```

There seem to be different versions of ActiveRecord installed on our system. But how can we use them in our Ruby programs? Until RubyGems

---

[33]If you're trying to install Gems on a computer in your company, you probably have to specify a proxy server:
```
mschmidt:/tmp>gem install -p http://proxy:port rake
```

actually becomes the Ruby packaging standard, you have to call require 'rubygems' whenever you want to use a Gem.[34]

```
require 'rubygems'
require 'active_record'
```

Note that even though the Gem is called *activerecord*, we require the 'active_record' module and not 'activerecord'.

If you don't want to add require 'rubygems' to all of your programs, you can invoke the Ruby interpreter and use the -r option:[35]

```
ruby -rubygems . . .
```

Even better, set the RUBYOPT environment variable:

```
mschmidt:/tmp> export RUBYOPT=rubygems
```

If you want to use a particular version of a Gem, you have to use the require_gem(gem,*version_requirements) function:

```
irb(main):001:0> require 'rubygems'
=> true
irb(main):002:0> require_gem 'activerecord', '= 1.11.1'
=> true
irb(main):003:0>
```

In this case we loaded version 1.11.1 of ActiveRecord. If we try to load a version that is not installed on our system, RubyGems complains with an informative error message:

```
irb(main):003:0> require_gem 'activerecord', '= 1.11.0'
Gem::LoadError: RubyGem version error: activerecord(1.11.1 not = 1.11.0)
```

To specify a particular Gem version, you have to pass a list of version requirements to require_gem(). Every version requirement consists of an operator and a version number. The operators are =, !=, >, >=, <, <=, and ~>. Most of them should be self-explanatory, so the following:

```
require_gem 'activerecord', '> 1.1'
```

loads the most current ActiveRecord Gem whose version is greater than 1.1. If instead we'd used the following:

```
require_gem 'activerecord', '> 1.1', '<= 1.2'
```

---

[34]RubyGems is currently in transition. It is very likely to become built in to a future version of Ruby, but until then it allows you to write your require statements as if it already were the standard tool. Someday you only have to remove all the require 'rubygems' statements.

[35]Yes, there is a file called ubygems.rb.

RubyGems would load the most current ActiveRecord Gem in the version range 1.1–1.2.

However, the ~> operator (read: approximately greater than) looks unfamiliar. It's called the *pessimistic operator*, because it makes the pessimistic assumption that major releases of software are often incompatible with former releases. Using that reasoning, it's optimistic to do the following:

```
require_gem 'activerecord', '> 2.1'
```

because this may end up loading ActiveRecord version 18.7.1, which may no longer support some of the methods that you're using in your script. A more pessimistic approach would be to constraint the version number to start 2:

```
require_gem 'activerecord', '> 2.1', '< 3.0'
```

That's what the pessimistic operator does. The following is (in effect) identical to the previous code:

```
require_gem 'activerecord', '~> 2.1'
```

RubyGems provides many more useful features for the Gem user. You can also write your own Gems. All this isn't necessary to get your enterprise integration software up and running, but if you want to become a real Ruby hacker, you'd better read the RubyGems manual.

Conclusion

When creating open source software that will be disseminated via Internet, RubyGems is the best choice today—it has been designed for this specific purpose. For the deployment of enterprise software, setup.rb is still a useful tool. setup.rb dictates a directory layout you have probably used anyway, and there is no reason why setup.rb and RubyGems should not coexist peacefully.

6.5 Project Automation with Rake

In the lifetime of every software project there comes a point when you have to automate things. It might be sufficient to run the compiler manually and to copy the resulting executable to its final destination by hand if you have to compile only two files. But as soon as the number of source files reaches a critical mass (i.e., which only takes three files or so), you'd better think about automating tasks such as compiling, linking, packaging, and so on.

When developing software, impatience is a good guide. Whenever you're working with a compiled programming language such as C/C++, Java, or C#, you think about project automation automatically to decrease compile time. It does not make sense to compile every single file every time. Instead, you want to compile only those files that are newer than their corresponding binary objects. Integrated Development Environments (IDEs) such as Eclipse and tools such as make manage these steps for you.

With interpreted languages like Ruby this compilation and build management isn't necessary. There are, however, still some tasks that have to be managed the "make way". For example, if you use SOAP, you'd like to call wsdl2ruby.rb (see Section 5.3, *Web Services Description Language*, on page 210) only when it's necessary.

Also, compiling files is not the only task that can be automated in a typical software project. Usually, you have to generate documentation using rdoc, package and deploy your software, and run all unit tests. Often, these tasks depend on each other and have to be performed in a particular order.

Many project automation tools exist: make,[36] Ant,[37] and A-A-P,[38] to name a few. Although they differ slightly in functionality, they have one thing in common: their input file formats are rarely convenient. For example, make depends on significant whitespace characters, and Ant expects you to write bloated XML documents. For simple tasks, that is OK, but as soon as you have to implement some logic, you're doomed.

Jim Weirich was fed up with this situation. Because he likes Ruby, he has developed a project automation tool called rake.[39] Jim did not invent yet another input file format. Instead, he used Ruby to drive his build tool. This Ruby lives inside things called *Rakefiles*.

Rakefiles

Before this section gets too theoretical (after all, this is a pragmatic book), we'd better run rake and see what happens:

```
mschmidt:/tmp> rake
```

---

[36]http://www.gnu.org/software/make
[37]http://ant.apache.org
[38]http://www.a-a-p.org
[39]http://rake.rubyforge.org

```
rake aborted!
No Rakefile found (looking for: rakefile, Rakefile, rakefile.rb, \
Rakefile.rb)
/usr/local/lib/ruby/gems/1.8/gems/rake-0.6.2/lib/rake.rb:1373:in \
   'load_rakefile'
```

rake automatically searches for an input file called rakefile, Rakefile, rake-file.rb, or Rakefile.rb. Because it searches for files with the extension .rb, we conclude that it expects a Ruby file. Let's create our first Rakefile:

```
puts 'Hello, Rake!'
```

And run rake again:

```
mschmidt:/tmp> rake
(in /tmp)
Hello, Rake!
rake aborted!
Don't know how to build task 'default'
```

We're getting closer. rake has executed our Ruby code but complains that we did not specify a task called default. So, what is a rake task and what is the default task?

Rakefiles consist of ordinary Ruby code that uses a set of methods and classes defined by rake. Typically, a Rakefile contains several tasks. Each has a name and is associated with a block of Ruby code. Tasks can depend on other tasks—a task may have some prerequisites that have to be fulfilled before it gets executed. If you do not specify a task to be executed, the task called default is run. Tasks can be defined with the task(args,&block) method. Here's the new version of our Rakefile:

```
task :default do
  puts 'Hello, Rake!'
end
```

This time everything works as expected:

```
mschmidt:/tmp> rake
(in /tmp)
Hello, Rake!
```

In most Rakefiles the default task doesn't have code in its body (rake calls this body an *action*). Instead, the default task will list other tasks as dependencies, and these tasks will run by default when rake is executed without any overriding parameters.

Let's refactor our Rakefile and store it in a file called hello.rb:

File 104

```
Line 1   # The refactored Rakefile.
  -      task :default => [:hello]
```

Some Syntax Notes

Rakefiles tend to look nice. In part, that's because they use some of Ruby's syntactic sugar. Two things often confuse inexperienced Ruby programmers when they work with rake:

- The prerequisites of a task are passed as a hash with the => notation:

```
task :default => [:hello]
```

This is the same as this

```
prerequisites = Hash.new
prerequisites[:default] = [:hello]
task(prerequisites)
```

- Because of the different precedence of do/end blocks and their curly counterparts ({ }), you have to be careful when using the latter. The following statement produces a parse error:

```
task :default { puts 'Hello, Rake!' }
```

The code block is associated with the :default symbol and not with the task() method. Put :default into parentheses and everything is fine again:

```
task(:default) { puts 'Hello, Rake!' }
```

I recommend not using the curly braces syntax in Rakefiles.

```
    desc 'Prints a nice greeting!'
5   task :hello do
      puts 'Hello, Rake!'
    end
```

This way we can reuse the ingenious hello task, and we can run it separately: rake -f hello.rb hello.[40] The default task was reduced to a list of dependencies that consists of only a single element in our case.

In addition, we have written a description for the hello task with the desc task. These descriptions will be output when you pass the -T option to

---

[40]It's possible to specify a list of tasks on the command line that should be executed: rake task1 task2....

rake. With -f you can set the Rakefile to be used and the -P option will print all tasks and their prerequisites:

```
mschmidt:/tmp> rake -f hello.rb -T
(in /tmp)
rake hello  # Prints a nice greeting!
mschmidt:/tmp> rake -f hello.rb -P
(in /tmp)
rake default
    hello
rake hello
```

Tasks and Actions

Having a mechanism for defining tasks and their dependencies is useful. It's even more useful that you can implement the actions needed when executing in the same Ruby code. And, to get you started, rake comes with a lot of useful predefined tasks. We'll use one of these, PackageTask, to create a package of the Ruby files belonging to our status monitor. Here's the content of the lib directory:

```
mschmidt:~/work/sm> ls lib
StatusMonitor.java             status_monitor.rb
status_monitor.pm              status_monitor_client.rb
```

We'd like to create a .tgz file that contains all the Ruby files in the lib directory (along with the directory itself). The Rakefile that does this looks like this:

File 105

```
Line 1    require 'rake'
          require 'rake/packagetask'
          include Rake

5         SM_VERSION = '0.0.1'

          PackageTask.new('sm-ruby', SM_VERSION) do |p|
            p.need_tar = true
            p.package_files.include('lib/**/*.rb')
10        end
```

First we load the two libraries we need to use the standard rake tasks. In line 7 we define the *package* task with PackageTask. Its constructor expects the name of the file to be created and the version information that should be appended to the file name. The rest is defined in a code block that gets the current PackageTask instance. By setting the need_tar attribute to true, we tell the task that we want to have a .tgz file. package_files is an instance of class FileList that we set to all .rb files below the lib directory (see Section 6.5, *File Lists*, on page 316, for details). To find the name of the task and usage, it's -T to the rescue:

```
mschmidt:~/work/sm> rake -T
(in /Users/mschmidt/work/sm)
rake clobber_package   # Remove package products
rake package           # Build all the packages
rake repackage         # Force a rebuild of the package files
```

Obviously, rake defines three tasks automatically for us as soon as we define a package task. So, let's use them:[41]

```
mschmidt:~/work/sm> rake package
(in /Users/mschmidt/work/sm)
mkdir -p pkg
mkdir -p pkg/sm-ruby-0.0.1/lib
rm -f pkg/sm-ruby-0.0.1/lib/status_monitor.rb
ln lib/status_monitor.rb pkg/sm-ruby-0.0.1/lib/status_monitor.rb
rm -f pkg/sm-ruby-0.0.1/lib/status_monitor_client.rb
ln lib/status_monitor_client.rb \
  pkg/sm-ruby-0.0.1/lib/status_monitor_client.rb
cd pkg
tar zcvf sm-ruby-0.0.1.tgz sm-ruby-0.0.1
sm-ruby-0.0.1/
sm-ruby-0.0.1/lib/
sm-ruby-0.0.1/lib/status_monitor.rb
sm-ruby-0.0.1/lib/status_monitor_client.rb
cd -
mschmidt:~/work/sm> ls pkg
sm-ruby-0.0.1           sm-ruby-0.0.1.tgz
mschmidt:~/work/sm>
```

To execute the package task, rake calls standard Unix commands such as cd, ln, and rm. Do you need a .zip file, too? Add p.need_zip = true to the PackageTask task, and run it again:

```
mschmidt:~/work/sm> rake package
(in /Users/mschmidt/work/sm)
cd pkg
zip -r sm-ruby-0.0.1.zip sm-ruby-0.0.1
  adding: sm-ruby-0.0.1/ (stored 0%)
  adding: sm-ruby-0.0.1/lib/ (stored 0%)
  adding: sm-ruby-0.0.1/lib/status_monitor.rb (deflated 43%)
  adding: sm-ruby-0.0.1/lib/status_monitor_client.rb (deflated 50%)
cd -
mschmidt:~/work/sm>
```

---

[41]At the time of writing, rake has some problems with Ruby 1.8.4. If you run into any problems (such as "no such option: noop"), try to install the latest version, gem update rake.

rake creates the .zip file and is clever enough to realize that the .tgz file does not have to be created again. Anyway, we will clean up our mess:

```
mschmidt:~/work/sm> rake clobber_package
(in /Users/mschmidt/work/sm)
rm -r pkg
mschmidt:~/work/sm>
```

But what if you want to have different package tasks? Maybe we need one that creates the status monitor files for Ruby programmers, and another one that creates it for Java programmers? rake automatically gives the package task a name, and there is no way to set it. But rake *namespaces* has a much better solution: *namespaces*:

File 107

```
Line 1    require 'rake'
    -     require 'rake/packagetask'
    -     include Rake
    -
    5     SM_VERSION = '0.0.1'
    -
    -     namespace :ruby do
    -       PackageTask.new('sm-ruby', SM_VERSION) do |p|
    -         p.need_tar = true
   10         p.need_zip = true
    -         p.package_files.include('lib/**/*.rb')
    -       end
    -     end
    -
   15     namespace :java do
    -       PackageTask.new('sm-java', SM_VERSION) do |p|
    -         p.need_tar = true
    -         p.need_zip = true
    -         p.package_files.include('lib/**/*.java')
   20         p.package_files.include('build.xml')
    -       end
    -     end
```

You can wrap any task in a namespace. Rake automatically puts this namespace in front of the task name (separated by a colon). This time we have defined two package tasks, one for the Ruby package and one for the Java package. You can use them like this:

```
mschmidt:~/work/sm> rake -T
(in /Users/mschmidt/work/sm)
rake java:clobber_package    # Remove package products
rake java:package            # Build all the packages
rake java:repackage          # Force a rebuild of the package files
rake ruby:clobber_package    # Remove package products
rake ruby:package            # Build all the packages
rake ruby:repackage          # Force a rebuild of the package files
```

rake comes with a lot of standard tasks:

- The file task creates a file from a list of other files. In C/C++ projects, for example, an executable is built by linking a list of object files:

```
file 'game' => %w(aliens.o joystick.o screen.o sound.o) do |t|
  sh "c++ -o #{t.name} #{t.prerequisites.join(' ')}"
end
```

Whenever one of the object files is more recent than our executable, the game file is rebuilt. We build it by invoking the C++ compiler with the sh() method. This method, which comes with rake, simply executes shell commands. The code block gets passed the task, and we use some of its properties (the task's name and prerequisites) to create the command-line string.

Note we did not specify how to create the object files themselves. You could do this with a file task for every object file, but we'll show you a better way using the rule task.

- The rule task specifies what rake should do if it encounters a file name that has no task associated with it. For example, you can define how to create .o files from .cc files:

```
rule '.o' => ['.cc'] do |t|
  sh "c++ -c #{t.source} -o #{t.name}"
end
```

You can access the names of both the source and the destination files in the task's action. We use them to invoke the C++ compiler with rake's sh() method. rule works recursively; if it cannot find the .cc file it needs, it would try to find a rule for creating .cc files. This is useful when you're working with code generators such as lex and yacc.

Regular expressions can be used to specify the output files, and the source files can be determined by a code block. Our last rule was an abbreviation for the following:[42]

```
rule(/.o$/ => [ proc { |dest| dest.sub(/\.[^.]+$/, '.cc') } ]) do |t|
  sh "c++ -c #{t.source} -o #{t.name}"
end
```

- The directory task creates paths in the file system. For example, the :default task in the following Rakefile:

---

[42] In this case it's necessary to put the arguments of rule() in brackets.

File 103

```
require 'rake'
data_dir = 'pkg/test/data'
task :default => [data_dir]
directory data_dir
```

will create the directory pkg/test/data if it does not already exist.

- The clean and clobber tasks can be used to clean up the working directory. clean removes all *temporary* files that have been
  created during the build process, and clobber removes *all* files
  that have been added to the original package. The files to be
  removed are specified by the file lists CLEAN and CLOBBER, respectively. (CLOBBER always contains all the files in CLEAN.)

```
require 'rake/clean'
CLEAN.add('**/*.o')
CLOBBER.add('**/*~', '**/*.bak', '**/*.tmp')
```

- RDoc is the de facto standard for documenting Ruby code. The
  RDocTask task runs the rdoc command to create documentation
  from the comments in your source files. A typical RDocTask looks
  as follows:

```
Rake::RDocTask.new(:docs) do |rd|
  rd.main = 'README.rdoc'
  rd.rdoc_files.add('README.rdoc', 'lib/**/*.rb')
  rd.options << '--all'
end
```

  In this case we gave the RDocTask the name docs. Rake automatically creates two additional tasks called clobber_docs (remove the
  generated documentation) and redocs (force a rebuild of the documentation) for us.

- You can create a Gem for your project with GemPackageTask. It
  works exactly like PackageTask, except that it expects a Gem specification:

File 106

```
Line 1  require 'rubygems'
     -  require 'rake/gempackagetask'
     -  include Rake
     -
     5  SM_VERSION = '0.0.1'
     -  gem_spec = Gem::Specification.new do |s|
     -    s.name = 'sm'
     -    s.version = SM_VERSION
     -    s.platform = Gem::Platform::RUBY
    10    s.files = FileList['lib/**/*.rb']
     -    s.requirements << 'none'
     -    s.require_path = 'lib'
```

```
-        s.autorequire = 'status_monitor_client'
-        s.summary = 'Status monitor for PragBouquet applications.'
15       s.description = 'Use the status monitor to report errors.'
-      end
-
-      GemPackageTask.new(gem_spec) do |pkg|
-        pkg.need_zip = true
20       pkg.need_tar = true
-      end
```

The preceding Rakefile creates a .tgz, a .zip, and a .gem version of our status monitor package:

```
mschmidt:~/work/sm> rake package
(in /Users/mschmidt/work/sm)
mkdir -p pkg
mkdir -p pkg/sm-0.0.1/lib
rm -f pkg/sm-0.0.1/lib/status_monitor.rb
ln lib/status_monitor.rb pkg/sm-0.0.1/lib/status_monitor.rb
rm -f pkg/sm-0.0.1/lib/status_monitor_client.rb
ln lib/status_monitor_client.rb \
  pkg/sm-0.0.1/lib/status_monitor_client.rb
cd pkg
tar zcvf sm-0.0.1.tgz sm-0.0.1
sm-0.0.1/
sm-0.0.1/lib/
sm-0.0.1/lib/status_monitor.rb
sm-0.0.1/lib/status_monitor_client.rb
cd -
cd pkg
zip -r sm-0.0.1.zip sm-0.0.1
  adding: sm-0.0.1/ (stored 0%)
  adding: sm-0.0.1/lib/ (stored 0%)
  adding: sm-0.0.1/lib/status_monitor.rb (deflated 43%)
  adding: sm-0.0.1/lib/status_monitor_client.rb (deflated 50%)
cd -
  Successfully built RubyGem
  Name: sm
  Version: 0.0.1
  File: sm-0.0.1.gem
mv sm-0.0.1.gem pkg/sm-0.0.1.gem
mschmidt:~/work/sm> ls pkg/
sm-0.0.1         sm-0.0.1.gem     sm-0.0.1.tgz     sm-0.0.1.zip
```

You can find more tasks on the Internet. For example, there are tasks that create code statistics or publish files with ssh. Before you write a new task, find out whether someone else had a similar problem and solved it already.

File Lists

Managing software projects often comes down to managing files. Files have to be created, removed, and compiled. Files depend on each other. So it's only natural that rake supports the handling of file lists with a separate class called FileList.

FileList objects are arrays with some additional methods for managing files specified by file name patterns. These patterns are evaluated lazily—when the first object is requested from a FileList object. In a typical Java project, you will probably find a file list that looks like this:

```
files = FileList['build.xml', 'lib/**/*.jar', 'src/**/*.java']
```

Once a FileList has been created, more files can be added with both the add(*filenames) or include(*filenames) method:

```
files.add('README')
files.include('MANIFEST')
```

If you pass an array to any of these methods, every element of the array is added to the file list. Excluding files is possible, too:

```
files.exclude('src/**/Test*.java')
```

By default, file lists will ignore files:

- Containing CVS or .svn in the file path
- Ending with .bak or ~
- Named core

You can clear the default exclude pattern with the clear_ignore_patterns() method. Calling select_default_ignore_patterns() sets it back to the initial default value.

When automating software project tasks, you often have to rename files or change their extensions. FileList supports these actions, too:

File 108

```
Line 1    files = FileList['lib/**/*.rb']
     -    puts "Original files:"
     -    puts files
     -    puts
     5
     -    backup_files = files.gsub(/$/, '.bak')
     -    puts "Backup files:"
     -    puts backup_files
     -    puts
    10
     -    rhtml_files = files.ext('.rhtml')
     -    puts "rhtml files:"
     -    puts rhtml_files
```

This prints the following (for the directory of the status monitor):

```
Original files:
lib/status_monitor.rb
lib/status_monitor_client.rb

Backup files:
lib/status_monitor.rb.bak
lib/status_monitor_client.rb.bak

rhtml files:
lib/status_monitor.rhtml
lib/status_monitor_client.rhtml
```

FileList has more interesting methods. Look at them before you start working with rake. It's an independent class, and maybe you can use it in your own projects, too.

Conclusion

rake is well accepted in the Ruby community, is actively maintained, and will certainly become more and more popular (perhaps even outside the Ruby world). Interestingly, most of the rake tutorials you can find on the Internet concentrate on topics such as building C/C++ programs. That's nice for demonstrating some of rake's features, but it's a bit misleading, too. rake is in an early stage of development and does not work well with tools such as GNU's autoconf, which are important when building portable tools. At the moment I recommend not using Rake for anything other than Ruby projects.

Rake might not even be an optimal choice for all Ruby projects. One of the biggest advantages of the Java build tool ant is that it offers useful commands such as ftp and scp that are independent of the underlying operating system. Hence, you do not have to write and maintain .sh and .bat versions of the same build and deploy tools.

Unfortunately, rake does not work this way. It calls the tools it needs with the system() call. If no tar command is found in your path, the PackageTask won't work. For development teams that are working on different operating systems, it might be better to use a platform-independent tool such as ant (even though its input files are a pain to maintain).

6.6 Testing Legacy Applications

One of the biggest problems when working with existing enterprise software is that it is often undocumented and cannot be tested automatically. Whenever you add a column to a database table or change a configuration file, you have to ask yourself whether everything else is still working as expected.[43] Most legacy code does not have unit tests because unit testing wasn't widely used back in the eighties and nineties (and because programming languages such as C and C++ don't make it as convenient as, for example, Ruby does). So, before you change something in an existing infrastructure, you had better find a way to check whether everything still works afterward.

Usually, it's a good compromise to create a tool that performs a system test instead of creating unit tests from scratch. If, for example, you have an executable program that expects an input file and sends output to another file, you can easily create a test tool. Such tools always work the same way:

1. Create input files for all the things you want to test.

2. Run your program with every input file and store the program's output for every test case separately.

3. Check whether the output files are correct—that they contain the expected results. You have to do this manually, but only once.

4. Whenever you change the program, run it again with all the input files, and check whether the current output matches the reference output files you created in the preceding steps.

Let's create a tool that performs these steps. We'll use YAML to describe our tests (see Section 3.5, *YAML Ain't Markup Language (YAML)*, on page 141, to learn more about YAML):

File 155
```yaml
- cmd: 'echo Hello'
  out: 'echo_test.out'
- cmd: 'date -u'
  out: 'date_test.out'
```

Every test case is defined by the executable that should be run and by the output file that should be created or compared to. For demonstration purposes we chose to test the echo and date commands. Our test tool looks like this:

File 156
```ruby
Line 1   require 'yaml'
   -     require 'logger'
   -     require 'fileutils'
   -
```

---

[43]And you know it probably isn't!

Executing External Programs

You'll usually use one of the following methods to execute external programs from your Ruby programs:

- system( ) runs a command and sends its output to STDOUT— the command's output and the calling program's output go to the same channel. It returns true if the command was found and could be executed successfully; otherwise, it returns false:

```
mschmidt:/tmp> irb
irb(main):001:0> system('ls /etc/rc*')
/etc/rc                  /etc/rc.netboot
/etc/rc.common           /etc/rc.shutdown
=> true
irb(main):002:0> puts $?.exitstatus
0
=> nil
```

- %x (and the backquotes—some people call them *backticks*) run an external program and return its standard output as a string. Depending on the command you're calling, this string can contain newlines:

```
mschmidt:/tmp> irb
irb(main):001:0> %x(env | grep TERM)
=> "TERM_PROGRAM=iTerm.app\nTERM=vt100\n"
irb(main):002:0> $?.exitstatus
=> 0
irb(main):003:0> `cat /etc/passwd | wc -l`
=> "      36\n"
irb(main):004:0> $?.exitstatus
=> 0
```

In all cases the command string will be interpolated; i.e., all expressions and escape sequences are expanded before the command is called. The exit status of all these functions can be found in the global variable $?, which is an instance of class Process::Status.

```ruby
 5  class TestTool
 -    attr_accessor :create_reference
 -    attr_accessor :reference_dir, :output_dir
 -
 -    def initialize(options)
10      @create_reference = options[:create_reference]
 -      @reference_dir = options[:reference_dir]
 -      FileUtils.mkdir_p(@reference_dir) if @create_reference
 -      @output_dir = options[:output_dir]
 -      FileUtils.mkdir_p(@output_dir)
15      @logger = Logger.new(options[:logfile])
 -    end
 -
 -    def process(input_file)
 -      @logger.info("Processing #{input_file}.")
20      test_suite = YAML::load_file(input_file)
 -      test_suite.each do |test_case|
 -        command = test_case['cmd']
 -        output_file = File.join(@output_dir, test_case['out'])
 -        process_test_case(command, output_file)
25      end
 -    end
 -    def process_test_case(command, output_file)
 -      begin
 -        output = exec_command(command)
30        @logger.info("Storing output in #{output_file}.")
 -        File.open(output_file, 'w') { |f| f.write(output) }
 -        reference_file = File.join(@reference_dir, output_file)
 -        if @create_reference
 -          FileUtils.mkdir_p(File.dirname(reference_file))
35          FileUtils.cp(output_file, reference_file)
 -        else
 -          if !FileUtils.compare_file(output_file, reference_file)
 -            @logger.warn("#{output_file} differs from reference file!")
 -          else
40            @logger.info("#{output_file} is correct.")
 -          end
 -        end
 -      rescue Exception => ex
 -        puts ex.backtrace
45        @logger.error(ex.to_s)
 -      end
 -    end
 -    def exec_command(command)
 -      @logger.info("Running #{command}.")
50      output = `#{command}`
 -      raise "An error occurred: #{$?}!" if $? != 0
 -      output
 -    end
 -  end
```

Although the program nearly fills a single page in this book, it is all you need to perform a system test for typical command-line programs. In the initialize() method we store some configuration data: the variable @create_reference specifies whether the test tool was started to create the reference output files or whether it should check that the system to be tested still produces the expected results. @reference_dir contains the directory where the reference files are stored, and @output_dir points to the directory the output files for a test run are written. Finally, we create a Logger for writing the test log.

process(input_file) reads one of our YAML test suites. For every command and its output file it calls process_test_case(command,output_file). This method is the heart of our TestTool class. It executes the program to be tested and stores its output in the output file. If the test tool is in "create reference data" mode, it copies the output file to the directory containing the reference data. Otherwise, it compares the current output file with the reference file.

It's time for a first test run. Let's create the reference data for our little test suite:

```
Line 1    tt = TestTool.new(
    -         :reference_dir => './reference',
    -         :create_reference => true,
    -         :output_dir => './output',
    5         :logfile => 'test_tool.log'
    -     )
    -     tt.process('suite1.yaml')
```

In the log file we'll find the following messages (I've adjusted the output for brevity):

```
INFO -- : Processing suite1.yaml.
INFO -- : Running echo Hello.
INFO -- : Storing output in ./output/echo_test.out.
INFO -- : Running date -u.
INFO -- : Storing output in ./output/date_test.out.
```

Nothing special happened—all we did was create the reference data. echo_test.out contains "Hello\n", and date_test.out contains something like "Sun Jan 29 08:04:52 GMT 2006\n."

Now let's perform our first system test:

```
Line 1    tt.create_reference = false
    -     tt.process('suite1.yaml')
```

This is what we find in our log file:

```
INFO -- : Processing suite1.yaml.
INFO -- : Running echo Hello.
INFO -- : Storing output in ./output/echo_test.out.
INFO -- : ./output/echo_test.out is correct.
INFO -- : Running date -u.
INFO -- : Storing output in ./output/date_test.out.
WARN -- : ./output/date_test.out differs from reference file!
```

As expected, the echo command produces the same output as before, but our test case for the date command failed—which comes as no surprise, because time flies....

Finally, we add a nice command-line interface to our TestTool class:

File 157

```
Line 1   require 'getoptlong'
    -    require 'test_tool'
    -
    -    tt_options = {
    5      :reference_dir => './reference',
    -      :create_reference => false,
    -      :output_dir => './output',
    -      :logfile => 'test_tool.log'
    -    }
   10
    -    begin
    -      options = GetoptLong.new(
    -        ['-create-reference', '-c', GetoptLong::NO_ARGUMENT],
    -        ['-reference-dir', '-r', GetoptLong::OPTIONAL_ARGUMENT],
   15        ['-output-dir', '-o', GetoptLong::OPTIONAL_ARGUMENT],
    -        ['-logfile', '-l', GetoptLong::OPTIONAL_ARGUMENT]
    -      )
    -
    -
   20      options.each_option do |name, value|
    -        case name
    -        when '-create-reference'
    -          tt_options[:create_reference] = true
    -        when '-reference-dir'
   25          tt_options[:reference_dir] = value
    -        end
    -      end
    -    rescue Exception => ex
    -      puts "#{File.basename($0)} usage: ..."
   30    end
    -
    -    test_tool = TestTool.new(tt_options)
    -    ARGV.each do |input_file|
    -      test_tool.process(input_file)
   35    end
```

Now we can run it like this:

```
mschmidt:/tmp> ruby test_tool_runner.rb -c suite1.yaml
mschmidt:/tmp> ruby test_tool_runner.rb suite1.yaml
```

Admittedly, the first version of our test tool is pretty simple, but it's a good basis for more sophisticated solutions. For example, you could add preconditions for each input file that create a particular state in a database or generate some test data. Sometimes it even makes sense to define a complete *domain-specific language* (DSL) to describe your test cases. In addition, you don't have to restrict yourself to running executable programs. You can also test HTTP or SOAP services, or you can test Java programs with Rjb (see Section 5.4, *Bridging the Gap*, on page 230).

The quality of a test tool mainly depends on the quality of the test suite, not on the quality of the tool itself. Only an extensive test suite will give you the confidence to make changes. It does not have to be complete right from the beginning—even a small test suite might reveal bugs quickly—but it should grow over the time.

Conclusion

Although this book tries to show that Ruby is a full-blown programming language that can be used for implementing nearly all of your system architecture, we should never forget that it's also a perfect language for little scripts that can simplify your working life. In particular, when testing applications, it can greatly increase your productivity.

Appendix A

Resources

A.1 Bibliography

[Fow03]   Martin Fowler. *Patterns of Enterprise Application Architecture*. Addison Wesley Longman, Reading, MA, 2003.

[Ker04]   Joshua Kerievsky. *Refactoring To Patterns*. Addison-Wesley, Reading, MA, 2004.

[Sim02]   John E. Simpson. *XPath and XPointer*. O'Reilly & Associates, Inc, Sebastopol, CA, 2002.

[Ste98]   W. Richard Stevens. *Unix Network Programming, Volume 1: Networking APIs: Sockets and Xti*. Prentice Hall, Englewood Cliffs, NJ, second edition, 1998.

[STK02]   James Snell, Doug Tidwell, and Paul Kulchenko. *Programming Web Services with SOAP*. O'Reilly & Associates, Inc, Sebastopol, CA, 2002.

[TFH05]   David Thomas, Chad Fowler, and Andrew Hunt. *Programming Ruby: The Pragmatic Programmers' Guide*. The Pragmatic Programmers, LLC, Raleigh, NC, and Dallas, TX, second edition, 2005.

[TH05]   David Thomas and David Heinemeier Hansson. *Agile Web Development With Rails*. The Pragmatic Programmers, LLC, Raleigh, NC, and Dallas, TX, 2005.

Index

Symbols

* (select nodes XPath), 122
+ symbol (YAML), 143
- - double hyphen (daemons), 284
- symbol (YAML), 141, 143
. abbreviation (XPath), 123
.. abbreviation (XPath), 123
// abbreviation (XPath), 123
: character (LDIF), 56
: symbol (YAML), 143
[] (predicates XPath), 122
character (LDIF), 56, 59
$KCODE, 245
%x (Ruby), 319
| (ICU4R), 253
| (XPath), 125

A

A-A-P, 307
Abstraction layers, 26
Accessors, 35
Active Record (Fowler), 34
ActiveDirectory (Ruby/LDAP interface), 62
ActiveLDAP, 71–79
  accessors for attributes, 75
  ActiveLDAP::Base, 74
  ActiveLDAP::Base.connect() method, 73
  additional features, 77
  allow_anonymous option, 74
  :attribute, 75
  attributes as array, 77
  attributes as string, 77
  :attrs parameter, 76
  base option, 74
  :base parameter, 76
  belongs_to() method, 78, 79
  bind_format option, 74
  :class_name parameter, 78

classes parameter, 75
connect() method, 74, 75
cosine schema, 72
CRUD (Create, Retrieve, Update, and Delete), 77
delete accounts, 77
DN (distinguished names), 75
dnattr parameter, 75, 76, 78
:filter parameter, 76
find() method, 75, 76
find_all() method, 75, 76
:foreign_key parameter, 78
gidNumber attribute, 78
Group object, 75
has_many() method, 78, 79
initialize, 73
keys, 75
ldap_mapping() method, 75
:local_key parameter, 78
nis schema, 72
object relationships, 77
:objects, 75
password_block option, 74
posixAccount object class, 72
posixGroup object class, 72
prefix parameter, 75, 76
rootdn, 74
:scope parameter, 76
search() method, 76
tag with description, 77
:value, 75
ActiveRecord, 34, 49–52
  accessors, 35
  add_column() method, 49
  add() method, 44
  add_flower() method, 45
  add_index() method, 49
  :all option, 36

API specification, implementing, 203, 204

attributes, 35

background, 34

belongs_to() method, 43

code block, 45

connect to database, 34

create_table() method, 49

CRUD (Create, Retrieve, Update, and Delete), 33, 37

delete rows, 36

down() method, 49

drawbacks, 51

drop_table() method, 49

errors, 47

execute() method, 49

find() method, 36, 37, 51

gem, 35

has_and_belongs_to_many() method, 39, 43

has_one() method, 43

id column, 36

JOIN, 40

join tables, 38, 39f, 39–42

Logger class, 158

macros, 43

many-to-many relationship, 38, 39, 42

method_missing() method, 37

name derivation, 35

pattern definition, 31

print_report() method, 45

push_with_attributes() method, 41

read rows, 36

remove() method, 45

remove_column() method, 49

remove_index() method, 49

rename_column() method, 49

reset_column_information() method, 50, 51

Ruby, 203, 204

Ruby mapping, 42

RubyGems, 304

save!() method, 48

save() method, 47

security, 37

SELECT, 40

serve() method, 158

set_primary_key(), 36

SQL, 40

SQL statements, 37

status monitor database, accessing, 157

table names, 38

tables, relationships, 38

to_s(), 35

transaction() method, 45

transactions, 45

up() method, 49–51

update rows, 36

validate() method, 47

validation, 47–48

see also ActiveLDAP

add() method, 316

add_flowers() method, 202

add_method() method, 209, 210

add_servant() method, 209, 215

Addresses

add recipients to existing book, 66

customer address book, 56

directory layout with LDAP, 57

layout of book, 60f

mass mailing, 21

storing, 13

user id, 65

Agile Web Development with Rails (Thomas), 52, 175

Ant, 175, 307

Aoki, Minero, 291, 299

API (application program interface)

Oracle, 12, 14

Arrays

XML-RPC, 186

Artificial primary keys, 30, 31, 237

ASCII characters, 167

AT cellular command interface, 161

authenticate() method, 178, 179, 217

autocommit, 23

autocommit feature, 23

Autogenerated identifiers, 28, 30

Automatic management system, 29

Automation, *see* rake

B

basic_auth() method, 178

Berger, Daniel, 285

Berkeley DB (bdb), 57

Binary data, 161

Binary values, 65n

bind() method, 233

Bind variable (SQL), 22

Black, David A., 302

BLOB (binary large object), 14
body() method, 166
Brannan, Paul, 302
Build processes, 289–306
Builder, 93–97

C

C++ (CORBA services), 236
call() method, 190
call2() method, 190
canonical_log() method, 275
CGI (common gateway interface), 173
CGI Handler (WEBrick), 175f
Character sets, 244–258
    collation, 247
    I/O classes, 254–256
    ICU4R, 251–254
    jcode, 249–250
    sort order, 247
    string to uppercase, 247
    Unicode, 251
Character-Separated Values, see CSV
    (comma-separated values)
chop!() method, 249
chop() method, 249, 254
classname() method, 235
clear_ignore_patterns() method, 316
CLOB (character large object), 14
code() method, 166, 167
Code block
    ActiveRecord, 45
    LDAP (Lightweight Directory Access
        Protocol), 63, 64
    Ruby, 16, 68
Columns
    constraints on, 46, 47
COMMIT command, 23
Configuration (Log4r), 275–281
Configuration files, 127
connect() method, 14, 26
Connection handling (with GServer),
    148
Connection object, 14, 27, 28
Constraints, 46, 47
CORBA, 181
    binary messages, 227
    C++, 226
    C++ services, 236
    client, implementing, 228–230
    HTTP server, via WEBrick, 235–236

IDL (interface definition language),
    210, 224
IDL compiler, 226
.idl file, 225
IIOP (Internet inter ORB protocol),
    224
interface definition (SMS service),
    224
interfaces, 224
introduction to, 223
Java client, 226
Java SDK, 226
OMG (object management group),
    223
ORB (object request broker), 224
orbd, 228
overview, 225f
Ruby access, 224
Ruby Java Bridge, 230–235
skeletons, 224, 226
SmsServer class, 228
stubs, 224, 226
text messages, 227
Coupon application, 10–24
    mass mailing, 21
    security, 20
    statistics, 24
    workflow, 10f
create() method, 32, 188, 219
create_address_book() method, 199
create_connection() method, 26
create_recipient() method, 199, 200
create_flower() method, 202, 206
create_mail() method, 160
create_recipient() method, 199
create_rpc_driver() method, 215
create_session() method, 217
CRUD (Create, Retrieve, Update, and
    Delete), 33, 51
    REST, 201f
CSV (comma-separated values),
    135–141
    accessors, 138
    code block, 136
    CSV library, 136
    CSV::Reader class, 136
    CSV::Writer class, 136
    data, generating, 136
    defined, 135
    delimiters, 135, 136
    expressions, regular, 136

fs (field separator), 136
generate() method, 136
mailing program, 20
new() class, 138
open() method, 137
parse() method, 137
PragBouquet mailing, 10
processing, 136–138
product classes, 137
rs (record separator), 136
stream parameter, 136
strings, 136
Struct class, 137, 138
to_sym() method, 137
Cursors, 15, 16
Custom databases, 12
Customers
   address book, 56
   address databases, 13
   order tracking, 97–104
   payment application (e-score), 85
   privacy, 18
   statistics, 21, 24
   tracking, 21

D

Daemons, 282–284
   - - (double hyphen), 284
   absolute path, 284
   command-line options, 284
   control scripts, 283, 284
   debugging, 284
   introduction to, 282
   logger, 284
   Ruby package, 283
DAP (Directory Access Protocol), 52
Data binding, 104
Data Definition Language (DDL)
   statement, 49
Database driver, 26
Database interface (DBI), 26
Database.instance.connect() method, 31
Database.instance.connection() method,
   31
DatabaseHandle, 26
Databases, 9–79
   abstraction layers, 28
   accessing, 9
   artificial primary keys, 30, 31
   autogenerated identifiers, 29
   automatic management system, 29

C/C++, 29
column constraints, 47
columns, automatic increments, 36
content maintenance, 48
CRUD (Create, Retrieve, Update, and
   Delete), 33
customer, 12
customer addresses, 13
data constraints, 46
directories, 52
drivers, 26
Embedded SQL, 29
id values, 33
introduced, 9
migrating data, 29
modeling one-to-one relationship, 42
multiple vendors, 9, 28
MySQL, 18, 157
objects, 33
password for writing to, 57
replacing and moving, 28
resource management, 25
schema maintenance, 48
singleton object, 25
stock management, 43, 45, 46
subselects, 28
transactions, 30
vs socket, 148
writing data, 22
Date formats, 256–258
Dates, 28
Davidson, James Duncan, 134
:days, 17
DBI (database interface)
   abstraction layers, 26, 29
   block syntax, 27
   connect(), 26
   connection object, 28
   database driver, 26
   DatabaseHandle, 26
   DBI.connect() method, 27
   drivers for, 29
   native drivers, 26
   performance, 29
   prepared statements, 31, 32
   select_all() method, 27
   StatementHandle, 26
DBI.connect() method, 27
DDL (Data Definition Language)
   statement, 49
debug() method, 269

delete!() method, 249

delete() method, 249, 254

delete_address_book() method, 197

delete_card() method, 183, 189

delete_recipient() method, 197

Delimiters (in CSV), 135

Deployment processes, 289–306
  introduction to, 289

Descendant-or-self axis, 120

Deserialization, 104

Directory
  entries, 52
  LDAP (Lightweight Directory Access
    Protocol), 56
  services, 62
  structure, 52

Directory Access Protocol (DAP), 52

Distributed applications, 181

DN (distinguished names), 55, 59, 61,
  63, 66, 67, 75

do_DELETE() method, 197

do_GET() method, 169, 170, 177

do_POST() method, 170

do_PUT() method, 170

DOM, 82, 99

downcase() method, 248, 250

draw_card() method, 182, 189

DRb (distributed Ruby), 237–241

DRb.start.service() method, 237

Drewry, Will, 71

dRuby (distributed Ruby), 237–241
  DRbUndumped class, 240
  remote reference, 239
  security, 241
  uses for, 240

DSL (domain-specific language), 323

Duck typing, 151, 152

Dynamic languages
  DBI (database interface), 26
  objects, 152

E

e-mail
  status monitor, 160
  to-SMS-gateway, 161

E-score application, 85

E-score architecture, 86f

each_char() method, 250, 252

each_word() method, 252

each_hash() method, 19

Electric XML library, 82

encode() method, 166

encoded() method, 160

Encodings, 244–258
  I/O classes, 254–256
  ICU4R, 251–254
  Unicode, 249–251

End User License Agreements (EULA),
  290

Enterprise integration, 3
  databases, 5
  defined, 3
  Ruby standards, 4
  tools, 5

Enterprise software, 2–3
  defined, 2
  dynamic languages, advantages, 3–4
  replacing and moving databases, 28
  requirements of, 2–3
  vs other software, 2

error() method, 269

EULA (end user license agreements),
  290

exec() method, 15, 16, 28, 173

execute() method, 28

F

fatal() method, 269

Fatal application errors, 161

fetch(), 15

fmt() method, 253

fork method, 285

format() method, 274

Format specifiers (Log4r), 272f

Formatters (in Log4r), 271–274

Fowler, Chad, 302, 303

Fowler, Martin, 2, 31, 34

func() method, 32

G

get_instance() method, 193

GET request, 164, 170

get_report() method, 202, 286

get_uid() method, 195

gettext() method, 258

Greeting Card Architecture, 183f

Groovy, 231

GServer, 148–152
  duck typing, 151
  join() method, 149
  puts() method, 151, 152
  readline() method, 151

serve() method, 149, 151
start() method, 149

H

Hansson, David Heinemeier, 34
Hash, 20
   in MySQL, 19
   LDAP, 66, 68
Header handlers, 219
Hook Script API, 300
HTTP, 148
   + sign, 163
   add new entries, 198
   authentication, 215
   basic authentication, 177
   client library, 165
   CRUD, mapping to REST, 201f
   delete methods, 197
   GET request, 166
   international phone numbers, 163
   key,value pairs, 168
   layer for CORBA, 224
   location header, 199
   map address book to, 191–201
   method handler, 194
   modify entries, 199
   POST command, 167
   proxy servers, 171
   remote procedure calls, 161–166
   SMS interface with, 161
   status code, 163, 167
   testing, 164
   URL, use of, 196
   URL-encoding, 163, 166
   WEBrick, 170
HTTP service status monitor, 168–170

I

I/O classes, 254–256
i18n (internationalization), 243–244
   encoding for source code files, 246
   encoding for textual data, 244
   J2EE, 256
   .NET, 256
   tips and tricks, 263
   see also l10n (localization)
i18n_read() method, 256
ICU (and ICU4R), 251
ICU4R, 251–254
   |-characters, 253
   chop() method, 254

delete() method, 254
   disadvantages of, 254
   each_char() method, 252
   each_word() method, 252
   fmt() method, 253
   iterate over characters, 252
   sprintf() method, 253
   to_u() method, 251
   to_s() method, 252
   tr() method, 254
   u() method, 251
   URegexp class, 251
   UString class, 251, 252
IDE (integrated development
   environments), 307
IDL (interface definition language), 210,
   224
IIOP (Internet inter ORB protocol), 224
import() method, 232, 233
index() method, 248
info() method, 269, 271
initialize() method, 33, 169, 193, 275,
   321
inspect() method, 249
install_service() method, 287
instance_eval() method, 241
instance_variable_set method, 241
International Component for Unicode
   (and ICU4R), 251
International I/O, 254–256
Internationalization, 243–244
   see also Localization
*Internet Assigned Numbers Authority
   (IANA)*, 53
_invoke() method, 235
IPC (interprocess communication), 181

J

J2EE
   i18n, 244, 256
Java
   Ant, 134
   Electric XML library, 82
   encoding of types, 235f
   exception, 234
   JNI (Java natural interface, 231
   JRuby, 231
   JVM (Java virtual machine),
   231–233
   rjb (Ruby Java Bridge), 231

RMI (remote method invocation),
181, 223
Ruby Java Bridge, 230–235
Ruby, embed code in, 226
Ruby, integrating, 223–235
status monitor client library,
153–155
toString() method, 152
XmlSchema files, 126
yajb (yet another Java bridge), 231
jcode, 249–250
advantages of, 250
chop!() method, 249
chop() method, 249, 254
delete!() method, 249
delete() method, 249, 254
each_char() method, 250
jcount() method, 250
jlength() method, 250
squeeze!() method, 249
squeeze() method, 249
succ!() method, 249
succ() method, 249
tr!() method, 249
tr() method, 249, 254
tr_s!() method, 249
tr_s() method, 249
Unicode, 251
jcount() method, 250
jlength() method, 250
JNI (Java natural interface), 231
join() method, 149
Jython, 231

K

Kain, Jim, 12
Key/value pairs
XML-RPC, 186
Key:value pairs (in LDAP), 59
Kilmer, Richard, 302

L

l10n (localization), 243–244
tips and tricks, 263
last_insert_id() method, 29
LDAP (Lightweight Directory Access
Protocol), 52–79
: character (LDIF), 56
character (LDIF), 56
ABSTRACT, 54
ActiveLDAP, 71–79

add() method, 66
add recipients to an existing book,
66
address book layout, 60f
address books, 57
arrays, 64, 65
attribute modifications, 65
attributes, 53, 55, 65
attributes_only, 64
AUXILIARY, 54
-b uid option, 61
base_dn, 63
Berkeley DB (bdb), 57
binary values, 65n
bind() method, 63, 66
cn (common name), 55
code block, 63, 64, 68
connection object, 63
core schema, 53, 57
create entries, 64
create() method, 65
database password, 57
delete() method, 70
DESC keyword, 53, 54
directory entries, 52
directory layout, 57
directory structure, 58
DN (distinguished names), 55, 59,
61, 63, 66, 67, 70
each() method, 68, 69
each() method (private), 68
each_recipient() method, 68
EQUALITY, 54
filter, 63
hash, 66, 68
hashes, 64
initialize() method, 65
inject() method, 69
key:value pairs, 59
LDAP::Conn.add() method, 66
ldapadd command, 59
LDAP::Conn.modify(), 70
LDAP::Mod, 65
LDAPv3 service, 63
LDIF, 69
LDIF (LDAP Data Interchange
Format), 56, 69
MAY, 54
MUST, 54
NAME keyword, 53, 54
nil, 64

object classes, 53, 55
(objectclass=*) option, 62
OID (object identifier), 53
OpenLDAP, 57
options, 61
overview of, 52–56
print method, 67, 68
RDN (relative distinguished names), 55
root DN, 66
root entry, 55
root node, 57
Ruby/LDAP, 62–71
-s base option, 61
-s one option, 61
-s sub option, 61
schemas, 53
scope, 63
search filter, 63
search() method, 63, 64
seconds, 64
sn attribute, 68
sort_attribute, 64
sort_proc, 64
STRUCTURAL, 54
SUBSTR, 54
SUP keyword, 53
SYNTAX keyword, 54
udn() method, 67
uid attributes, 58, 59
useconds, 64
User class, 65
-x option, 61
ldapsearch command, 60
LDIF (LDAP Data Interchange Format), 56
LDIF (LDAP Data Interchange Format) file, 58–59
Legacy applications, testing, 317–323
    DSL (domain-specific language), 323
    executing external programs, 319
    log file, 321
    reference data, 321
    test log, 320
    TestTool class, 321
    tools for, 318
length() method, 245, 249
listFiles() method, 233
load() method, 232
load_xml_file() method, 276
load_xml_string() method, 276

Localization, 243–244
Location paths, 119
Location steps, 119
Log files, 264
Log4r, 267–282
    app logger, 279
    attributes, 278
    canonical_log() method, 275
    child loggers, 270
    configuration, 275–281
    configuration sections, 278
    Configurator, 275
    console outputter, 278
    db logger, 279
    debug() method, 269
    default levels, 269
    error() method, 269
    fatal() method, 269
    format() method, 274
    format exceptions, 273
    format specifiers, 272f
    formatters, 271–274
    hierarchy of levels, defining, 269, 270
    info() method, 269, 271
    initialize() method, 275
    level names, 270
    Log4r classes, require, 279
    Log4r objects, 278
    logfile outputter, 278
    vs Logger, 265, 282
    Logger class, 268–271
    Logger with two outputters, 277
    Outputter class, 268
    outputters, 274–275
    PatternFormat class, 271, 273
    printf() method, 271
    Ruby gem, 268
    super() method, 275
    timestamps, formatting of, 271, 273
    to_s() method, 271
    usec() method, 273
    vs Logger, 266, 267
    warn() method, 269
    XML configuration, 275, 276
    XML outputters, 276f
    XML parameters, 280
    YAML, 279–281
    YAML configuration, 275
    see also Logger
Logger

vs Log4r, 282
Logger class, 264–267
　configuration options, lack of, 266
　to files, 265
　IO object, logging to, 266
　log level, 265
　log lines, 266
　vs Log4r, 265
　new() method, 265
　rotating loggers, 266
　strftime() method, 267
　timestamp format, 267
　vs Log4r, 267
　vs Logger, 266
Logging, 264–282
　daemons application, 284
　drawbacks, 281
　to files with Logger, 265
　Log files, purposes of, 264
　log levels, 265
　Log4r, 267–282
　Logger class, 264–267
　with Logger, 282
　test tool logger, 321
login() method, 216, 217
log() method, 153, 155, 157
Lugovoi, Nikolai, 251

M

Macdonald, Ian, 62, 71
Machine objects, 258
make, 307
Martin, Robert, 148
Masahiro, Tomita, 18
Masato, Yoshida, 12, 251
McLean, Grant, 126
Megginson, David, 99
message() method, 166
method_missing() method, 189
Mind Electric, 82
Mixed content, 103
mount() method, 178
mount_proc() method, 178
Mower, Matt, 18
Mutoh, Masao, 258
MySQL
　background information, 18
　databases, 157
　portable statements, 28
　PragBouquet database, 11
　prepared statements, 19, 32

Ruby/MySQL, 18
　singleton, 31
　table, moving to Oracle, 27
MySQL/Ruby, 18

N

n_() method, 261
Nakamura, Hiroshi, 136, 207
.NET
　i18n, 256
　i18n support, 244
　XmlSchema files, 126
Netscape (Ruby/LDAP interface), 62
Networks
　ASCII, 167
　background information, 147–148
　e-mail, 160
　proxy servers, 171
Neumann, Michael, 187
new() method, 14, 26, 265
new_with_sig() method, 234, 235
Node sets (XPath), 120
num_rows() method, 20

O

Object identifier (OID), 53
Object-relational mappers, 29–52
OCI (Oracle Call Interface), 14
OID (object identifier), 53
OMG (object management group), 223
on_init() method, 208
on_simple_inbound method, 219, 221
One-to-one relationship, 42
only_at() method, 274
OpenLDAP, 57
　code block, 63
　connection object, 63
　ldapsearch command, 60
　LDAPv3 service, 63
　Ruby/LDAP interface with, 62
　see also LDAP (Lightweight Directory
　　Access Protocol)
OpenSSL, 162
Oracle
　autogeneration feature, 29
　connection object, 23
　cursors, 15
　DBI (database interface), 27
　grouping SQL statements, 23
　migration to MySQL, 29
　optimization, 16

portable statements, 28
PragBouquet database, 11
SQL*Plus, 11
Oracle (Masato), 12
Oracle Call Interface (OCI), 14
ORB (object request broker), 224
Ordering process, stock, 42
Outputters (Log4r), 274–275, 276f

P

parse() method, 17, 28
parse_recipient() method, 199
parse_user() method, 199
Patterns of Enterprise Application Architecture (Fowler), 2, 31
peer_cert() method, 162
Perl
    dynamic language, advantages, 4
    status monitor client, 155–156
    XML::Simple, 126
    YAML, 141
PHP (YAML), 141
Placeholders, 17, 37
Portable object, 258
Portable object template, 258
Portable software, 29
Portable statements, 28
PragBouquet (example company)
    address book add entries, 198
    address book delete method, 197
    address book modify entries, 199
    API of stock class, refactoring, 202
    authentication for stock control server, 215–222
    automated ordering, 49
    convert customer addresses into XML, 86
    coupon application, 10–24
    customer account data, 71
    customer address book, 56
    DBI (database interface), 26
    e-score application, 85
    e-score architecture, 86f
    greeting card application, 181–191
    greeting card architecture, 183f
    greeting card printing (daemons process), 283
    infrastructure, 6n
    Java client, 153
    map address book to HTTP, 191–201
    mass mailing program, 10

OpenLDAP server, 71
orders, automatic management system, 29
overview, 5–6
performance of XML processing, 104
Perl client, 155
remote procedure calls, 161–166
Ruby client, 153
server for greeting card application, 187–191
service control panel observer, 288f
SMSC, 161–166
sorting customer list, 18
status monitor clients, 152–157
status monitor, create, 149–152
status monitor, services test, 285
stock management, 43, 45, 46
tracking orders, 97–104
user accounts (web), 71
Predicates, 122
Prepared statements, 16, 19
Primary keys, artificial, 30
print() method, 189
print_card() method, 183, 189
print_report() method, 202
printf() method, 256, 271
Privacy, 18
process() method, 321
process_test_case() method, 321
Programming Ruby (Thomas), 5, 148
proxy() method, 190
proxy2() method, 190
puts() method, 151, 152, 264, 282
Python
    dynamic language, advantages, 4
    YAML, 141

Q

query() method, 19
Query execution plan, 16

R

RAA (Ruby application library), 290
rake, 306–317
    -T, 311
    actions, 310–315
    classes, 308
    clean task, 314
    clear_ignore_patterns() method, 316
    clobber task, 314
    directory task, 313

file task, 313
file lists, 316–317
file name patterns, 316
FileList class, 316
GemPackageTask, 314
IDE (integrated development
     environments), 307
lib directory, 310
libraries, 310
managing files, 316
methods, 308
namespaces, 312
package tasks, 311
pros and cons, 317
rakefiles, 307–310
RDocTask, 314
rule task, 313
select_default_ignore_patterns() method,
     316
sh() method, 313
standard tasks, 313
syntax, 309f
task() method, 308
tasks, 308, 310–315
tutorials, 317
Unix commands, 311
RDN (relative distinguished names), 55
readline() method, 151, 152
Refactoring to Patterns (Kerievsky), 97
RELAX NG (Regular Language for XML,
     New Generation), 130–132
   < characters, 132
   comments, 132
   compact syntax, 130
   parsing, 132
   read_doc() method, 132
   syntax styles, 130
   translate requirements into XML
        syntax, 131
   validate against schema, 131
   whitespace, 132
   XML header, 132
   XML syntax, 130
Remote procedure calls
   testing, 164
Remote procedure calls (HTTP)
   SMSC, 161–166
remove_flowers() method, 202
require_gem() method, 305
REST (Representational State
     Transfer), 196

add new entries, 198
CRUD mapping, 201f
delete methods, 197
location header, 199
modify entries, 199
standards, 201
reverse() method, 248, 249
REXML
   support for RELAX NG, 130
   array parameter, 116
   attlistdecl() method, 108, 113
   attributes accessor, 100
   block parameter, 116
   cdata() method, 107, 112
   characters() method, 112
   children, 100
   comment() method, 106, 107, 112
   comments in RELAX NG, 132
   doctype() method, 107, 112
   DTD handling, 115
   each_element() method, 100, 101
   elementdecl() method, 108, 112
   elements, 100
   end_document() method, 111
   end_element() method, 112
   end_prefix_mapping() method, 112
   entity() method, 108
   entitydecl() method, 108, 113
   instruction() method, 107
   invoke stream parser, 105
   listen() method, 116–117
   listener parameter, 116
   method_missing() method, 105, 109
   new() method, 100
   notationdecl() method, 108, 113
   processing_ method, 112
   read_doc() method, 132
   RELAX NG (Regular Language for
        XML, New Generation), 130–132
   REXML::StreamListener, 109
   root() method, 100
   root element, 100
   SAX2, 111–117
   start_document() method, 111
   start_element() method, 112
   start_prefix_mapping() method, 112
   stream parsing, 104–111
   support for RELAX NG, 132
   symbol parameter, 116
   tag_end() method, 106, 107, 111
   tag_start() method, 106, 111

text() method, 106, 107, 111
UTF-8 character set, 93
validating documents, 130
whitespace, 132
XML header, 132
XML processing, 98
XML, turn objects into, 194
xmldecl() method, 105, 106
xpath() method, 125
XPath support, 118, 125
  see also RELAX NG (Regular
    Language for XML, New
    Generation)
REXML::StreamListener, 109
Rjb::import(classname), 234
RMI (remote method invocation), 223
ROLLBACK, 23
Root DN (distinguished names), 66
RPC (Sun's remote procedure call), 181
Ruby, 151
  $KCODE, 245
  %x, 319
  connect() method, 14
  ActiveLDAP, 71–79
  ActiveLDAP Gem, 73
  ActiveRecord, 157, 203, 204
  ActiveRecord Gem, 35
  add() method, 316
  address book, 57
  API of Rjb library, 232
  Application Archive, 4
  artificial primary keys, 237
  attlistdecl() method, 108, 113
  authenticate() method, 217
  Authenticator class (SOAP), 216
  basic_auth() method, 178
  body() method, 166
  build and deployment processes,
    289–306
  Builder, 93–97
  cdata!() method, 96
  cdata() method, 107, 112
  central installation, 290
  character set encodings, 254–256
  character sets, 244–258
  characters() method, 112
  chop!() method, 249
  chop() method, 249, 254
  classes for storage, 102
  clear_ignore_patterns() method, 316
  code() method, 166, 167

code block, 16, 68
comment!() method, 96
comment() method, 106, 107, 112
compilation and build management,
  307
CORBA access, 224
CORBA binding, 226
CORBA to HTTP via WEBrick,
  235–236
create server automatically from
  class, 209
create_mail() method, 160
create_session() method, 217
Daemons package, 283
daemons, 282–284
database drivers, 26
Date class, 256
date formats, 256–258
DateTime class, 256
DBD modules, 26
DBI (database interface), 26
declare!() method, 96
delete!() method, 249
delete() method, 249, 254
deserialization, 104
Distributed Ruby (DRb), 181
do_GET() method, 169, 170, 177
do_POST() method, 170
do_PUT() method, 170
doctype() method, 107, 112
downcase() method, 248, 250
DRbUndumped class, 240
dRuby (distributed Ruby), 237–241
duck typing, 152
dynamic language, advantages, 3–4
each_char() method, 250, 252
each_parcel() method, 104
each_word() method, 252
echo command, 322
echo server (example), 148
elementdecl() method, 108, 112
encode() method, 166
encoded() method, 160
encodings, 244–258
end_document() method, 111
end_element() method, 112
end_prefix_mapping() method, 112
entity() method, 108
entitydecl() method, 108, 113
exec() method, 15, 16
executing external programs, 319

factory classes, 219

fmt() method, 253

fork() method, 285

Gem, 126

generate code, 212

gettext() method, 258

header handler (SOAP), 220

HTTP client library, 165

HTTP server, 176

HTTP services, accessing, 161–168

HTTP services, creating, 168–170

I/O classes, 254–256

i18n, 250, 263

i18n support, 244

i18n_read() method, 256

Iconv, 255, 256

ICU4R, 251–254

indent option, 94

index() method, 248

initialize() method, 104, 169, 321

InputStream, 255

insert tags for XML, 95

inspect() method, 249

install_service() method, 287

instruction() method, 107

iterators, 15

Java exception, simulate, 234

Java interface, associate Ruby class, 233

Java type encoding, 234

Java, integrating, 223–235

jcode, 249–250

jcount() method, 250

jlength() method, 250

JRuby, 231

JVM (Java virtual machine), 232, 233

l10n, 263

language translation, 258

LDAP, 67

Legacy applications, testing, 317–323

length() method, 245, 249

load_xml_file() method, 276

load_xml_string() method, 276

Log4r, 267–282

Logger class, 264–267

Logger class, 158

logger object, 150

login() method, 217

mapping from ActiveRecord, 42

margin option, 95

message() method, 166

method_missing() method, 94, 105, 109

migration advantages, 49

modeling one-to-one relationship, 42

mount() method, 178

mount_proc() method, 178

MySQL support, 18

MySQL/Ruby, 18

n_() method, 261

NET::SMTP, 160

network services, creating, 238

new() method, 14, 265

notationdecl() method, 108, 113

object-relational mappers, 34

objects, 152

only_at() method, 274

OpenSSL, 162

Oracle modules, 12–14

pack() method, 93

parcel tracking with REXML, 102

peer_cert() method, 162

prepared statements (in MySQL), 19

process() method, 321

process_test_case() method, 321

processing_instruction() method, 112

protocol standards, support, 181

puts() method, 151, 264, 282

RAA (Ruby application library), 290

rake, 306–317

rake syntax, 309f

readline() method, 151

remote reference with dRuby, 239

require_gem() method, 305

REST support, 201

reverse() method, 248, 249

REXML stream parser, 105

Rjb methods, 234

Rjb signature, rules for, 234

rjb (Ruby Java Bridge), 231

Ruby Java Bridge, 230–235

Ruby-GetText, 258–260

Ruby/Java hybrid, 232

Ruby/LDAP, 62–71

Ruby/MySQL, 18

RubyGems, 302–306

rule() method, 313

security with dRuby, 241

select_default_ignore_patterns() method, 316

send() method, 161
send_sms() method, 166, 167
send_mail() method, 160
SequenceManager class, 238
serve() method, 151, 169
Services (for Windows), 284–289
setup.rb, 291–302
sh() method, 313
singleton object, 25
skeleton (server), 214
SOAP soap4r library, 206
sprintf() method, 253
squeeze!() method, 249
squeeze() method, 249
start() method, 166, 288
start_document() method, 111
start_element() method, 112
start_prefix_mapping() method, 112
status monitor, 149
status monitor client, 153
Status MonitorClient, 153
stop() method, 289
strftime() method, 257, 267
String objects, 246
Struct class, 102
succ() method, 249
sudo command, 294
support for DTD, 81
support for validation, 81
support for XSLT, 81
system() method, 132, 133, 297, 317, 319
tag() method, 89–91
tag_end() method, 106, 107, 111
tag_start() method, 106, 111
target!() method, 94
target option, 94
task() method, 308, 309
TCP servers, creating, 148
TCPSocket, 153
test tool logger, 321
test tool, creating, 318
test tool, example, 318–320
test_stock_service() method, 286
TestTool class, 321, 322
text!() method, 96
text() method, 103, 106, 107, 111
thread-safe, 238
Time class, 256
time formats, 256–258
tmail library, 291

to_u() method, 251
to_xml() method, 92
to_event() method, 104
to_s() method, 102, 252, 282
to_upper() method, 263
to_xml() method, 87, 88, 93
tr!() method, 249
tr() method, 249, 254
tr_s!() method, 249
tr_s() method, 249
U*, 248
u() method, 249, 251
Unicode, 251
Unicode strings, manipulating, 250
unpack() method, 93, 248
unsigned integer values representing UTF-8* characters, 248
upcase method, 246, 250
UString, 249
UTF-8 strings, 248
validating XML documents, 130
validation, 47
variables in Log4r configuration files, 280
vs C++, 152
vs Java, 152
WEBrick, 168–175
WEBricklets, 175–177
win32utils, 285
write() method, 92
.wsdl files, 213–215
wsdl2ruby.rb, 212
X.509 certificate, 162
xml_in() method, 128, 129
XML parsers, 82
XML support, 81
xmldecl() method, 105, 106
xmlrpc4r, 187–191
XmlSchema files, 126
XmlSimple, 126
yajb (yet another Java bridge), 231
YAML, 141–146
YAML test suite, 321
yield() method, 104
see also RubyGems
Ruby Application Archive, 4
Ruby Application Library (RAA), 290
Ruby Java Bridge, 230–235
Ruby on Rails, 34, 57
Ruby-GetText, 258–260
    array syntax, 262

machine object (.mo) file, 260, 261
parameters, 259
plural forms, 262
portable object (.po) file, 260, 262
test example, 261
translation example, 259–260, 262
Ruby/LDAP, 62–71
  attributes parameter, 76
  base_dn parameter, 76
  directory service, 62
  filter parameter, 76
  scope parameter, 76
Ruby/MySQL, 18
Ruby/OCI8 (Takehiro), 12
Ruby/OCI8 driver, 14
Ruby9i (Kain), 12
RubyForge, 4
RubyGems, 302–306
  ActiveSupport, 304
  compared with setup.rb, 306
  documentation system, 303
  .gem file, 303
  gem list, 302
  Gems server, 304
  how to use, 303
  invoke Ruby interpreter, 305
  list option, 304
  open source software, 306
  operators, 305
  pessimistic operator, 306
  proxy server, 304
  rake command, install, 303
  require 'rubygems', 305
  root user, 304
  sudo command, 304
  update option, 304
  user guide, 303
  version requirements, 305
  versions, 305
rule() method, 313
Russel, Sean, 82, 114

S

SAX2, 82, 111–117
  background information, 111, 114
  code block, 114, 115
  compared with REXML Stream
    Parsing, 114
  parsing example, 113
  text nodes, 114, 115
  whitespace, 115

Schemas, 53
  maintaining, 48
  validating with xmllint, 132
  validating XML documents, 131
Security
  authentication for stock control
    server, 215–222
  coupon application, 20
  dRuby (distributed Ruby), 241
  HTTP basic authentication, 177
  password (LDAP), 57
  prepared statements, 16
  SQL, 16
  SQL injection, 32, 37
  SSL (secure sockets layer), 162
  WEBrick, 178
Seki, Masatoshi, 237
select_all() method, 27
select_default_ignore_patterns() method,
  316
send() method, 161
send_sms() method, 166, 167
send_mail() method, 160
sendBinarySms() method, 227
sendTextSms() method, 227
serve() method, 149, 151, 158, 169
service_init() method, 286
service_main() method, 286
Services (for Windows), 284–289
  absolute file name, 287
  control scripts, 285
  external control, consequences of,
    287
  introduction to, 282
  logging, 286
  service control panel observer, 288f
  service names, 287
  starting a service, 288
  stock server, 286
  stopping a service, 289
  uninstall a service, 289
  win32utils, 285
  Windows interface, implementing,
    285
  working directory, 286
  see also Daemons
set_price() method, 202, 211, 212
setup.rb, 290–302
  alternatives to, 302
  compared with RubyGems, 306
  create MySQL database, 299

directory layout, 298
directory mapping, typical, 298f
directory names containing blanks, 297
execute Ruby scripts, 300
global options, 294
Hook Script API, 300
lib/sm directory, 300
options, complete list, 295
status monitor package, 299
subdirectories, 298
task-specific options, 294
test status monitor installation, 301f
testing installation, 300
tmail library, 291
usage, 297
SGML (Standard Generalized Markup Language), 83
sh() method, 313
Short message peer-to-peer protocol (SMPP), 161
Short message service center (SMSC), 161
   HTTP, 161
Short messages (SMS), 161
Simple data types (XML-RPC), 185f
simulate_request() method, 152
Singleton, 127
Singleton objects, 25, 31
Small, John W., 148
SMPP (short message peer-to-peer protocol), 161
SMS (short messages), 161
   binary data, 161
   international phone numbers, 163
   status monitor testing, 164f
   testing (HTML page), 164
   textual data, 161
SMSC (short message service center), 161
   HTTP, 161
   testing, 164
SOAP, 148, 181
   authenticate() method, 217
   authentication for clients, 216
   authentication for stock control server, 215–222
   Authenticator class, 216
   background information, 204–209
   child, 206
   create_session() method, 217

elements, 205
header, 218
header handler, 220, 221
headers, 219, 222
headers (transport for meta information), 216
industry standard, 222
languages, programming, 212
login() method, 217
messages, 212
method parameter, 205
mustunderstand, 219
Response, 206
return value, 206
skeleton (server), 214
soap4r, 222
soap4r Ruby library, 206
textual protocol, 223
W3C specification, 204
.wsdl files, 215
WSDL (Web Services Description Language), 210–215
XML-RPC comparison, 204
XmlSchema, 212
soap4r, 207
   authentication for HTTP, 215
   factory classes, 219
   header handlers, 219
   headers, 217, 219
   proxy, 209
   server instance, 208
   SIGINT signal, 208
   SOAP::RPC::StandaloneServer, 208
   test client, 208
   web service creation, 207
   wsdl2ruby.rb, 212
soap4r library
   parameters, 208
Sockets, 148–160
esprintf() method, 253
SQL
   autocommit, 23
   bind variable, 22
   embedded, 29
   injection, 16, 32, 37
   joining tables, 15
   portable statements, 28
   SELECT option, 62
SQL statements
   bind parameters, 22
   grouping in Oracle, 23

strings, 20
SQL*Plus
    PragBouquet coupon application, 11
    statistics for coupon application, 24
squeeze!() method, 249
squeeze() method, 249
SSL (secure sockets layer), 162
Standard Generalized Markup
        Language (SGML), 83
Standard product, 12
start() method, 149, 166, 288
StatementHandle, 26
Statistics, 21
Status Monitor
    class, 155
    clients, creating, 152–157
    creating, 149
    duck typing, 151
    e-mail, 160
    fatal application errors, 161
    features, adding, 157
    HTTP service, 168–170
    log() method, 153, 155, 157
    package withsetup.rb, 299
    serve() method, 151
    services test, 285
    simulate_request() method, 152
    STDOUT, 149
    StringIO, 151
    telnet, 150
    test installation of, 301f
    testing remote procedure calls, 164f
    V0.0.1b, 149
    web access, 168
Stock management, 43, 45, 46
stop() method, 289
Stream parsing, 99, 104–111
    defined, 105
strftime() method, 256, 257, 267
StringIO, 151, 152
Structs, 186
Subselects, 28
succ!() method, 249
succ() method, 249
super() method, 275
Syntax for dates, 28
syslogd, 149
system() method, 317, 319
system method, 297

Tables
    constraints on, 46, 47
    joining with SQL, 15
Takehiro, Kubo, 12, 14
task() method, 309
Tateishi, Takaaki, 62
TCP server, creating, 149
TCPSocket, 153
telnet, 150, 163
test_stock_service() method, 286
throw() method, 234
Time formats, 256–258
tmail, 291–294
    C extensions, 293
    configuring, 293, 294f
    copy to Ruby library directory, 293
    directory names containing blanks,
        297
    downloading from Internet, 292f
    global options(setup.rb), 294
    incompatibilities, 293
    installation, 291, 296f
    library, 291
    root password, 294
    setup, 295f
    setup.rb, 291, 292
    sudo command, 294
    task-specific options(setup.rb), 294,
        295
to_u method, 251
to_cn() method, 195
to_s() method, 35, 252, 271, 282
to_upper() method, 263
to_xml() method, 193–195
Torres, Leon, 268
toString() method (in Java), 152
tr!() method, 249
tr() method, 249, 254
tr_s!() method, 249
tr_s() method, 249
Tree parsers, 98–104
    DOM, 99
Tree structure, 83f
    XML, 83

u() method, 249
u method, 251
Uehlinger, Thomas, 283
Unicode, 251

Unique IDs, 30
Unix daemons, 283–284
Unix Network Programming (Stevens),
    148, 283
unload() method, 233
unpack() method, 248
upcase method, 246, 250
URL encoding, 166, 167
usec() method, 273

V

Validation, 47
Vim, 175

W

W3C, 81, 99
Wall, Larry, 156
warn() method, 269
WEBrick, 168–180
    Apache web, 178
    attributes, 172
    authenticate() method, 178, 179
    CGI scripts, executing, 173
    CGIHandler, 173, 174, 175f
    cookies, 172
    dispatching, 170
    ERBHandler, 175
    exec() method, 173
    FancyIndexing, 178
    FileHandler, 175
    GET request, 173
    HandlerCallback, 178
    hash objects, 172
    HEAD command, 172
    header, 172
    htpasswd, 178
    HTTP basic authentication, 177
    HTTP requests (rules), 170
    HTTP server, implementing, 235–236
    HTTPAuth, 177
    HTTPRequest, 172
    HTTPResponse, 172
    map address book to HTTP, 191–201
    methods, 172
    OPTIONS command, 172
    POST requests, 173
    query, 172
    security, 178
    serving files, 173
    servlet creation, 193
    WEBricklets, 175–177

xmlrpc4r, 188
WEBricklets, 175–177
Weirich, Jim, 93, 302, 307
why the lucky stiff
    (YAML parser), 141
Widenius, Monty, 18
win32utils, 285–289
    get_report() method, 286
    install_service() method, 287
    Logger, 286
    service_init() method, 286
    service_main() method, 286
    start() method, 288
    StockServerObserver, 286
    stop() method, 289
    test_stock_service() method, 286
Winer, Dave, 183
WSDL (Web Services Description
    Language), 210–215
    elements, 210, 211
    generate code, 212
    interface, 211
    interface description, 210
    service binding, 212
    service description, 210
    XML namespaces, 210
wsdl2ruby.rb, 212

X

X.500 directory specification, 52
X.509 certificate, 162
XML, 81–146
    alternatives to, 134–135
    attributes, 84
    attributes vs elements, 84–85
    automation, 126
    Builder, 93–97
    cdata!() method, 96
    CDATA section, insert, 96
    characteristics of, 81
    comment!() method, 96
    data binding, 104
    declare!() method, 96
    deserialization, 104
    document processing, 97–117
    documents, generating, 85–97
    DTD, 107, 108
    DTD declarations, inserting, 96
    indent option, 94
    international character sets, 81
    listener class, 108, 109

margin option, 95
method_missing() method, 94
mixed content, 96, 103
nesting, 84
notations in DTD, 108
overview of, 83–85
pack() method, 93
parameters in Log4r, 280
parsing schemes, 98
REXML, processing with, 98
REXML::StreamListener, 109
SAX2, 111–117
SAX2 parser, example, 113
serial processing, 105
SGML, 83
startElement() method, 84, 85
stream parsers, 98, 99, 104–111
strings to generate documents, 86
tag() method, 89–91
target!() method, 94
target option, 94
text!() method, 96
to_xml() method, 87, 88, 92, 93
tracking orders, 97
tree parsers, 98–104
unpack() method, 93
validating documents, 129–134
W3C, 81, 99
well-formedness, 83
when to avoid, 134–135
whitespace, 132
widespread use of, 81
write() method, 92
XML::Simple (Perl module), 126
xmllint, 132–133
XmlSchema files, 126
XmlSimple, 126–129
XPath, 117–126
XSL (eXtensible Stylesheet
    Language), 135
YAML, 141–146
see also XML-RPC, see also
    XmlSimple, see also XPath, see
    also YAML (YAML Ain't Markup
    Language)
XML-RPC, 181
architecture, 184, 184f
arrays, 186
data types, 186
faults, 186, 187
overview, 183–187

s/RPC2, 189
services, 189
simple data types, 185f
SOAP comparison, 204
structs, 186
textual protocol, 223
xmlrpc4r, 187–191
xmllint, 132–133
xmlrpc4r, 187–191
    default handler, 189
    delete_card() method, 189
    draw_card() method, 189
    print() method, 189
    proxy, 190
    server reference, 190
    server types, 190
    WEBrick, 188
XmlSchema files, 126
XmlSimple, 126–129
    arrays, 128
    attribute values, 128
    elements, 128
    hashes, 127, 128
    IO object, 129
    key_attr option, 128
    nil, 129
    production base password
        (accessing), 128, 129
    string, 129
    xml_in() method, 128, 129
    XML source (for xml_in() method), 129
XPath, 117–126
    != (not equal to), 124f
    * symbol, 118, 122
    . abbreviation, 123
    .. abbreviation, 123
    // abbreviation, 120, 122, 123
    = (equal to), 124f
    [] predicates, 122
    | (union operator), 125
    > (greater than), 124f
    >= (greater than or equal), 124f
    < (less than), 124f
    <= (less than or equal), 124f
    ancestor axis, 123
    ancestor-or-self axis, 123
    attribute axis, 123
    axes, 120, 123f
    boolean, 122, 124
    boolean functions, 125
    boolean operators, 124f

child axis, 123
compared with Unix, 120
context, 120
defined, 117
descendant axis, 123
descendant-or-self axis, 120, 123
each() method, 118
expressions, 119
first() method, 118
following axis, 123
following-sibling axis, 123
functions, defining, 124–125
location paths, 119
location steps, 119
lvalue op rvalue, 122
match() method, 118, 119
methods (REXML), 118
namespace axis, 123
namespaces, 118
node set functions, 124
node sets, 101, 119, 120, 122
nodes, 120
number functions, 125
parent axis, 123
preceding axis, 123
preceding-sibling axis, 123
predicates, 122
REXML support for, 125
root element, 119
self axis, 123
string functions, 124
tracking results, 121f
tree structure, 120, 121f
xpath() method, 125
XPath and XPointer (Simpson), 118

Y

YAML (YAML Ain't Markup Language),
141–146
- symbol, 141
. (period), 143
: (colons), 143
array elements, 141
arrays, 144
begin attribute, 145
Boolean values, 143
data (serializing, deserializing), 145
data types, 142
dates, 144
encodes objects, 145
end attribute, 145
excl attribute, 145
expressions (regular), 145
Float objects, 143
Hash objects, 142, 143
hashes, 144
indentation, 144
integer objects, 143
key/value pairs, 143, 144
leading spaces, 144
Log4r, 279–281
objects (yamlfied), 144
parser, 141
Range objects, 145
Ruby array, 141
sign characters, 143
string object, 142
Struct objects, 144
symbols, 143
timestamps, 144
to_yaml method, 142

Facets of Ruby Series

All Ruby programmers need the definitive book on the Ruby language. Learn how to use Ruby to write exciting new applications. And if you're thinking of using Ruby to create Web applications, you really need to look at Ruby on Rails.

Programming Ruby (The PickAxe)

• The definitive guide for Ruby programmers. • Up-to-date and expanded for Ruby version 1.8. • Complete documentation of all the built-in classes, modules, and methods. • Complete descriptions of all ninety-eight standard libraries. • 200+ pages of new content in this edition. • Learn more about Ruby's web tools, unit testing, and programming philosophy.

Programming Ruby: The Pragmatic Programmer's Guide, 2nd Edition
Dave Thomas with Chad Fowler and Andy Hunt
(864 pages) ISBN: 0-9745140-5-5. $44.95

Agile Web Development with Rails

• The definitive guide for Rails developers. • Tutorial introduction, and in-depth reference. • All the scoop on ActiveRecord, ActionPack, and ActionView. • Special *David Says...* content by the inventor of Rails. • Chapters on testing, web services, Ajax, security, e-mail, deployment, and more.

Agile Web Development with Rails
Dave Thomas and David Heinemeier Hansson, with Leon Breedt, Mike Clark, Thomas Fuchs, and Andreas Schwarz
(560 pages) ISBN: 0-9745140-0-X. $34.95

The Pragmatic Bookshelf

The Pragmatic Bookshelf features books written by developers for developers. The titles continue the well-known Pragmatic Programmer style, and continue to garner awards and rave reviews. As development gets more and more difficult, the Pragmatic Programmers will be there with more titles and products to help programmers stay on top of their game.

Visit Us Online

Enterprise Integration with Ruby

pragmaticprogrammer.com/titles/fr_eir
Source code from this book, errata, and other resources. Come give us feedback, too!

Register for Updates

pragmaticprogrammer.com/updates
Be notified when updates and new books become available.

Join the Community

pragmaticprogrammer.com/community
Read our weblogs, join our online discussions, participate in our mailing list, interact with our wiki, and benefit from the experience of other Pragmatic Programmers.

New and Noteworthy

pragmaticprogrammer.com/news
Check out the latest pragmatic developments in the news.

Save on the PDF and other Ruby Books

Save more than 60% on the PDF version of this book. Owning the paper version of this book entitles you to purchase the PDF version for only $8.50 (regularly $21.50). That's a saving of more than 60%. The PDF is great for carrying around on your laptop. It's hyperlinked, has color, and is fully searchable. Buy it now at pragmaticprogrammer.com/coupon

Contact Us

Phone Orders:	1-800-699-PROG (+1 919 847 3884)
Online Orders:	www.pragmaticprogrammer.com/catalog
Customer Service:	orders@pragmaticprogrammer.com
Non-English Versions:	translations@pragmaticprogrammer.com
Pragmatic Teaching:	academic@pragmaticprogrammer.com
Author Proposals:	proposals@pragmaticprogrammer.com